Italian Novels of Peasant Crisis, 1930–1950

Italian Novels of Peasant Crisis, 1930–1950

Bonfires in the night

Brian Moloney

FOUR COURTS PRESS

Set in 10 on 13 Janson for
FOUR COURTS PRESS LTD
7 Malpas Street, Dublin 8, Ireland
e-mail: info@four-courts-press.ie
http://www.four-courts-press.ie
and in North America
FOUR COURTS PRESS
c/o ISBS, 920 N.E. 58th Street, Suite 300, Portland, OR 97213.

A catalogue record for this title
is available from the British Library.

ISBN 1–85182–880–x

Printed in England
by Antony Rowe Ltd, Chippenham, Wilts.

Contents

Acknowledgments

The research on which this book is based has been supported by grants from the University of Hull and the British Academy, which are gratefully acknowledged.

In the course of researching and writing this book, I have incurred many debts. David Fairservice spurred me on by most generously giving me a copy of the first edition of Ignazio Silone's *Fontamara*. Cormac Ó Cuilleanáin heroically read and made useful comments on the whole book. A number of other colleagues have either read and commented helpfully on early versions of chapters or have in discussion or correspondence made useful suggestions. I am indebted in these and other respects to Sergia Adamo, Dick Andrews, Judith Bryce, Luciano Cheles, Paul Ginsborg, Jim Hagan, Gareth Steadman Jones, Russell King, Laura Lepschy, Gerald Mangan, Gaetano Maruca, Philip Morgan, the late Tom O'Neill, Dachine Rainer, Judy Rawson, Doug Thompson and George Talbot. I owe much that is good in this book to them, but must accept sole responsibility for errors of fact or interpretation.

A number of friends in Italy have been generous with their hospitality and company: Elio and Silvia Silvestri; Silio and Simona Pispisa; Lazzaro and Emilia Papagallo; Frank and Melba Woodhouse; Virgil Kingsley; and Christine Wilding. I am grateful to them all.

I also owe a debt of gratitude to unfailingly helpful members of staff at a number of libraries, particularly the Brynmor Jones University Library at Hull; the Biblioteca Nazionale Centrale, Florence; the Biblioteca Nazionale Vittorio Emanuele, Rome; the Biblioteca di Storia Moderna e Contemporanea, Rome; the Biblioteca Emilio Sereni, Rome; the Fondazione Carlo Levi, Rome; the Biblioteca Giustino Fortunato, Rome.

An earlier version of chapter 13 appeared in *Spunti e Ricerche* 17 (2003), pp. 27–40, and an early version of chapter 14 was published in '*Onde di questo mare*': *Reconsidering Pavese*, edited by Rossella Riccobono and Doug Thompson (Troubador: Market Harborough, 2001), pp. 111–20.

A NOTE ON TRANSLATIONS

This book is addressed to a wide audience, consisting not only of Italianists, who will want quotations from Italian literary texts to be in the original Italian, but also historians, sociologists and others, who may be glad to have quotations translated. All translations used in this book are by myself.

Introduction: Bonfires in the night

In Ignazio Silone's *Fontamara*, the Impresario diverts the stream that irrigates the peasants' meagre plots of land. Berardo advises them that arson is their only method of obtaining restitution of the water: 'Mettetegli fuoco alla conceria e vi restituirà l'acqua senza discutere. E se non capisce l'argomento, mettetegli fuoco al deposito dei legnami' [Set fire to his tannery and he'll give you your water back without any discussion. And if he doesn't understand that argument, set fire to his wood store] (Silone 1998, 74). Those particular bonfires do not take place, but later, when the Impresario illegally takes possession of common land on which the peasants had previously grazed their sheep, Berardo burns down the new fence. Fire is a traditional form of peasant protest.

In addition, two of the novels to be discussed in this book, both published in 1950, end with memorable images of a bonfire. In Francesco Jovine's *Le terre del Sacramento*, the peasants of Morutri have engaged in the reclamation of previously uncultivated land, from which they have been evicted by a combination of armed Fascists and *carabinieri*. Several of their number have been killed, and the women of the village sit round a fire lamenting their dead, who include the novel's young hero, Luca Marano;

> Piansero e cantarono grande parte della notte, rimandandosi le voci, parlando tra loro con ritmo lungo, promettendo il loro dolore ai morti. La notte era buia e le voci si perdevano sulla terra desolata oltre il circolo della luce che faceva il fuoco, ancora vivo (Jovine 1972, 251).

> They wept and sang for much of the night, taking up each other's cries, talking amongst themselves in slow rhythms, promising the dead all their grief. The night was dark and their voices were lost on the desolate land beyond the circle of the fire, which still burned.

There is a note of deep grief to Jovine's conclusion; the peasants' attempt to claim justice has failed; injustice cloaked in legality has apparently prevailed. Nevertheless, there is also an optimistic note to this conclusion; although the peasants' voices are not heard by any wider audience, the light of their fire continues to shine in the darkness, which does not overcome it. Given that Luca Marano is an ex-seminarian who has been strongly influenced by a highly

9

unorthodox priest, Don Giacomo Fontana, a former missionary in Egypt, we are certainly intended to catch an echo of the gospel according to St John 1: 5: 'The light shines in darkness, a darkness which was not able to master it', as well as a moving depiction of the southern Italian folk custom of the 'pianto funebre' or keening for the dead.

Jovine's optimism derives not from the historical context in which the action of his novel is set – 1921–2 and the rise of Fascism, with more than twenty years of Fascist rule still to come – but from the context in which it was published. By 1950, Fascism had been overthrown, democratic institutions restored, and the peasant movement was actively campaigning for agrarian reform. The past can therefore be represented and reinterpreted for the benefit of a new generation as part of an attempt to ensure that the errors and injustices of the past are not repeated. In the event, there was no major agrarian reform. Jovine's is a fine novel, but his optimism was premature.

Cesare Pavese's *La luna e i falò*, his last and most mature novel, published in the same year as *Le terre del Sacramento*, ends with the haunting image of the bonfire on which the partisans have burnt the body of Santa, whom they have executed for acting as a spy for the Fascists. Bonfires, in fact, are a recurring image in Pavese's novel, in which they have a dual significance. On the one hand, they are images of destruction and renewal; their significance owes much to folk custom and the observance of fire rituals at the winter solstice, as well as to Pavese's study of James Frazer's *The Golden Bough* and other, more modern works of social anthropology which he saw through the press while working for the publishing house of Einaudi. On the other hand, Pavese's bonfires may also be symbols of what Pavese called 'il selvaggio' [the wild], by which he meant those dark forces that constantly threaten to destroy the fragile constructs of civilisation. If there is an element of optimism in Pavese's novel, it is a very cautious one indeed, tempered by a keen awareness of humankind's capacity for evil. Darkness is also a recurrent symbol in *La luna e i falò*.

Other fires had for decades cast baleful shadows over the collective memory of the southern peasantry. In the course of the brutal campaign of 1861–5 to put down what some Italian historians have come to refer to as 'political brigandage' on the part of the southern peasantry, to be discussed in chapters 2 and 12, a number of villages were singled out for punitive treatment. The first step was for Piedmontese troops to surround the selected villages, cutting off all possible escape. Then the troops charged. Men were shot indiscriminately, including some known liberals; women were raped and then bayoneted. Houses were pillaged and then set alight. In one village, a group of women chose to die in a burning house rather than emerge to be raped (Martucci 1999, 296).

These images of bonfires burning in the night, then, offer a fitting title for this study of Italian novels of peasant crisis. Set mainly, but not exclusively, in the Fascist period, the novels to be discussed seek to record and interpret the past in the context of the present in which they were written and published, a context in which the past is seen as providing a warning not to repeat past injustices in a situation in which a new society is about to emerge.

We in our turn read with hindsight. We know that hope was aroused but not fulfilled; promises of agrarian reform were made but not kept. We interpret what we read, that is, in the light of our experience and knowledge of history, which in turn leads us to take account, in our reading, of the political and cultural experiences of the novelists concerned. Novels of peasant crisis can never attempt to provide a detached account of rural life, of the impact of Fascist ruralism and the postwar struggle for land ('la lotta per le terre'), since they are always, inevitably, interpretations of history weighted and coloured by both the ideological and the literary experiences of the novelists themselves. One of the main aims of this present study is to examine the ways in which those experiences shape the novels in question. That core principle of modern poetics, namely the distinction drawn between the authors of fictional narratives and their narrators, is not valid in the case of radical fiction that is the expression of its author's commitment (Visser 1996).

Most of the novels studied are set in the south of Italy. Historians have begun recently to speak not of 'the south', as of one uniform identity, but of 'the souths', emphasizing the varieties that exist between and within the regions of southern Italy. Novelists to a remarkable extent anticipated this development. Economic historians have also begun to speak of 'three Italies', rather than two: the northwest, characterized by industrial development; the centre-east, characterized by small enterprises; and the south, by underdevelopment (Bagnasco 1977). While this may be valid in general terms, the fact remains that, when I first visited the Langhe, where much of Pavese's fiction is set, only a few miles from prosperous Turin, official notices proclaimed that it was a 'zona economicamente depressa'.

There has recently also been discussion of southern Italy in terms of 'orientalism', prompted by Edward Said's influential *Orientalism*, first published in 1978, in which Said applied to the Orient the notion of discourse as defined by Foucault in *The Archaeology of Knowledge* (1969). According to Said, 'the Orient was almost a European invention' (Said 1991, 1), a literary construct, one might say. Orientalist texts, for Said, are not 'natural' depictions of the Orient, but 'representations' of it. Westerners therefore approach the Orient 'through experiences that belong to the realm of ideas and myths culled from texts, not empirical reality' (Said 1991, 80). It follows that 'the Orient that appears in Orientalism, then, is a system of representations formed by a whole set of forces that brought the Orient into Western learning, Western consciousness, Western Empire' (Said 1991, 202–3).

Said's work has provoked considerable disagreement, not least among historians of the British Empire; nevertheless, Pietro Bevilacqua has consistently argued that the 'southern question' is a constructed representation of the south (Bevilacqua 1996, 81–92 and 1997). In fact, the south was often represented in the nineteenth century as a 'liminal space between Europe, Africa and the Orient', with the result that representations of southern Italy and the Orient sometimes intersect (Moe 2002, 3, 73–6). Consequently there have been significant attempts to apply Said's notion of Orientalism to Italy's southern problem (Chu 1998, Schneider 1998), leading to discussion of it in terms of 'Orientalism in one country'. John Dickie has written that 'more work needs to be done before Said's Orientalism can be translated into the Italian context', particularly because 'at the very least since 1876, the South has not been subordinated to the North or to the state in a way which one could even remotely describe as imperialistic' (Dickie 1999 (1), 81). Perhaps not: but distinguished Italian *meridionalisti* such as Gaetano Salvemini have used the Marxist-Leninist term, 'internal colonisation', to describe central government policies in the post-Risorgimento period. Recent research has shown that Garibaldi could in fact rely on the support and cooperation of the Piedmontese government. His famous 'Thousand' were swollen to 20,000 by Piedmontese veterans and regular troops. His campaign more closely resembled an undeclared war by the Piedmontese government against the Kingdom of the Two Sicilies than has been admitted (Martucci 1999, del Longo 2001, 75). Guido Dorso and others were not entirely wrong to describe the process by which Italy achieved unity as a 'conquista regia' [royal conquest] (Dorso 1972, 145–6). Conquest and colonialization may not for some time have been terms acceptable to modern historians as a description of the south, but they have been key features of its representation in southern discourse, as Tomasi di Lampedusa's *Il Gattopardo* shows. Fascist ruralism, with its imposition on the south of agricultural policies totally unsuited to it, was perceived as that same process carried to extremes.

If Orientalism, moreover, is a collective notion identifying 'us' Europeans as against all 'those' non-Europeans, as Said maintains, then the Italian south may become in turn a collective notion identifying the north – usually as progressive, hard-working, efficient and therefore deservedly prosperous. The political earthquake which shook Italy in 1992 and the emergence of the northern Leagues, have given fresh prominence to the topos of 'two Italies' – an organized, hard-working and prosperous north as opposed to a chaotic, corrupt and corrupting, essentially parasitic south. Some of the novels studied in this book seek to reverse the process and represent peasants as embodying – in ways to be discussed later – virtues which northerners lack and which therefore make the previously despised southerners morally superior to those who exploit them. Here lies the danger of replacing old Orientalisms with new.

In the case of Italy, moreover, another binary opposition comes into play, namely the urban versus the rural. The urban may be presented as either progressive or as corrupt, in which case the rural 'Orient' may be either backward, even savage, or the idyllic home of virtues lost to the city.

In any case, even when experience of the Italian 'Orient' is based on empirical reality and is not merely 'culled from texts', the way in which that experience is narrated must inevitably derive at least in part from other texts. Calvino observed, in his 1964 preface to *Il sentiero dei nidi di ragno*:

> Che i libri nascano sempre da altri libri è una verità solo apparentemente in contraddizione con l'altra: che i libri nascano dalla vita pratica e dai rapporti tra gli uomini (Calvino 1978, 16).

> That books are always born from other books is a truth only apparently in contradiction with the other truth: that books are born from practical life and relations between people.

The fact is that 'other books' always and inevitably shape the depiction or narration of practical life and human relations. Orientalism may be a fact of literary life and Said's 'natural' description, whether of the Orient or of the south of Italy, may be a chimera.

A second aim of this study, then, is to examine the ways in which the novelists concerned sought on the one hand to undermine or destroy certain literary stereotypes of the south or of rural Italy, which may still be current today, but, on the other hand, ran the risk of subjecting the south to another, more subtle process of 'orientalisation'.

Also implicit in the project is a third aim, namely that of continuing the process of breaking down the disciplinary fences separating literary and historical material, a process which, in a sense, was begun by the novelists themselves, who were using the novel as a way of analyzing history and conducting a political discussion.

Our texts refer to a social and historical reality outside themselves, an extra-text that they interpret and judge. The criteria by which they do so are provided by their authors' ideologies. It is my contention that the texts need to be read in the light of the extra-text as it has been interpreted and judged (or, one might say, narrated) by historians and sociologists, and also in the light of what we know or can reasonably deduce about the ideologies of the novelists concerned. We shall then be able to decide whether the novelists' interpretations of the extra-text have been pushed so far that they result in distortion or even in falsification of the extra-text, and, if so, to what end and with what effect.

Distortion or falsification may result from a number of causes. One is simple ignorance. Our authors were not themselves peasants. They may have lived or worked in rural Italy, but their direct experience of peasant life was necessarily limited, however much they may have tried to empathize with the peasants, even to identify with them. Levi, for example, is always aware of his outsider status, and of the prestige which it confers on him in the eyes of the peasants, as is John Berger in the Haute Savoie. As a *confinato*, moreover, Levi's movements were restricted and so he was prevented from seeing and describing the peasants at work in their distant fields. Do these limitations in any way invalidate Levi's account of southern village life, and, if so, to what extent? Jovine and Pavese lived mainly in cities, Rome and Turin respectively. However deep they felt their roots to be in the countryside, and however frequently they re-visited the country, there is a sense in which they are detached from rural life. Does this detachment have a negative effect on their art?

All art, moreover, involves a process of selection, arrangement and stylization which can in turn produce distortion, especially if, in the process, historical truth is sacrificed, intentionally or not, to the emotional or aesthetic effect which the work is intended to produce on the reader. Renato Fucini's fictional stone-breaker in his tale of that title, 'Lo spaccapietre', in *Le veglie di Neri* (1882) earns only eighty *centesimi* for his long day's laborious work. The author's notes on his conversation with the real stone-breaker on which the sketch is based show clearly that his wage was in reality ninety (Reidy 1974, 15). To reduce this worthy worker's wage by ten *centesimi* solely in order to squeeze an extra tear from the eye of a sympathetic but ill-informed reader is a piece of unacceptable trickery. This is no doubt a relatively minor point, but the test of their fidelity to history must be one of the criteria by which we judge texts which point so unequivocally to an historical extra-text. In the case of the five texts to be studied here, this means both assessing the accuracy with which they record the public events of the Fascist and the post-war periods, and the patterns of social relations in rural societies that have changed almost out of all recognition as a result of political and social change and rural depopulation.

It is my contention that the texts will yield richer meanings if they are set firmly in two contexts. The first is the historical context in which the action of the novel takes place. In this way we can understand, for example, how it is that Silone and Levi can offer such radically different views of peasant society as racked by conflict in one case and living in harmony in the other, and yet both offer accurate and convincing views. The second context is that of the date of publication of the novels, which in most cases is that of the post-war *lotta contadina*. Silone in the late 1940s can permit himself a cautious optimism which would have been out of place and unconvincing in 1933. Jovine's *Signora Ava* can offer no more than the remote but unlikely possibility that an individual might, if lucky, escape from poverty; his *Le terre del Sacramento* of 1950, on the other hand, is concerned with changing the social order for the benefit of an entire class. Pancrazi's view of Jovine as a nostalgic writer whose tone is predominantly picturesque seems to privilege only one aspect of his work and depends on taking his novels totally out of the context in which they were published (Pancrazi 1953). For this reason, this book will include brief chapters on the problem of the south (Chapter 2) and on Fascist ruralism (Chapter 3).

The emphasis in these novels is on the peasants' point of view. (In an interesting novel by Fortunato Seminara, *Il vento nell'oliveto* of 1951, the first-person narrator is a land-owner who is forced by striking labourers to increase wages: but that novel is, as far as I know, quite exceptional.) The result is that in these novels we see history from the margins, or as lived by the emarginated: 'la casa guardata dal cortile', in Silone's phrase [the house seen from the courtyard] (Silone 1999, 1375). Our authors are distrustful of both the grand structures of the traditional historical novel and the grand rhetoric of politics. One result of this is that they shed a vivid light on the history they depict and interpret. Nicola Chiaromonte, in *The Paradox of History*, writes:

> The reader may wonder why I have approached through works of fiction, rather than through theoretical treatises, the subject of the relation between history and the individual and the matter of the resurgence of the idea of fate in a world that seemed dedicated to the idea of progress. The answer is simple. It is only through fiction and the dimension of the imaginary that we can learn something real about individual experience. Any other approach is bound to be general and abstract (Chiaromonte 1970, 10–1).

In a similar vein, the historian Raymond Carr reported in the *Times Literary Supplement* of 23-29 June 1989 that Gerald Brenan once told him that he despaired of finding 'truth' with the methods of professional historians and that it could only be grasped by the unfettered imagination in novels. Could it be that Italian society first comes to grips with its traumas and problems through the novel? Walzer argues that social critics are most likely to be effective when they operate in what Gramsci calls the 'national-popular' mode (Walzer 1989, 223).

If that is indeed the case, then two further problems will have to be tackled in the course of this book. The first of these is the relationship of the particular to the general or universal: and the second is the relationship between our texts and the literary tradition, particularly the Italian literary tradition. Ruskin, in *Sesame and Lilies*, divided books into two categories: the books of the hour and the books of all time. This is what I mean by the particular and the universal. Our texts clearly tell us something important about a particular society at a particular time. Yet they clearly aspire to tell us something of universal significance as well. How can they reconcile both ambitions? The conventional answer to this question is simply to state that because they are so true to the particular they must also be true to the universal. Guglielmo Petroni, for example, says of Silone:

[...] egli infatti non si è mai distaccato dalla realtà del Meridione che è la sua stessa realtà, anche se vi ha aggiunto una consapevolezza di esperienza di grande vastità, ed è nella adesione diretta e ristretta a questa realtà che va spiegata l'indiscussa ed anche praticamente confermata universalità della sua narrativa (Petroni 1956, 72).

[...] in fact he has never detached himself from the reality of the south, which is his own reality, even if he has added to it a wide experience and awareness, and the indisputable universality of his fiction, which can be confirmed by the facts, is explained by his direct and limited attachment to this reality.

One can accept that the publication of *Fontamara* in some thirty or more languages confirms in practical terms the universality of Silone's novel; but I do not think it is enough to say that its universality lies in its fidelity to the local. To say that is merely to take refuge in paradox. But what is the alternative to paradox? This is a subject to which we shall return.

We now take it for granted that rural communities in many parts of the world, including Italy, have been studied by social anthropologists and ethnologists, some of whose studies will be referred to in this book. In fact, only one such study (by Charlotte Gower Chapman) had been carried out in Italy before the second world war, but it was not published until 1971 and so remained unknown (Raffa 1997). Our novelists' intimate knowledge of peasant society was based to a large extent on personal experience. Their depictions of peasant society are pioneering works. It is true that Levi had read something about the problem of the south before going into *confino* (or internal exile), but nothing had prepared him for the experience of the regular practices of magic and daily contact with witches. Silone, as a Communist Party activist, had written, before *Fontamara*, a number of studies of Fascist support in rural areas; Jovine carried out extensive research into the history of Molise; Pavese not only studied and theorized about myth himself, but, as an Einaudi editor, he saw through the press a number of important studies on the subject. Experience was supplemented by reading.

When novels claim to be based on historical and what we would now call social and anthropological research, it is important to ask how truthful and accurate are the depictions they offer of peasant society and whether ideological considerations or literary factors have led to any distortion or falsification of the truth that we may detect. Reviewing Caroline White's *Patrons and Partisans* in 1981, Desmond Gill praised her 'admirable refusal to exclude an appreciation of literary values from historiography', which he clearly considered exceptional (Gill 1981). Literary scholars ought equally to refuse to exclude historiographical values from their analyses; given that the history of Italy, and of the south in particular, is currently being radically revised, the process may yield interesting results. At the same time, they need to ask whether and to what extent literary influences may distort their representations of reality.

Authors continued to write about the peasant world after 1950, our *terminus ad quem*. One could have included chapters on Giuseppe Berto's *Il bandito* (1951), or Seminara's *Il vento nell'oliveto* (1951). But by 1960, industry and industrial society had become the central concerns of socially aware and politically committed novelists, and the peasant world, as in the novels of Carlo Sgorlon, came once again to be regarded as something whose inevitable passing was to be recorded and lamented.

CHAPTER 1

Italian novels of peasant crisis

PEASANTS AND PEASANT CRISIS

In 1974, David Craig published in the *Journal of Peasant Studies* an article 'Novels of Peasant Crisis', in which he drew attention to a number of novels which were published in the 1930s in Europe and the United States and dealt with the life of the peasantry. The novels concerned were: Lewis Grassic Gibbon's *Sunset Song* (1933), Ignazio Silone's *Fontamara* (1933), *A Price on his Head* (1933) by Anna Seghers, and *The Grapes of Wrath* by John Steinbeck (1939). By peasant crisis Craig meant 'a quake in the basis of the way of life which gives rise to a qualitative change in the condition of the people' – the qualitative change being always for the worse – and this group of novels, together with others which he did not discuss in any detail, such as Sholokov's *And Quiet Flows the Don* (1928–40), was seen by Craig as evidence of an unprecedented international concern with the plight of the peasantry on the part of writers able to use all the resources of modern literary artistry to create large and complex pictures of their themes.

'Peasant' is a term which it has always been difficult to define satisfactorily. Not for nothing did Theodore Shanin describe peasants as 'the awkward class' in his book of that title (Shanin 1972). Some time ago I attended a series of seminars which had been announced beforehand as dealing with 'peasant life'; but expert participants at the first meeting produced so precise a definition of the peasant that they were forced to conclude that there were almost certainly no inhabitants of any rural areas, anywhere, whom one could now call 'peasants'. The seminars were thenceforth described as dealing with 'rural life'. Craig, more pragmatic in his approach, defines peasants in Shanin's terms as:

> small agricultural producers who, with the help of simple equipment and the labour of their families, produce mainly for their own consumption and for the fulfilment of obligation to holders of political and economic power (Shanin 1971, 240).

Ian Carter defines the peasant as:

> a farmer working his holding with family labour as far as possible, growing his family's subsistence food crop as his highest priority, but

18

with a subsidiary cash crop for the market being grown alongside (Carter 1979, 4).

Colburn defines the peasant broadly as one who works in agriculture and has a subordinate position in a hierarchical economic and political order (Colburn 1989, ix).

In the case of Italy, however, and especially of southern Italy, the definition of peasant has to be extended specifically to include a kind of rural proletariat, the *braccianti*, day-labourers who owned no land at all but sold their labour to those who did, and the *mezzadri*, or share-croppers, who leased a family-sized holding and paid rent in kind, with a share of the crop. Systems of land tenure in Italy are not susceptible to generalized descriptions. Jacini wrote in 1884:

> It may well be said that Italian agriculture, more than any other in Europe, shows all the varieties of rural economy as practiced from Edin-burgh to Smyrna, from Stockholm to Cadiz; from the medieval latifun-dum, using the most primitive type of extensive cultivation, to one using the most advanced intensive forms of cultivation; from small-scale farm-ing of a single specialized crop to small-scale producers of everything; from an income of 5 lire per hectare of cultivated land to one of 2,000 lire per hectare; from the peasant-owner or long leaseholder to the casual day-labourer; from relative prosperity for agricultural workers of all classes, including the casual labourers, to the most squalid poverty among all workers, including owners and sharecroppers (cit. Clark 1984, 13).

It follows that the Italian peasants whose lives are depicted in the novels which I shall be discussing will include land-owning and landless peasants, as well as share-croppers, who are tenant farmers. Most will be characterized by their poverty and by the fact that they work the land, rather than by the system of land tenure under which they work. This is the broad sense in which the term *con-tadino* was used in Italy in the period with which I am concerned. Writing in *L'E-poca* in 1930, Arrigo Serpieri, Mussolini's Under-Secretary of State for Land Reclamation, defined *contadino* simply as 'chi lavora manualmente la terra'. As Eric Hobsbawm puts it: 'It may well be a complex matter for a zoologist to define a horse, but this does not normally mean that there is any real difficulty in recognizing one' (Hobsbawm 1973, 3).

This is to stretch the definition of peasant to make it more inclusive, taking into account the complexities of the Italian situation: but in the case of the other half of my term, 'crisis', I wish to be more restrictive. Craig's 'quake in the basis of the way of life which gives rise to a qualitative change in the way of life of the people' is too general to be helpful. In any walk of life a crisis may be – albeit rarely – a purely personal and private affair, as when a person is tormented by doubts about the existence of the God in whom he or she has hitherto firmly believed, or by remorse for some offence committed in the past and unknown to others. In peasant society, a crisis may affect the family work force, as when one indispensable member of that work force dies or has a serious illness or accident which not only prevents him or her from working but necessitates the hiring of temporary labour to keep the farm going, thus increasing expenditure without generating any corresponding increase in productivity or income. Such a situation could clearly inspire a moving novel or short story: in Verga's 'Nedda' (1874), the heroine's tragedy is brought about by the malaria which weakens her fiancé and causes him to fall from an olive tree, as a result of which he dies, leaving her to cope alone with her pregnancy and the death of their child. In the same author's *I Malavoglia*, the wreck of the ironically named fishing boat, *La Provvidenza*, provokes another such crisis. Indeed, what are known as rural novels often deal with such themes, as M.H. Parkinson has pointed out: 'A frequent structurally organizing device in rural novels is an intrusion from outside the closed community, the provoking of a sudden crisis (e.g. by Tess's loss of virginity [in Hardy's *Tess of the D'Urbervilles*] or by the avalanche in C.F. Ramuz's *Derborance*, 1936)' (Parkinson 1973, 166).

But the effect of such intrusions is to suggest that normally rural society is not only different from urban society but is also separated, even isolated from it, and self-sufficient. This is not in fact the case, as Craig's and Shanin's reference to 'obligation to holders of political and economic power' suggests. Peasantry in the modern world may sometimes appear to be isolated and backward, but it is inevitably connected to the rest of society by a complex network of links and relationships. At times there will be a relatively stable adjustment between national and local life, but at other times social, economic and political policies and changes that take place in national life will inevitably produce changes at the local level, and some of these changes will provoke crises in peasant society which make those fictional characters who are described as experiencing them seem typical or representative of their society as a whole. I therefore use the term 'peasant crisis' to denote the usually detrimental impact on peasant society of macro- rather than micro-politics, of national social, economic and political policies and changes. It follows from this that the novel of peasant crisis will differ from the rural novel in that the former lays considerable stress on the working conditions and lives of the peasantry. The latter does not, although peasants' leisure and private activities may be affected by the environment in which they work.

NOVELS OF PEASANT CRISIS: UNIFICATION TO FASCISM

Faced by change of the kind I have described, novelists may react in a number of different ways. Keith remarks that English regional writing has 'a constant pre-occupation [...] with change and the need to preserve memories of past ways of life' (Keith 1988, 55). English rural novelists wrote of a way of life that was vanishing before their eyes even as they wrote. Verga's preface to *I Malavoglia* has something of the same feeling about it. By 1930, and Alvaro's preface to *Gente in Aspromonte*, one has the impression that little has changed on the literary scene, although change continues inexorably to destroy traditional ways of life:

> Come al contatto dell'aria le antiche mummie si polverizzano, si polverizza così questa vita. È una civiltà che scompare, e su di essa non c'è da piangere, ma bisogna trarre, chi ci è nato, il maggior numero di memorie (Alvaro 1955, 13).

> Just as ancient mummies turn to dust on contact with the air, so this way of life is turning to dust. It is a vanishing culture. There is no point in weeping over it, but those who were born there must draw from it as many memories as they can.

Alvaro's language and imagery are as revealing as are Verga's. Just as progress, for Verga, is a great 'fiumana', an irresistible natural phenomenon, so too for Alvaro change is 'aria', which must, by definition, be both natural and fresh, since it reduces to dust a mummified culture which has somehow been artificially preserved. There is no point in shedding tears over the disappearance of what was, in any case, already dead and cannot be restored to life, still less offered as a valid alternative to what is replacing it. It follows that Alvaro is incapable of writing a novel of peasant crisis, since he sets out only to record and to give satisfying artistic shape to what he records:

> Non ho mai aspirato ad acquistare la figura dello scrittore meridionale [...] In altri termini, non mi sono mai proposto d'illuminare, se non nella sua sede, in qualche saggio o studio, la condizione della mia regione, la Calabria, né di illustrarne i problemi più o meno attuali. Non ho mai inteso impegnarmi socialmente, ma ritrarre la realtà, e trovare una dimensione poetica, cioè letteraria. Se è un difetto, è nella mia formazione umanistica (Alvaro 1956, 47).

> I have never aspired to the role of southern writer [...] In other words, I have never set out to shed light on the state of my region, Calabria, nor to illustrate its more or less present problems, except in the appropriate

place, in some essay or study. I have never sought to commit myself socially, but to portray reality, and find a poetic, that is, literary dimension for it. If this is a fault, it lies in my humanistic education.

Alvaro seems here concerned to avoid the issue of how – or even whether – a novelist can portray a problematical reality without in some way interpreting it. I use the term novel of peasant crisis to imply more than the act of depicting decline and disappearance and recording memories. It implies protest and the proffering of alternatives. Novels of peasant crisis are novels of social criticism in the sense in which Michael Walzer uses the term. They are written by mainstream critics who stand close to their audience, and, one might add, to those about whom they write; they elucidate the values that underline their complaints; and they are directed towards the future (Walzer 1989, 11–7). Novelists of peasant crisis may start from Marxist premises; but Marx and Engels' often quoted reference to 'the seclusion and ignorance of rural life' in Section 1 of *The Communist Manifesto*, seems to imply that peasants have no valid values of their own. Indeed, Marx consistently argued that any surviving peasants were destined to become proletarians. Novelists of peasant crisis, however, take a radically different view, as we shall see.

I find it difficult to believe, however, that there was in the 1930s any widely shared concern with the plight of the peasantry. It was after all in 1924 that the Polish Wladislaw Reymont was awarded the Nobel prize for his four-volume cycle *The Peasants*, first published 1904–9, but frequently reprinted during this period in several languages, including Italian. Reymont portrays the land as the source of strength. Certainly we are not likely to find a wave of Italian novels of peasant crisis written during the thirties. During most of that period, Mussolini's popularity was at its height in what historians have called 'the years of consensus', in the course of which much propaganda was devoted to projecting Fascist agricultural policy in such a way as to suggest that in the Italian countryside all was for the best in the best of all possible worlds. Silone's *Fontamara* apart, a good deal of Italian fiction from the 1920s to the mid-1940s either ignores the peasantry altogether or else gives an over-idealised picture of rural life and its supposed advantages and virtues. Some novels of this kind will be discussed in chapter 4.

There were of course a few notable exceptions. Fortunato Seminara's *Le baracche* was written in 1934, but was not published until 1942. Its sequel, *La masseria*, appeared only in 1951. Vittorini's *Conversazione in Sicilia* (1941), which was one of the most impressive novels written in Fascist Italy, gives a moving account of the narrator-hero's encounters first with a poverty-stricken and exploited Sicilian orange-picker, whose employers pay him with the oranges which neither they nor he can sell, and then with the sick and infirm of a remote village in the Sicilian mountains; but it is not a novel of peasant crisis. The novel emphasizes the way in which the narrator's encounters with suffering enable him to recover his sense of values and celebrates Vittorini's recovery of his sense of vocation as a committed writer; but the condition of the peasants is depicted by Vittorini as unchanging and static.

The relatively few other novels of the Fascist period which depict rural deprivation do so only, as it were, as a subsidiary or secondary theme. A notable exception, however, is Jovine's *Signora Ava* (1942), which is written in the nineteenth-century historical novel tradition and deals with Molise during the Risorgimento. It can, however, be read as an oblique comment on the so-called Fascist 'revolution', seen as peasant crisis.

So to what period should we look for Italian novels of peasant crisis? In Boccaccio's *Decameron*, the ignorance of rustics is the subject of comedy rather than the object of compassion. Angelo Beolco (1495/6–1542), known as Ruzzante after the peasant character he created and acted, dealt in his plays with the reality of poverty, hunger and war; but his was an isolated voice. The shepherds and shepherdesses of the pastoral tradition and of romance, who feature so prominently in Italian literature until the eighteenth century, have little or no connection with the harsh realities of rural life. The sheltered and happy rural community is an urban myth. It is not until we reach the Enlightenment and such writers as Pietro Verri (1728–97) that we find indignation and compassion expressed on behalf of the peasantry because of the wretched conditions in which they live and work:

> Vediamo il miserabile contadino, nude le gambe e scalzo; egli ha sul corpo il valore di tre o quattro lire e non più; egli mangia un pane di segale e di miglio; non beve mai vino; rarissime volte si pasce di carni; la paglia è il suo letto prima d'avere una moglie; un meschino tugurio è la sua casa; stentatissima è la sua vita e faticosissimi i suoi lavori. Egli si consuma e si logora sino all'ultima vecchiaia senza speranza di arricchire, e contrastando colla miseria per tutto il corso de' suoi giorni, null'altro bene raccoglie se non quello che accompagna una vita semplice e producono l'innocenza e la virtù. Egli non trasmette a' suoi figli altra eredità che l'abituazione al travaglio. Generazione d'uomini frugalissimi, che danno un valore alla terra ed alimentano la spensieratezza, l'ozio e i capricci della città! (Verri 1964, 164–5).

> Let us look at the poverty-stricken peasant, bare-footed and bare-legged; his clothes are worth two or three lire at the most; he eats rye- and millet-bread; he never drinks wine; he only occasionally eats meat; he sleeps on straw until he takes a wife; his home is a mean hovel; his life is full of poverty, his work laborious in the extreme. He wears himself out until extreme old age with no hope of becoming rich, fighting against poverty

throughout his life, with no other profit than that which comes from a simple life and is the product of innocence and virtue. He hands down to his children no inheritance other than the habit of hard work. This most thrifty and hard-working race of men adds value to the land and feeds the carefree idleness and whims of the city!

But this was in a fairly specialized economic treatise, Verri's *Della economia politica* of 1771, not in a work of narrative fiction written for a wide public, and Verri was probably right to assume that most of the inhabitants of Italy's cities knew little of the life of the peasants on whom their food-supply depended. A similarly compassionate view of the peasantry is to be found in Giuseppe Maria Galanti's *Descrizione dello stato antico ed attuale del contado di Molise* (1781), which was well known to Jovine. Similar sentiments had been expressed in La Bruyère's *Caractères* a century earlier. One notices, however, that Verri's attack on the luxury and corruption of city life makes him stress, polemically, the innocence and virtue of rustic life, thereby appearing almost to justify its poverty. The same is true of Verri's contemporary, the poet Parini (1729–99), whose occasional vignettes of the 'zappator' [farm-labourer] returning home to his Horatian 'parca mensa' [frugal fare], poor but honest, is part of his satire on the decadence of the aristocracy in *Il giorno*, as is his praise of the 'beata gente / che, di fatiche onusta, / è vegeta e robusta' [blessed people who, burdened with toil, are healthy and robust] in his ode, 'La salubrietà dell'aria', in which rice fields are seen as unhealthy, a source of malaria; but the poet's main objection to them is their proximity to the city of Milan, rather than any threat they pose to the health of peasants. The peasant family in the hills, on the other hand, in 'La vita rustica' is perfectly free, 'a nessun giogo avvinto' [bound by no yoke].

What are often referred to, somewhat patronizingly, as 'gli umili' [the humble] did not make an entrance into Italian literature in their own right until Manzoni wrote his *Fermo e Lucia* (1821–3), which he later revised as *I promessi sposi* (1827), the definitive version of which was published in 1840–2. But Manzoni's hero is far from being a poor peasant; indeed, it is doubtful whether a twentieth-century sociologist would describe him as a peasant at all. Renzo Tramaglino certainly owns land, 'un poderetto', or small farm, to cultivate which he employs labour, while his principal occupation is that of silk-weaver, 'di modo che, per la sua condizione, poteva dirsi agiato' [so that, for one of his class, he could be said to be well-off]. His betrothed, Lucia, works in the local silk-mill. She is described by Manzoni's narrator as 'una contadina', just as Renzo is described as 'un contadino', but we do not see her working the land, and she and her mother enjoy relative prosperity, for which they are only partly dependent on the land. The crisis which Renzo and Lucia face is not primarily economic, but personal, and by the end of the novel the qualitative change in their way of life has taken the form of greater prosperity. Even so, some of Manzoni's early critics doubted whether even these relatively well-off 'umili' were worthy protagonists of a serious work of literature. Meanwhile, Antonio Bicci's decorative drawings of Tuscan peasants, engraved by Carlo Lasinio (Florence 1796), were becoming much sought after as features of interior decoration, as they still are today.

Cesare Correnti, writing in the Milanese *Rivista Europea* in 1846, expressed the hope that there would soon be a literature inspired by peasant life (Paris 1977, 17). The rustic tales of Ippolito Nievo (1831–61) provide some of the first examples in Italian fiction of deep insights into the reality of peasant life, albeit still accompanied by a tendency to idealize poverty, but it is only in the post-Risorgimento period that we find full-length novels and short stories depicting life in the lower reaches of peasant society with a vivid and powerful realism that had few precedents in Italian literature, with works such as Verga's *Vita dei campi* (1880), *I Malavoglia* (1881), and *Novelle rusticane* (1883).

We shall see in chapter 2, which deals with the problem of the south, that the impact of the unification of Italy on the peasantry was disastrous, especially in the south. Denis Mack Smith has pointed out that 'although Italy was an essentially agricultural country, few deputies were much concerned about rural society' (Mack Smith 1969, 243). Cavour, Italy's first Prime Minister, never visited the south. There were, of course, exceptions, among them the conservatives Pasquale Villari (1826–1917), Sidney Sonnino (1847–1922) and Giustino Fortunato (1848–1932), who constituted the first wave of *meridionalisti*, or writers on the problem of the south. An English journalist caused offence when he asserted that foreign travellers were better informed about the south than Italy's governing class; but the comment was justified. It helped to provoke Franchetti into writing his *Condizioni economiche ed amministrative delle province napoletane* (1875). The writings of these first *meridionalisti* were soundly researched and vigorously argued, but since no government translated them into a programme of reform, they cannot be said to have had any great practical effect other than that they constituted a kind of initial stocktaking for the newly united nation and helped to make literate and responsible Italians more aware of the magnitude of the problem of rural poverty.

At almost the same time, naturalism became the dominant mode in the novel. And whereas in France the naturalists tended mainly to depict urban life, of both the working class and the bourgeoisie, in Italy the *veristi* and their successors tended to write mainly and most powerfully about rural life, with its shepherds, peasants and fishermen.

Naturally the *veristi* were never concerned exclusively with peasant society; Verga himself had originally planned a series of novels, after the manner of Zola's Rougon-Macquart cycle, although on a smaller scale, which would cover the whole social spectrum from the peasantry to the aristocracy. His ambitions in this respect were never realized, but other *veristi* dealt with the higher reaches of society – De Roberto in *I vicerè* (1894), and Capuana in *Il marchese di Roccaverdina* (1901). To some extent we can see the novels and short stories of the *veristi* and their successors as also enabling the newly united country, whose reading public was mainly northern and urban, to take stock of its constituent parts, bringing to the attention of their readers the rapidly-worsening plight of their fellow-citizens in a series of works which can be considered Italy's first novels of peasant crisis. Torraca was almost certainly not alone in 1885 in hoping that '*I Malavoglia* aiuteranno, al pari degli scritti dei Franchetti e dei Sonnino, a far conoscere le condizioni sociali della Sicilia' [*I Malavoglia*, like the writings of people like Franchetti and Sonnino, will help to make known the social condition of Sicily] (Torraca 1907, 382).

But here, as we read, we become aware of a paradox. The *veristi* depicted the consequences of the unification of Italy as a disaster for the peasants. On the one hand, the wealth and power of the landed gentry were increased, while on the other hand a punitively high level of taxation bore most heavily on those – the poor, and especially the peasants – who were least able to bear it. The result is that Verga, while apparently striving for a certain detachment, tends to appear to be politically conservative, nostalgically lamenting the sad decline of an earlier way of life and of values – especially the cult of family solidarity – which had great virtues but which were – regrettably – unable to survive under the new economic pressures, while at the same time the 'progress' which produces these pressures, is accepted as inevitable and even, in broad terms, desirable. Globalization is justified today in much the same terms. In Verga's case, the result is an unhistorical, or ahistorical 'still-life' account of Sicily. According to Pasquino Crupi, the critic Boutet was right to argue in *Don Chisciotte* in 1894 'che una cosa è la Sicilia sulla quale il Verga scrive e un'altra cosa ancora è la Sicilia vera sulla quale il Verga tace' [that the Sicily about which Verga writes is one thing, and the real Sicily about which Verga is silent is something different] (cit. in Crupi 1977, 12–3). Crupi goes on to argue that the negative view of emigration which Verga presents in *I Malavoglia* is an essentially conservative contribution to the debate on the subject which began after unification. Sciascia's strictures on Verga's view of a peasant uprising in the tale 'Libertà' make the same point about Verga's fundamental conservatism (Sciascia 1970, 79–84). A similar attitude to rural life in Sardinia is conveyed by the novels and tales of Grazia Deledda (1871–1936), who tends to depict Sardinian culture as unchanging, outside time, Homeric or biblical. Cirese is right to say that 'complessivamente la Sardegna della Deledda non è altra che la Sardegna della Deledda' [all in all, Deledda's Sardinia is just Deledda's Sardinia] (Cirese 1976, 45). A peasant class which is remote or quaint cannot be threatening. Particularly as these writers were interpreted by critics in the 1920s and 1930s, with little reference to their depiction of economic factors, readers tended to derive from their works a view of rural life akin to Richard Hoggart's vision of working-class life in northern England in the 1950s: 'in many respects a good and comely life, one founded on care, affection, a sense of the small group, if not of the individual' (Hoggart 1959, 37).

No doubt there is in all this a reaction to the growth of cities and the increasing sophistication of city life. A publisher's advertisement for Carolina Jaccone's *Il marito della Madonna* (1892) announced (on the cover of Luigi Coppola's *I misteri del Vomero* of the same year) that it would be the first of a series of 'novelle rusticane' in which

> [l]e passionali lettrici [...] troveranno dipinti degli affetti sani e forti, accanto alle pagine idilliche troveranno il dramma rusticano, senza nevrosi e senza spleen, e fa bene, fra l'aria viziata dai profumi languenti, respirare una boccata d'aria pregna d'ossigeno – d'aria dei monti.

> impassioned lady readers [...] will find portrayed strong and healthy emotions, alongside idyllic pages they will find rustic drama, without neuroses and without spleen, and it does one good, in air vitiated by languorous perfumes, to breathe a mouthful of air full of oxygen – of mountain air.

But the great agrarian crisis of 1880 and the social dislocation which it caused contributed greatly to the end-of-century crisis. It was in large measure this crisis which made more and more literate Italians aware that there was indeed a problem of rural poverty.

NOVELS OF PEASANT CRISIS: THE POST-WAR PERIOD

The second period to which we can look for a group of novels of peasant crisis is, not surprisingly, the period immediately following the second world war. Inevitably, given the circumstances prevailing in Fascist Italy, Silone's *Fontamara* was an isolated phenomenon. Jovine's *Signora Ava* is presented as an historical novel rather than as a novel of rural life. But with the end of the 'ventennio nero', the bleak twenty years of Fascist rule, writers were finally free to say clearly and openly things at which they had previously been obliged to hint by means of symbol or oblique satire: another period of stock-taking began, and the problems of rural deprivation and the south were aired in novels, pamphlets, essays and treatises. The impact of these publications on the Italian reading public was all the greater since, during the Fascist period, the problem of the south had been officially declared solved; Raffaele Ciascia, in volume XXIII of the prestigious Fascist-sponsored *Enciclopedia italiana*, pontificated:

> Tuttavia, di una 'questione meridionale' non si può più, oggi, legittima-
> mente parlare: e perché tante differenze sono scomparse e perché ormai
> sono in piena attuazione i provvedimenti del governo fascista che mira-
> no, intenzionalmente, a elevare il tono dell'Italia agricola specialmente
> meridionale. Ma più ancora, perché ogni traccia di contrasto, di antago-
> nismo, ogni senso di interessi diversi, sono scomparsi dagli animi per la
> fusione operata dalla guerra mondiale e dal fascismo (Ciascia 1949, 151).

> All the same, it is no longer legitimate today to speak of a 'southern prob-
> lem': both because so many differences [i.e. between north and south]
> have disappeared, and because the Fascist government's measures, which
> deliberately aim at raising the tone of Italian agriculture, especially in the
> south, are being fully implemented. But all the more because the sense of
> unity brought about by the world war and by Fascism has led to the dis-
> appearance from all minds of any trace of conflict, of antagonism, or any
> sense of a clash of interests.

Here we may hear the authentic voice of Fascism, which tended blandly to deny
the existence of problems rather than attempt to solve them. A periodical entitled *Questioni meridionali* (in the plural) was founded in the Fascist period precisely to make the point that there was no longer a *questione meridionale* in the
singular. Mussolini, in a phrase which he used for the first time in his speech 'Al
popolo di Palermo' on 5 May 1924, had resolved to 'andare verso il popolo' [to
go towards the people], which might at first have seemed to suggest an atten-
tiveness to their needs, a desire to hear what they had to say. Far from letting the
people speak, however, Fascism strove to make Italians conform to Mussolini's
image of them. Post-war novelists, on the other hand, were free to explore the
reality of an Italy which to all intents and purposes had become a country
unknown to most of its inhabitants.

   Ciascia's article was naturally reprinted in the 1949 edition of the *Enciclopedia
italiana*. The novels to be discussed must have come to some readers as a star-
tling revelation.

   The experience of war and civil war made it highly unlikely the period of
national stocktaking that followed the second world war would not merely
repeat that which had followed unification. In the heady excitement of the years
immediately following the liberation, there was a widespread and deeply felt
desire to re-examine the country's problems and to get off to a new start. The
experience of fighting a losing war on the side of German allies, who in 1943
became almost overnight a brutal occupying force, of division and of civil war,
had been traumatic. The country needed new ideals, which —were provided by
the 'valori della Resistenza' [values of the Resistance] a new constitution, and
new goals. The experience of Fascism and the war, and the state of post-war Italy

were described and analysed in countless publications. The problem of the south loomed large amongst those pressing for a solution, which must have come as a shock to those who had until now, in good faith, accepted the official Fascist version. Primo Levi, in his autobiography *Il sistema periodico*, has vividly described the effect in 1943 on a highly intelligent but previously blinkered young man of the discovery of an alternative view, of an intellectual opposition to Fascism. That experience must have been multiplied many times over the length and breadth of Italy from 1943 onwards.

Essays and treatises on the problem of the south and on the role of agriculture, northern and southern, in the Italian economy, rolled from the presses. Some, like Emilio Sereni's *La questione agraria nella rinascita nazionale italiana* (1946), even circulated widely in typescript before publication, such was the sense of urgency which prompted their authors. Some were new, written especially for the new circumstances. Others, like Guido Dorso's *La rivoluzione meridionale* (1944), were updated versions of works published earlier but about which there had inevitably been very limited discussion. And in one case a dead man spoke freely, and to an increasingly wide public, for the first time since his imprisonment by the Fascists in 1926. Three of the central themes of Gramsci's writings – the southern problem, the role of the intellectuals, and national-popular literature – greatly influenced political and literary debates in post-war Italy as his scattered essays were collected and re-published and his previously unknown prison writings were published for the first time. The problem of the south was once more a topic for free and open debate; the public came to understand that it was one of the continuities of Italian history, that it was, indeed, in the context of post-war reconstruction, one of the most urgent problems that Italy had to face.

This intellectual ferment was matched by a ferment of artistic creativity. Italo Calvino, in his 1964 preface to *Il sentiero dei nidi di ragno* has caught for a later generation the excitement of what it was like to be a young writer at that time, as have the respondents to Carlo Bo's *Inchiesta sul neorealismo* (Turin 1951). There was an urgency about the writer's task, to which the public seems to have responded by investing writers with a prestige they had not previously enjoyed. Franco Fortini, in his 1965 essay 'Per uno stato civile dei letterati' says of writers in the 1940s:

> Gli uomini delle parole, gli scrittori, furono investiti di una incredibile responsabilità pubblica [...] Uomini come Vittorini, Levi e, in misura minore, molti altri, si trovarono ad avere un'autorità morale che nessun scrittore aveva avuto dai tempi del bardo della democrazia o del poeta soldato (Fortini 1974, 24).

> Men of words, writers, were invested with an incredible public responsibility [...] Men such as Vittorini, Levi, and, to a lesser extent, many oth-

ers, found themselves having a moral authority which no writer had had
since the bard of democracy or the soldier-poet.

In some cases this prestige was no doubt a result of the writers' known participation in the resistance; in other cases it was probably a product of the intense
moral seriousness and integrity of their writings. It may also be that many members of the public now had Gramscian expectations of their writers and were
looking for a literature that would be truly national and popular. Whatever the
causes prompting the public esteem in which writers came to be held, it is clear
that Montale's pessimistic expectations of Italian literature were, for the time at
least, to be unfounded:

> Come la nostra lingua – fra le grandi lingue letterarie d'Europa – è quel-
> la che ha subito la più lenta evoluzione, così la nostra letteratura fu e resta
> e resterà probabilmente anche dopo il fascismo la letteratura più statica,
> la più indifferente alle contingenze della vita, l'interprete meno fedele dei
> tempi in cui nasce (Montale 1966, 20).

> Just as our language – amongst the great literary languages of Europe –
> is the one which has undergone the slowest evolution, just so our litera-
> ture was, remains, and probably will still remain after Fascism the most
> static literature, the one most indifferent to the circumstances of life, the
> least faithful interpreter of the times in which it is born.

'I tempi', however, the times, now urgently demanded interpreters, for this was
the period in which the peasants 'erupted into history', as the distinguished eth-
nologist Ernesto De Martino put it (cit. Cirese 1980, 217). Or, as Rocco Scotellaro wrote on behalf of the peasants of Lucania:

> È fatto giorno, siamo entrati in giuoco anche noi
> con i panni e le scarpe e le facce che avevamo (Scotellaro 1954, 150).

> Day has dawned, we have joined the game as well
> with our usual clothes and faces and shoes.

As the front line of the advancing allies moved northwards in 1943–5, so too did
a wave of peasant occupations, work-ins and strikes. Some uprisings were violent, with attacks on municipal offices to destroy tax records. It must have
seemed at first like a re-run of the period following the first world war, or even
of the previous century. Francesco Jovine wrote to Corrado Alvaro after reading
about the 'Red Republic' declared at Caulonia in Calabria in the spring of 1945:

> L'Italia liberata è oggi l'Italia rurale; ed è senza scarpe senza vestiti, senza
> strumenti di lavoro; da vent'anni dà pane e vino agli ufficiali del re e non

riceve nulla in cambio. Ho tristi presentimenti, caro Alvaro; ho letto nei giorni scorsi i fatti di Caulonia. Sono moti feroci, confusi, angusti che hanno gli stessi caratteri di quelli di un secolo fa; nei mesi scorsi in molti villaggi degli Abruzzi, i contadini hanno dato fuoco ai municipi distruggendo finanche i registri dello stato civile per tagliare ogni rapporto con la vita organizzata (Mauro 1974, 136–7).

Today, liberated Italy is rural Italy; and it has no shoes, no clothes, no tools to work with; for twenty years it's been giving bread and wine to the King's officers and receiving nothing in return. I have sad forebodings, my dear Alvaro; I've been reading in the papers about the events at Caulonia. These are fierce, confused, mean events which have the same characteristics as those of a century ago; in recent months, in many villages in the Abruzzi, peasants have been setting fire to the Town Halls, destroying even the electoral rolls, just to cut all ties with organized life.

In fact, there were in many cases significant differences between the peasant protests of 1943–50 and those of the nineteenth century, to which Jovine referred, and those following the 1915–8 war. The experience of war and the resistance had done much to raise the political consciousness of the peasantry. It was true that the resistance had not been a peasant movement, except in Emilia Romagna, but the peasants came into contact with the resistance fighters, who appropriated supplies from them, often giving them receipts which greatly exaggerated the amounts taken, thus enabling the peasants to cheat the authorities who were demanding fixed production quotas from them. Peasants hid escaping allied prisoners of war and air crew who had bailed out over enemy-occupied territory. They also concealed draft-dodgers, the 'renitenti alla leva' who refused to serve in Mussolini's army in the latter years of the war – including, of course, some of their own sons. Deceiving and defying authority in these ways helped to change the peasants' self-image. Then, the black market which flourished during and immediately after the war changed the relationship between townspeople and peasants, with the former almost in the position of supplicants and the latter exercising a new power and enjoying prestige.

The peasants, moreover, now had the vote, which they had not had until Giolitti extended the franchise in 1912, and their support was eagerly canvassed by the major political parties. The active Communist Party (PCI) in particular was quick to assist the organisation of peasant occupations and strikes, with the result that these were better led and had more clearly defined objectives than had ever been the case in the past. Communist and Socialist deputies, and even a Communist Minister of Agriculture in the first Parri government, ensured that the peasants had a voice in the capital. Even the Christian Democrat Party (DC). presented itself as a reforming party. It is not surprising that Guido Dorso argued that the post-war period represented for Italy an historic opportunity – 'un'occasione storica' – for solving the problem of the south.

Writers and artists responded to this situation imaginatively. Left-wing painters like Guttuso, Pirandello, Attardi, Capogrossi, Leonardi and others associated themselves with striking *braccianti* and painted their occupations of the fields. Novelists too wrote of the peasant movement. Amongst them, four stand out: Carlo Levi, whose *Cristo si è fermato a Eboli* was published in 1945, Ignazio Silone, who published much-revised versions of *Fontamara* in 1945, 1947 and 1949, Francesco Jovine, whose *Le terre del Sacramento*, published shortly after his death in 1950, is now recognised as one of the finest achievements of neo-realism, and Cesare Pavese, whose *La luna e i falò*, published in 1950 shortly before his death, is his most mature work.

It could perhaps be argued that *Cristo si è fermato a Eboli* is not a novel at all, but an autobiographical sketch covering one year (1935–6) in the author's life, or even a kind of documentary work. This is not a serious objection to its inclusion in this present study. Italian critics generally follow Levi in referring to it as a novel, or an essay-novel, a non-fictional or documentary novel of the kind to which we have by now become accustomed and is sometimes known as 'faction'. In so far as Levi is a conscious literary artist, shaping and ordering his material (and, in the process, taking liberties with the facts of his biography) in order to produce his effects, *Cristo si è fermato a Eboli* can for our purposes be treated as a novel. And since the names of Silone, Levi and Jovine are so often linked by historians of literature, it would be out of the question to omit Levi. In fact, it is Pavese who might at first seem to be the odd man out, since *La luna e i falò* is not about the south but is set in the north, in Piedmont: unless, that is, one is prepared to use the term south in a very broad sense indeed. Ernesto De Martino, in *Sud e magia* writes: 'ovviamente nel binomio "sud e magia" il termine "sud" non ritiene il valore di una designazione meramente geografica, ma politica e sociale' [obviously, in the dual concept "north and south" the term "south" does not have the value of a merely geographical designation, but a political and social one] (De Martino 1987, 8). I admit that I would have some difficulty in thinking of, say, Friuli, in the north, as being in the south simply on the grounds of its poverty. The binary opposition here is between city and country. Nor is the action of *La luna e i falò*, unlike that of the other texts, set solely or mainly in the Fascist period.

But poverty and rural deprivation are not confined to the south. Bigongiari observes that with Pavese the southern problem becomes a northern one (Bigongiari 1956, 110). Pavese in his early collection of poems, *Lavorare stanca* (1936) had consistently stressed themes of rural poverty and deprivation and, influenced by American writers such as Anderson, Lewis, Faulkner and Steinbeck, had between 1930 and 1950 written a number of stories featuring the poverty of rural life. It is my contention that in *La luna e i falò*, his last and also his finest and most complex work, Pavese offers a perceptive analysis of the tensions lying just below the surface of post-war Italian society, particularly of rural Italy. He shows, too, how these tensions had their origins in pre-war society, and argues that it is as essential for a society as for an individual to base its future on a clear understanding of its past. *La luna e i falò* also has the advantage of being the only major novel of peasant crisis dealing with sharecropping (*mezzadria*), setting poor peasants alongside rich peasants. Bonaviri's *La contrada degli ulivi* (1958), set in Sicily during Fascism and the war, depicts chronic poverty rather than crisis.

A similar emphasis on the importance of understanding the parallels and contrasts between the past and the present in order to rectify the injustices of the past underlies much of the fiction of the post-war years. Given the disconcerting continuities of Italian history – between the liberal state and Fascism, and between Fascism and the post-war republic – this concern with the resemblances between past and present and the need to avoid repeating the errors of the past is amply justified. When Silone published *Fontamara* in 1933, he was writing urgently about the present, for the novel's action is set in 1929, when Mussolini's power and prestige were at their height. He was protesting against injustices for which he could foresee no immediate remedy: hence the bleak note of tragedy on which the first version of the novel ends. But when he, Levi and Jovine wrote or re-wrote their books after the war, they were writing about the past, but with obvious reference to the new present, in which a growing peasant movement was producing situations which seemed to many – as we have seen in the case of Jovine's letter to Alvaro – to reproduce episodes from Italy's troubled past.

Vittorini had already warned his fellow-writers that they should not see themselves solely as chroniclers, that merely recording the past was not in itself a worthwhile operation. We see this doctrine exemplified in *Conversazione in Sicilia*, when Silvestro is introduced to Ezechiele the saddler. As his name suggests, Ezechiele is a prophet-like figure and, as such, he can speak to Silvestro only through an intermediary. Like Silvestro, he is well aware of 'il mondo offeso' [the offended world], and he seeks to record the offences committed against humanity. At this point the reader becomes aware of a contradiction: this prophet-figure is concerned only with the past. The present has no interest for him, and its offences are dismissed as 'piccolezze' [petty matters]. He has no concern at all with the future. His form of opposition to oppression and injustice is dismissed as inadequate (Hanne 1975).

The novelists with whom I am concerned are also aware of the inadequacy of simply recording the past. Their texts deal with the past, but also point to an extra-text, the non-fictional world outside the text, which is the reader's present, as well as to a future in which the injustices of the past and present should be righted. Here we find ourselves on largely uncharted and frequently shifting ground, since the relationship between text and extra-text is complex and subtle and, in the case of our texts, largely unexplored. We now turn to that extra-text.

CHAPTER 2

The problem of the South

As Cavour saw the situation in 1861, the newly united Kingdom of Italy was faced with a number of seemingly intractable problems, three of which have dominated Italian politics until comparatively recently. These were: firstly, the problem of the 'terre irredente' [unredeemed lands] which either had a mainly Italian-speaking population or lay within what the government of the day regarded as Italy's 'natural' boundaries; secondly, the problem of the Roman Catholic church, which as a temporal power still ruled Rome and had always opposed unification; and thirdly, the problem of internal assimilation or the creation of a sense of national unity and identity which would replace regional or municipal loyalties. Even in the immediate post-world war two period, these problems were regarded as far from being completely solved.

The question of Italy's northern frontiers was finally resolved only in 1954, when the boundary between Italy and Yugoslavia was re-defined. The problem of the new state's relations with the church had been partly resolved in 1929 with the Lateran Treaty, under the terms of which the Vatican officially recognized for the first time the legitimacy of the new state, which in turn recognized Roman Catholicism as its official religion. The Concordat, as the treaty is known, was modified in 1985. The image of unification as redemption is an example of the sacralization of political discourse, which has an influence on some of the novels to be discussed and to which we shall return in later chapters; while tensions between what is seen as the established (and therefore compromised and worldly) church and authentic gospel values also provide rich themes for novelists.

It cannot be said even now, however, that the problem of national unity and identity has been completely resolved. Cavour, Italy's first Prime Minister, was aware of the imbalances and disparities, possibly social and economic as well as political, between north and south, but he never visited the south to see things for himself; it thus remained for him a literary construct, as it were. The south first came to be seen as a 'problem' in the wake of the 1848 uprisings, as discontented southern exiles began to make the plight of their fellow-countrymen (Petrusewicz 1998, 47–8) more widely known, but for most northern Italians the gravity of the problem of the south came as a more gradual, and consequently even more unpleasant discovery as a result of unification. Indeed, that the south came to be seen as constituting one problem, in spite of Jacini's report, cited in

34

chapter 1, may be a political consequence of the absorption into unified Italy of the Kingdom of the Two Sicilies, seen as a single block of territory and therefore presenting one problem.

Mack Smith sums up the reasons for this in his comments on the 1860 debates in the Turin Parliament:

> The task of solidifying a national consciousness was obviously going to prove so difficult that a conspiracy of silence was beginning even now about the 'southern question'. The need to create a sentiment of common nationality was so urgent in people's minds that all talk of provincial differences and rivalries had to be kept to a minimum (Mack Smith 1985, 328).

The south had been described in ancient times as the garden of the world. Sicily was described by Cato as the Republic's granary, a comment echoed by Jordanes, a sixth-century historian of the Goths, by whose day the agriculture of mainland Italy had already gone into decline. Deforestation began in mainland Italy in the late Empire, resulting in an extensive erosion of topsoil against which the ancient world had no technical remedy. The same period also saw the abandonment of much arable land and pasture. But the notion of the south's agriculturally based prosperity continued to flourish, unchecked by mere reality. Vincenzo Cuoco in his *Saggio storico sulla rivoluzione napoletana* (1801) described the south as possessing the most fertile soil and the most mild climate, while Pietro Colletta, in his *Storia del reame di Napoli dal 1734 al 1825* (1834) went so far as to assert that it had a rich soil and a wanton climate [terra ubertosa sotto un ciel lascivo]. Who should know better than they, who were fiercely patriotic historians of their region? Small wonder then that this view of the south persisted well into the nineteenth century, with Ruggiero Bonghi (1826–95) describing the south as 'the garden of the Hesperides', and Quintino Sella (1827–84) asserting its exceptional natural richness. These views of the south help to set both Verga's novels and short stories and the writings of the early *meridionalisti* in an interesting perspective. The grinding poverty they revealed must have come as an unwelcome shock to many of their readers. Giustino Fortunato commented in a speech first published in 1911:

> Nel felice giorno del patrio riscatto [...] nessuna precisa nozione del passato, nessuna vera coscienza del presente; tutta l'Italia credemmo fatta ad una immagine e similitudine, e il Mezzogiorno, semmai, in condizioni di natura assai piu favorevoli: che solo ingiuria o incuria di uomini avevano danneggiato [...]. Tutti credevano che la terra promessa, colma di tutti i doni celesti, a' quali male aveva solo corrisposto la fiacchezza degli abitanti, fosse appunto il Mezzogiorno [...] (Fortunate 1973, 543–4).

> On the happy day of the fatherland's redemption [...] no precise notion of
> the past, no clear awareness of the present; we believed all Italy made in
> one image and likeness, and the south, indeed, in a much more favourable
> natural condition, which only man's abuse or neglect had harmed [...].
> Everyone believed that the south was the promised land, full of all the
> gifts of heaven, to which only the indolence of its inhabitants had failed
> to respond.

At the time of unification, economic differences between north and south
were in fact much less marked than they were to become later: the chief differences lay in history, in social structures, and in population patterns. Historians
are divided over the question of when the ancient prosperity of southern Italy
began to decline. What is clear is that by the nineteenth century, three main
types of agricultural development had emerged in Italy. The northern valleys and
plains were generally (but not exclusively) characterized by large and medium-
sized properties, with relatively high capital investment, and were farmed preva-
lently by waged labour. The hill country of northern and central Italy was characterized mainly by the family farm, run mostly on the sharecropping system.
The prevalent (but again, not exclusive) farm of the centre-south, the south and
the islands was the great estate, or *latifondo*, which is closely related to the strict
form of feudalism and baronial privileges imposed by the Normans in the twelfth
century, and which successive rulers in the south failed to bring under their own
control, while in the rest of Italy feudalism lost power as the cities and city-states
gained power and autonomy (Campagna 1967, 54–5). Originally, those who held
large estates, or groups of estates, were themselves vassals or tenants, but certainly by the thirteenth century the fields of southern Italy had become allodial
tenures, held absolutely in free tenure by their lords, while the peasants working
on them lived in servitude.

In 1559 the treaty of Câteau-Cambrésis established Spanish hegemony in the
peninsula. Intellectually and culturally, Italy was cut off from the Franco-Ger-
man mainstream of the European tradition, while the Italian economy experienced a sharp decline followed by a long period of stagnation, which came to an
end only with the treaty of Aix-la-Chapelle in 1748. The Kingdom of the Two
Sicilies remained in Bourbon hands, while Lombardy became an Austrian possession, and Tuscany was eventually made over to Pietro Leopoldo, the younger
son of the Empress Maria Theresa. New rulers brought with them new men, or
promoted them from amongst groups of their subjects who, since they came
from a lower social class, had not previously been thought suitable for high
office. New ideas were absorbed, mainly from abroad, administrations were
modernized and social reforms were promulgated. Italy emerged from its back-
water to enter once more the mainstream of European culture.

But although the need for economic reform had been urged in Naples – by Antonio Genovesi and his followers – earlier than in other states, new ideas were regarded there with distrust and suspicion. The Bourbon monarchy remained rigidly conservative and oppressive, the feudal aristocracy grasping and corrupt, hostile to change. The mentality of the southern landowners was very different from that of their counterparts in the north. The former belonged to a long-standing feudal aristocracy, whereas the northern landowners were by and large a relatively new class who had moved into land ownership in the seventeenth and eighteenth centuries. Consequently they were willing to introduce new crops and new methods of cultivation, whereas southern landowners engaged in tradi-tional forms of extensive cultivation or leased out land at very high rates. Given the excess population in the south, which led to wages being kept low, and the general scarcity of natural resources and therefore of alternative forms of employment for the peasantry, they felt no need to improve their estates. It is these circumstances which explain the emphasis placed polemically by Cuoco and Colletta on the natural fertility of the soil: they were determined to place the blame for southern poverty not on nature, nor on the people, but fairly and squarely on the shoulders of the ruling classes who had failed to improve their land and who had kept their peasants in abject poverty.

Peasants on the great estates did not own land, tools, or animals, or owned at most only a small plot in or near the villages in which they lived and on which they produced for their own consumption. They worked as individuals, rather than as members of a family unit, and were not expected to have particular skills or any understanding of agriculture. By virtue of immemorial tradition, they had access to common land for pasturage and firewood rights in the forests: these were known as the *usi civici*, and have sometimes been seen as vestiges of the pre-Roman pastoral communities. In exchange for produce and labour from the peasants, the medieval baronial lords had provided a measure of security and administered a kind of justice. This paternalistic feudalism depended for its suc-cess and continuity on a recognition by both parties that the delicately balanced relationship on which it was based served a useful purpose and was part of the 'natural' order of things. In fact, the system had become subject to periodic strains, most noticeably during the eighteenth century, in some cases as a result of the decadence and inefficiency of the traditional landowners, in others, fewer in number, as a result of the introduction of new capital and more modem farm-ing methods. In modem times, of course, the landowners had ceased to admin-ister justice, but they still continued to exact their dues from the peasants.

Feudalism was officially abolished by Napoleon in August 1806, when parcels of land from the great estates and from village-owned common land were dis-tributed among the peasants. Poverty or crop failure soon compelled the latter to sell out, with the result that the great estates not merely reconstituted them-

selves, but often increased in size. In the process most residual traces of the paternalistic tie between lord and peasant finally disappeared, with the result that the
barons, whether old or new, came to be seen by the peasants as oppressors and
exploiters, and their land holdings as illegal usurpations: and, since the landed
proprietors had monopolistic powers over men and things, the social relations
between them became more unambiguously ones of lordship and servitude.

It should be remembered, however, that alongside the great estates there also
existed in the south large areas of what came to be known as *latifondo contadino*,
consisting, that is, of small farms owned by peasant families. This is the characteristic system of Carlo Levi's Gagliano, in *Cristo si e fe'ato a Eboli*, and which has
been seen as occupying more land than the great estates (Rossi-Doria 1956, 16).
There were also areas in the south characterized by *mezzadria*: Giuseppe
Bonaviri's *La contrada degli ulivi* (1958) describes the cycle of deprivation in the
life of a sharecropping family in Sicily.

Unification did nothing to improve matters; rather, its immediate effect was
to exacerbate the problem. The newly unified state – in order to balance its
budget – imposed a punitively high level of taxation, and the poorer peasants
were forced to switch from subsistence farming to cash crops.

One tragic result of the tensions generated in the Risorgimento period was
the rustic guerrilla warfare which became rife in the years 1861–5 and which is
referred to so frequently in the novels of Silone, Levi and Jovine, providing the
subject matter for the most powerful pages of the second part of *Signora Ava*. It
took 100,000 regular troops to put down what historians customarily refer to as
'banditry' or 'brigandage', inadequate though that term is as a recognition of the
social issues involved in what became in effect a traditional form of social protest
in the south, rather than – or as well as – a form of criminality (Jovine made the
point that he preferred to speak of 'peasants' rather than 'bandits' when referring
to the events of the 1860s and used the term 'political brigandage' to distinguish
it from the criminal variety (Jovine 1970, 638 and n. 5), as some recent Italian
historians have done. Had he lived long enough, he would probably have welcomed the term 'social banditry' coined by Eric Hobsbawm in 1959 (Hobsbawm
1963, 1–29), to which we shall return in chapter 12. Both troops and peasants
fought with a ruthless savagery in a series of campaigns in which more soldiers
died than in all the wars of unification. There was bitter irony in this, for
Garibaldi had originally made a bid for popular support by promising land redistribution and cheaper food. In other words, he promised social as well as political revolution, thus provoking the suspicion and hostility of Cavour and northern moderate liberals. The landowners, however, were naturally on the side of
'law and order' when faced with a threat of this kind and gave their support to
Turin in exchange for the maintenance of the existing social order: the cynical
perception of Tomasi di Lampedusa's Tancredi, in *Il gattopardo*, that everything

must change in order for everything to remain the same, is firmly grounded in history. 'By its own logic, therefore, a movement which had grown out of peasants rebelling against landowners ended up on the side of the landowners against the peasants – indeed, this was one important reason for its success' (Mack Smith 1969,42). Carlo Levi describes brigandage as the peasants' fourth national war (Levi 1965, 158) and reports that famous brigands were still folk heroes.

Unification was thus achieved without the support or consent of the peasantry and resulted in a worsening of their living and working conditions. For this reason, later writers such as Gobetti and Gramsci often speak of the Risorgimento as a 'failed revolution', in which political change was achieved without social change, in a pattern of events which was later to be repeated in the so-called revolution of the Fascists. 'To complete the process of unification, the common people had to be brought into the mainstream of national life. This was a lesson to be learned, and reluctance to learn it was to bring severe trials upon Italy in the next ninety years' (Mack Smith 1969, 43).

The nation's heavy indebtedness and the consequently high levels of taxation which were the legacy of the wars of unification led the government to attempt to solve recurrent financial crises – as governments often do – by short-term measures. In 1857 an act was passed enabling the government to sell off the vast areas of land which had accumulated in mortmain through possession by charitable trusts and the church. The object of the sale was to realize the maximum profit as soon as possible, in order to reduce the burden of the cost of the Risorgimento. This meant the sale of large units of land to wealthy buyers with ready cash. So much land was put on the market between 1867 and 1876 that prices fell, with the result that hasty privatization wasted a valuable national asset. Prices did not fall so far, however, that they came within range of the peasants' purchasing power; the sales were conducted at public auctions, and few peasants had either the money or the courage to bid against local notables. Verga's Mastro-Don Gesualdo, who has made his money in the building trade, is such an exception, in the novel of the same name: chapter I of part II describes his purchase of the former common land in spite of the opposition of the local aristocracy. The ancestors of Don Carlo Magna, in *Fontamara*, had acquired much of their land in the same way. A nickname which appears at first to link him with the heroes of epic and romance thus has an ironic dimension, especially as it turns out that he is so called because whenever peasants call to see him, his maid tells them (in dialect) that he is eating: 'Don Carlo? Magna!' (Silone 1933, 28). The estate which is the subject of contention in *Le terre del Sacramento* was also formerly church-owned land.

Another example of short-term profit-taking with disastrous consequences – this time by private enterprise – was further deforestation, mainly in the south. Between 1860 and 1880, large areas of forest were felled for railway sleepers and industrial purposes, resulting in further soil erosion. An agrarian Commission of Inquiry in the 1880s estimated 'that 10,000 hectares in Basilicata were permanently under water because of deforestation, and malaria became a far greater scourge' (Clark 1984, 15). Peasants also contributed to the damage, since they were driven to cultivate farther up the mountain-sides than ever before, as Silone's Berardo Viola later is, in *Fontamara*.

The lot of the peasantry was further depressed by the re- introduction in 1869 of the detested tax on the grinding of wheat and corn. This tax, which dated back to medieval times, had always been unpopular, and its restoration led to a wave of rioting in which, in the space of a fortnight, 250 people were killed and 1,000 wounded (Mack Smith 1969, 87).

Economic policies which encouraged the development of the emerging industries of the north also tended, naturally and inevitably, to depress the south still further, since Cavour's reduction of customs duties had operated only to the benefit of northern Italy. By 1865 the loss of industrial protection had caused many southern factories to close. Another case in point is the tariff war with France of 1887–92. By the mid-1880s, the government wished to increase tariffs once more, partly in order to raise extra revenue, partly in order to protect industry against competition from cheaper foreign imports. Experts were generally agreed that agriculture would suffer as a result of protectionist policies, but the big land-owners were now alarmed by the collapse in cereal prices resulting from the easy availability of transatlantic grain. Together with the industrialists, they saw the protectionist measures through Parliament in an alliance which foreshadowed that of Fascist Italy. The price of grain, and therefore of bread, rose again, so that the large southern landowners, as producers, gained and the peasants, who were the largest consumers of bread and farinaceous foods, lost; while the south became a captive market for goods produced in the north which could no longer be exported as freely as before. The use of the concept of 'internal colonization' to describe the relations between north and south has its origins in this situation. Capital for investment, meanwhile, was naturally attracted to the north and to industry, rather than to the south and to agriculture, and the southern problem grew more acute. On the one hand Italian industry, based mainly in the north, enjoyed between 1881 and 1887 its first boom: overall production rose by 37 per cent, with an annual growth rate of 4.6 per cent, while prices were protected by customs barriers. On the other hand, agriculture entered a crisis caused by vast imports of Russian and American grain. Corn prices fell by 30 per cent between 1880 and 1887. The cultivation of corn, oil and vegetables as well as cattle-breeding all suffered in the agricultural crisis of the 1880s. Viticulture was the only sector to expand, largely as a result of the phylloxera that was devastating French vineyards. When the tariff war with France of 1887 deprived Italy of 40 per cent of its foreign trade, and threw viticulture into danger as well, the scene was set for an end-of-century crisis of appalling magnitude. It is not surprising that the effect of measures and policies such as these was to create a vast rural proletariat, which sought change through violence or through emigration. Peasant poverty did not exist in isolation: it existed in relation to and as a result of wealth and prosperity – the wealth of the southern landowners and the prosperity of the developing north. It was no doubt this extreme rural poverty that enabled some new *latifondi* to emerge in the second half of the nineteenth century – in the Tavoliere of Puglia, for example, and on the Fucino plain, to the north of which Silone sited his imaginary village of Fontamara.

The nineteenth century was marked by persistent unrest. The brigandage of the early 1860s was put down, but sporadic rioting remained a feature of rural life for the rest of the century. In reaction to the grist tax, for example, there was in 1868–9 a series of riots in which Town Halls were attacked and tax records destroyed. It was the memory of these riots which prompted Jovine's gloomy letter to Alvaro (chapter 1). Other forms of crime were at a high level, for theft was endemic – of wood for fuel, for example, of hay, of vegetables. The peasantry saw themselves not as committing crimes in such acts but as maintaining their own anarchistic version of the suppressed *usi civici*, the loss of which contributed to a widespread sense of injustice. 'Rural theft' was important to the family budget, given the level at which most of the peasantry lived, and Clark comments that 'thousands of peasants were imprisoned each year for acts which they regarded as perfectly justified' (Clark 1984, 70). Given the general lack of education among the peasantry on the one hand, and the state of the law on the other, there was no way in which this general popular discontent could be channeled into constructive forms by means of trade unions. Not only were attempts to organize them into unions met by the peasants with a good deal of suspicion and passive resistance, but in any case emigration was taking away many of their most likely natural leaders. Consequently agricultural unions were for the most part a northern phenomenon. The years 1891–3, as a result of the fall in the prices of wine, citrus fruits and sulphur, saw the growth of the Sicilian *fasci*, a combination of trade union and mutual benefit society. In 1893, the movement spread to the countryside, where it got out of control and led to violence. Peasants were wounded in clashes with police, and the *fasci* were forcibly suppressed.

Because the northern peasantry was more organized, the north initially supplied most emigrants, although the south eventually came to supply most of them. In the period 1876–80, an average of 109,000 Italians emigrated each year, but only 21 per cent came from the south. By 1890, the southern share of this human traffic was increasing, stimulated by the agricultural crisis of the tariff war, and by 1905–13, about half the emigrants were southerners; in some of their most deprived villages of the south the offices of the emigration agencies were almost the only signs of modern civilization. Some of the emigrants went to other European countries on a temporary or seasonal basis, but the percentage going to destinations across the Atlantic, mainly to the USA, rose steeply, from 24 per cent in 1876–80 to 58 per cent in 1886–90. By 1914 there were between 5 and 6 million Italians living abroad, as compared to 35 million in Italy, 3.5 million of them in the USA. 'No other country except Ireland could show an exodus on so dramatic a scale' (Seton-Watson 1967, 313). Adult males would leave first – about four fifths of emigrants were males, mainly between twenty and fifty years old – and later they would send for their wives or, if unmarried, would ask their families to choose a bride for them and send her out. Such a population loss was bound to have consequences, both good and bad, at home. Writers on the problem of the south hoped that the reduction of surplus labour would compel landowners to improve wages and working conditions, and would encourage technical progress. Any rise in wages, however, was not significant in the south as a whole, while the overall decline in population led to marginal land going out of cultivation, especially in Basilicata and the Sila plateau in Calabria. It is, however, likely that emigration, by drawing off some surplus labour, reduced the level of outbreaks of violence of the kind which characterized 1893 and 1898.

Another factor which probably contributed to the reduced level of unrest is that it was generally the peasants with most initiative who left, with the result that those remaining, often the poorest of the poor, often deprived of their natural leaders, were less likely to press their claims for change or to protest. In his account of the effects of Enclosure on English field labourers, E.P. Thompson writes of 'the fatalism of the cottager in the face of an ever-present power' and of the rural poor being confronted by 'an alien culture and an alien power' (Thompson 1968, 240). The words seem eminently applicable to the southern Italian peasantry. Patience and endurance were their defensive reaction to apparently irremediable wrongs.

Annual remittances and savings sent home by emigrants, however, mainly to the south, were beneficial. Indeed, the remittances sent home produced eventually a larger sum than the annual income from tourism (Seton-Watson 1967, 315–17) and represented a significant part of the national income. But when emigrants eventually returned home, they came back having acquired new ideas about living standards and about what constituted a living wage, and were a new source of discontent.

There was therefore some improvement in conditions in the south between 1900 and 1915, greater than in the previous forty years, but the problem was still acute. Unemployment and under-employment were still rife, and the liberalizing tendencies of the Giolittian era, with its extension of the suffrage, legalization of the unions, and its policy of wage concessions, applied more to the north than to the south. Most capital investment took place in the northern industrial triangle of Milan/Genova/Turin, or in the land reclamation projects of the Po valley. Thus the regions of the south still paid more in taxation than they received in government expenditure, therefore subsidizing northern development.

Giustino Fortunato was right to pray, in 1908, that nothing would induce the United States to close its doors (Seton-Watson 1967, 317), but it was the 1914–18 war which first saw the enforced return of Italian emigrants from other European countries, often in great distress. The catastrophe feared by Fortunato came later, in 1921. In 1913, a total of 377,000 Italians had emigrated to the USA: with the Immigration Acts of 1921 and 1924, the Italian quota was reduced first to 40,000 and then to 4,000. Other countries followed the American example, with the result that in a short time the number of old emigrants returning to Italy exceeded the number of new ones leaving. The flow of remittances home was greatly reduced and the standard of living in emigration areas declined once more. The subsistence economy of mountain areas in particular 'quite simply could not cope with the extra mouths it had to feed' (Ginsborg 1990, 35). Both Silone and Levi comment with feeling on the depopulation and disruption of family life caused by emigration: Levi's Gagliano had 1,574 inhabitants when he was there, with a total of 1,964 in the commune as a whole, but he estimates that there were 2,000 *gaglianesi* living in America (King 1988). The absence of any comment by Silone and Levi on the benefits – however limited – of emigration can be explained by the fact that they were writing of a period when the escape-route was closed and the flow of remittances greatly reduced. There is in fact, relatively little 'emigration literature' written and published in Italy: De Amicis's *Sull'oceano* (1889) shows much more sympathy towards disappointed middle-class idealists than it does towards the peasants, whose confused notions of geography and mispronunciation of standard but to them unusual words like 'emigrazione' provoke merely patronizing amusement. Francesco Perri's *Emigrant* (1928), published under the pseudonym of Paolo Albatrelli, on the other hand, is a searing denunciation of Calabrian backwardness. Return migration has become an important recurrent theme in narrative and is now becoming a subject of serious study. The first-person narrator of Pavese's *La luna e i falo* is a migrant who returns to his native Piedmont after an absence of several years in America.

If emigration came eventually to be seen as a source of shame, it was partly on religious grounds, for those who returned were often no longer good Catholics but Protestants, even Penticostalists, and partly on nationalistic grounds. If Italian peasants needed land, should the state not provide it for them in Libya, Eritrea or (later) Abyssinia? Nationalists resented the drain of youthful energy and enterprise to other countries, and bitterly described Italy as a proletarian nation, rich only in one resource, namely labour – an attitude which can be detected early in Celletti's novel *Tre tempi* (1938). Criticism of the emigration phenomenon thus turned into support for colonial expansion, regardless of the fact that the climate and soil of the projected colonies were worse than those in parts of southern Italy.

The first world war, not colonial wars, transformed the attitudes of many peasants. Like emigration, conscription into the army solved the problem of surplus labour in the countryside. Poor peasant farmers in northern Italy, working family farms, suffered greatly because they could not afford to lose any part of their labour-force, just as Verga's Malavoglia family suffered as a result of post-Risorgimento conscription, but in the south production remained almost as high as ever. True, food prices rose with inflation, but so too did income. Debts were reduced, even paid off, and peasants began to think for the first time that owning their own land was a realistic possibility. Meanwhile, those peasants who were at the front met men from other parts of Italy; their horizons were broadened, their political awareness increased. The troops were poorly paid, and their discontent was increased by the knowledge that their wretched half *lira* per day compared very badly with the average of 6.4 *lire* per day of urban factory workers, many of whom went on strike for more. Emilio Lussu relates in his autobiographical *Un anno sull'altipiano* (1937) an episode in which an older peasant-soldier is given a five-*lire* tip by his colonel because of the part he has played in the singing during a march to the front. There is irony in Lussu's account of the colonel's pleasure in finding the troops 'cosi allegri' [so merry], and even more in Zio Francesco's statement that he had never before been able to earn five *lire* in a single day:

> Mai nella mia vita, io ho guadagnato cinque lire in una volta. Mai guadagnato cinque lire, neppure in una settimana. Tranne nel periodo della mietitura, falciando a cottimo, dalla prima luce del giorno fino al crepuscolo (Lussu 1975, 33).

> I've never earned five *lire* at one go in all my life, never. Never earned five *lire*, not even in a week. Except at harvest-time, on piece-work, reaping from first light till dusk.

One needs to remember that at least 58 per cent of the army, possibly more, was drawn from the peasantry and that the peasants served mainly in the infantry, where the losses were inevitably highest (Sabbatucci 1974, 3). They regarded factory workers not as their natural allies in any class struggle, but as selfish and privileged shirkers (*imboscati*). This needs to be borne in mind when reading, say, Gramsci on the subject of the need for an alliance between workers and peasants, and Silone's Berardo (in *Fontamara*) on the inability of peasants and city-dwellers ever to understand one another. Poor pay, inadequate equipment and leadership, as well as heavy losses, all stimulated a festering discontent among the troops: low morale, as well as inefficiency, turned defeat at Caporetto in October 1917 into a rout which was halted only by the swollen flood-waters of the River Piave. The government weathered the resulting crisis, setting up a new Propaganda Service to raise the army's morale. Its propaganda campaigns, to which writers contributed, were designed to reach even – perhaps especially – the lowest social classes and were therefore very specific, promising to break up the *latifondi* and redistribute the land, to compel cultivation of uncultivated land, and to provide social security and credit for veterans when the war was won. Already in the early stages of the war the government had in fact sought to maintain food production by authorizing the use by agricultural cooperatives of uncultivated land. Occupations had begun at Lazio in the autumn of 1916, and the return of demobilized troops after the war increased the political tension, especially as the troops had, during the last two years of the war, been subjected to a propaganda campaign designed to raise their morale and to increase their political awareness of the causes for which they were fighting. They returned home convinced that the *patria* was now in their debt, and that they would be paid with land, to which they now had a right. That a revolution had meanwhile taken place in Russia – where, the peasants heard it rumoured, a new era for the peasants had begun – increased tension further. Would a revolution also take place in Italy?

CHAPTER 3

Fascist agricultural policy: ruralism

We have already seen that the government of the newly united Italy saw itself as being faced by three daunting problems, namely the question of Italy's 'natural' frontiers; the Roman question; and the problem of creating a sense of national unity. Later, it was said of the Risorgimento that it had 'made Italy', and that the time had come to 'make the Italians'. The full gravity of the problem of the south, in the sense of the economic and social disparity between the two halves of the peninsula was not at first perceived clearly, and indeed it was so exacerbated in the course of the second half of the nineteenth century that it was an important factor in the crisis which marked the end of the century.

Initially, the creation of a sense of national unity was given a high priority. Cavour never formulated a clear, positive policy towards the southern problem, and his example was followed by his successors. Any moves towards local or regional autonomy were suppressed in favour of a policy of centralization, while debates about regional differences had to be kept to a minimum. In Parliament – which in any case, whether it met in Turin, Florence, or Rome, was remote from the south – a conspiracy of silence, which lasted until the 1870s, muffled discussion of the 'southern question'. Even the term 'question' was a euphemism, of course, which helped to conceal the seriousness of the problem. Not that one need believe that the conspiracy was solely in bad faith: we have already seen why it was (chapter 2) that many northerners could believe in all sincerity that the south included some of the most fertile regions of Italy, but that their natural riches had been squandered either by corrupt and incompetent rulers or by a feckless and idle population.

The problem of the south did not go away: it grew worse as the policy vacuum and the centralization of power in the distant capital enabled the landlord class, clinging tenaciously to its privileges, to exert an even tighter control than before over the peasantry. Naturally the south became an object of study, not only on the part of some of those southern intellectuals and politicians anxious to win a better deal for their regions or towns, but also on the part of the better-informed and more socially aware northerners. Rossi-Doria (1956, 3) sees three generations of *meridionalisti*, led successively by Giustino Fortunato (1848–1932), a right-wing Deputy and Senator, Gaetano Salvemini (1873–1957), a socialist and a distinguished historian, as well as a close friend of Fortunato and a courageous opponent of Fascism, and Guido Dorso (1892–1947), whose views will be discussed in chapters 9–10 in relation to *Cristo si è fermato a Eboli*.

Some of Fortunato's numerous essays and speeches on the south were collected and published in the two volumes *Il Mezzogiorno e lo stato italiano*, which fully reveal both the strengths and the limitations of his position. He took up Cavour's point about the complexity of the southern problem, and, fiercely criticizing the ignorance of the northerners, argued that the south would make or break Italy. It was impossible, he maintained, for a state to be great and prosperous when one half of it was backward and poverty-stricken:

> Chi mai avrebbe osato dire che mezza Italia, poco difforme dalla Turchia ad essa così prossima, fosse chiamata a viaggiare con l'altra come un vaso di terracotta accanto ad uno di ferro? (Fortunato 1973, 544)

> Who would have dared to say that half Italy, not unlike nearby Turkey, would be called to travel with the other half, like a vase of clay next to one of iron?

The image, Manzonian in origin, is singularly unfortunate, since it suggests that the south is weak and liable to break – or else that unity will not hold.

Fortunato was well aware of the extent and causes of the social discontent which so often broke out in insurrection: as early as 1879 he warned that he 'could hear in the lowest strata of society the deep rumble of an earthquake, the dull thunder as of an imminent storm' (Fortunato 1982, 17). At times, one hears in his words the authentic voice of the enlightenment, as when he wrote that the peasants – whom he pointedly referred to in parliament as 'our fellow-citizens' – were still alien to political life and worn down by poverty. They had, he observed, no share in what they produced, and ate nothing but dry black bread. He was clear-sighted enough to realize, at an early stage, that Fascism was not the revolution it claimed to be, but a revelation – a revelation, that is, of Italy's old defects and vices. But Fortunato had grown up with the Risorgimento: a passionate believer in unification, he was unable to see what benefits might result from decentralization, and still looked for help from a state that showed few signs of being either willing or able to provide it, a point on which Guido Dorso and his associates, including Carlo Levi, strongly criticized him.

There was, moreover, one respect in which Fortunato's views were deeply, almost deterministically pessimistic. In his anxiety to refute the old myths of the south as enriched by nature but impoverished by man, he stressed the virtues of the peasantry and their capacity for work, explaining the backwardness of southern agriculture as due in part to inadequate management, and in greater part to the natural infertility of the soil and the hostility of the climate, which implied that the south's problems were, in the final analysis, insoluble. The title of one of his most frank essays is, indeed, 'Necessaria povertà del Mezzogiorno'. He became known as 'il politico del niente' because he saw no remedy for the problems of the south. Benedetto Croce pointed out in his *Storia del Regno di Napoli* that Fortunato's views led inevitably to a kind of materialistic determinism, and Carlo Levi's Signor Orlando, with his desolate 'Niente', is a clear reference to Fortunato's views (Levi 1965, 195).

The state was not, however, entirely inactive. Faced with a problem of such complexity and magnitude, the government did what governments tend to do when they do not know what to do: it set up a Commission of Inquiry. *La giunta per la inchiesta agraria e sulle condizioni della classe agricola* is generally known as the Jacini Inquiry after its Chairman, the conservative Senator and Lombard landowner Count Stefano Jacini (1827–91). Jacini had written extensively on agriculture, and he was a natural choice as Chairman. The Commission worked from 1877 until 1885, and its report was published between 1881 and 1886 – years in which the *veristi* were publishing fiction with a rustic setting – in twenty-six volumes containing just under 15,000 pages. Jacini's final report has been described as 'a classic statement of the liberal, free-trading view' (Clark 1984, 12), and it was significant that it was followed by an Appendix by another Commissioner, the politically radical ex-Garibaldino Agostino Bertani. Jacini realized that the peasants aspired to change and to improvements in their living and working conditions, and argued for the provision of decent housing in the countryside. But although social conditions in the rural areas, north and south, figured largely in the Report, Jacini gave it a mainly technical thrust, urging modernization and mechanization of a kind that could be provided only by the large landowners, and therefore within the existing social structures. Bertani, on the other hand, wanted to give the Inquiry a more socially committed thrust, turning it into an inquiry mainly into the living conditions of the peasant masses. His Appendix was in a sense the defensive move of a defeated man: where Jacini urged mechanization, Bertani asked the government to ensure that the interests of the peasants and day-labourers would be protected. In the last analysis, however, Jacini pinned his hopes on the conviction that industrial and commercial wealth would create rural wealth. And so indeed it did: but in the absence of social change the main beneficiaries were the *latifondisti*, not the peasants, whose lot could be improved only by emigration. The Jacini report gathered dust on library shelves, but some of its attitudes seem to anticipate Fascist rural policy: another of those disconcerting continuities of Italian history.

It is not part of my present purpose to give an account or explanation of the rise to power of Benito Mussolini – merely to describe the impact on rural society of Fascist policies. We have seen that the disturbed conditions prevailing during the first world war and the immediate post-war period seemed propitious for change in the south, especially in the light of the promises of land made by government to servicemen: but for a variety of reasons little real change – let alone revolution – came about in the long term.

Occupations of land by the peasants began during the war and continued afterwards. Peasants who had been induced to fight for their country by propaganda naturally wanted satisfaction on their return home. Their bitterness and impatience were increased when they realized that the temporary closure of the emigration routes during the war years had resulted in a renewed surplus of labour, while valuable jobs were being taken by Austrian prisoners of war and by convicts who had been drafted in to work the land in their absence. Was the government merely being slow to make good its wartime promises of land, or had it never had any intention of doing so? Natural suspiciousness suggested to peasant leaders that the latter was the case, but in any event the peasants felt that their needs were too urgent to allow them to wait long for an answer, with the result that the years 1919–21 were what amounted to a period of agrarian revolt, as a fresh wave of occupations took place – usually, but not invariably, of uncultivated land. This is the period in which Jovine sets *Le terre del Sacramento*, which deals with the reclamation and occupation of uncultivated land. There were also, during these years, a series of attacks on local government offices, on which peasant hostility traditionally focused since taxes were levied locally, often by such means as a retail consumption tax on basic items such as flour, bread and pasta – which the *signori* avoided by the simple expedient of buying wholesale. The Socialist Salvemini, who was later forced into exile on account of his opposition to Fascism, greeted the risings of 1919–21 with enthusiasm, seeing them as indications in the peasantry of a new political awareness. And in that the peasants were now more active and politically somewhat more sophisticated, this post-war period is often seen as a watershed in the history of the peasant movement, and is depicted as such by Jovine. This peasant activism seems to have taken the authorities by surprise, although it should not have done: intelligence reports compiled during the war had warned the Ministry of the Interior that the troops would demand an equitable division of the land on their return home, and Fortunato had written to Giolitti in 1917 about the 'pericoloso stato d'animo del nostro contadiname' [dangerous state of mind of our peasantry] (Bogliari 1980, 261–2).

It was now clear that the peasant movement was too powerful, too widespread and too spontaneous to be dealt with simply by the repressive measures which had been used in the past to quell the sporadic and isolated uprisings which had violently punctuated southern history since unification. The government adopted instead a policy of non-intervention, while local authorities and landowners showed themselves willing to make – or in the absence of effective means of repression were compelled to make – concessions on such matters as wages and conditions of employment and tenancy which they had not made in the past and would be unwilling to make again until faced with a second and even graver post-war crisis in the 1940s. Fear of the 'red menace' was a powerful factor in 1920s politics throughout Europe, and probably both ministers and landowners had in mind the possible effects on the Italian working classes, rural and urban, of the news of the Soviet revolution. They were therefore prepared to give the peasants, at any rate for the time being, something of what they wanted. In September 1919 and April 1920 the Visocchi and Falcioni decrees allowed Prefects to recognize, initially for a period of four years, occupations by ex-servicemen of previously uncultivated land. The landowners felt that the government was weak and, in so far as it was not prepared to defend private property, was acting against their interests, as they perceived them. In reality, the Visocchi decree did no more than prolong the wartime legislation authorizing the use by agricultural co-operatives of uncultivated land. In 1920, however, these temporary occupations were made permanent by Micheli, the then Minister of Agriculture, who was a member of the Catholic Popular Party. In 1921, he guaranteed all agricultural jobs until the end of 1922. The traditional alliance between government and landowners had, temporarily, broken down.

The reasons for this breakdown are to be sought in the electoral reforms of 1919, which introduced for the first time unrestricted adult male suffrage and proportional representation. This is another factor in Jovine's choice of period for the action of *Le terre del Sacramento*, in which Enrico Cannevale proposes to stand as a Socialist candidate in the elections. In the local elections of 1920, the Socialists and the Popolari did well. In the same year Giuseppe Micheli became Minister of Agriculture. It is noteworthy that land for the peasants was part of the programme of the initial *Fasci di combattimento* founded in Piazza San Sepolcro in Milan on 23 March 1919, which is often regarded as the inauguration of the Fascist movement. On 27 January 1921, Mussolini announced in *Il Popolo d'Italia* that Fascism meant 'land for those who till it', which proved an effective slogan for winning rural recruits (Seton-Watson 1967, 574). In the light of later developments, and especially in view of the way in which these developments were treated in the novels we are considering, it is worth quoting from this article:

> Di fronte al problema agrario, la posizione del fascismo tendenzialmente
> è questa: la terra a chi la lavora e la fa fruttare [...] Il fascismo non solo non
> deve contrastare, ma aiutare le masse agricole a togliersi la secolare e sacra
> fame della terra (De Felice 1966, 55).

> Faced by the agrarian problem, the potential policy of Fascism is this: land
> to those who work it and make it productive [...] Fascism must not only
> not oppose but help the rural masses to satisfy their ancient and sacred
> hunger for land.

Indeed, this was more than a slogan: Fascist syndicates even took over some estates in Liberal or Catholic areas in the north after 1922, selling or leasing them to local landless peasants, who in consequence often lost whatever Socialist leanings they might have had and supported the regime.

Unfortunately for the peasant movement, however, the peasants had little real power. They were not united: nor were they organized effectively. There were divisions and antagonisms between the *Opera nazionale combattenti* and the *Federterra* which frequently – as on the Fucino plain – frustrated reform plans (Sabbatucci 1974, 195). The former was the ex-servicemen's association, whose leaders were often men from the urban middle classes, out of touch with peasant feelings and incapable of leading a mass movement, particularly on a national scale. *Federterra* sought – unsuccessfully – to represent the peasantry as a whole, and could not accept that there should be discrimination in favour of war veterans. Their aim was bound to be justice for all peasants, but realization of their goals was further impeded by traditional differences between north and south, with peasant trade unionism inevitably being stronger in the north, by divisions between Catholics and Socialists, by the social stratification which is typical of Mediterranean peasant societies, and by the lack of political and ideological leadership from southern intellectuals – a problem which was to occupy Dorso and Gramsci. No policy was formed that was capable of introducing coherence and coordination into what remained, particularly in the south, a series of local outbreaks.

The landowners, sensing that the government was weak and that the peasant movement, in its divided state, was less of a threat than had at first seemed to be the case, combined to launch their own counter-offensive, in which they resorted without scruple to remarkable extremes of violence, even recruiting criminals for the purpose. Rural *squadrismo*, the use of hired squads of enforcers to harass one's opponents, was not an invention of the Fascists, since it had been a feature of rural life for decades. Snowden, writing about Puglia, states that:

> Force was no accidental feature but rather an integral part of labour discipline. Latifundism was fundamentally a labour repressive system of production. As political resistance to the system began increasingly to threaten the continuation of profit, deference and hierarchy, violence escalated (Snowden 1985, 3).

In fact, recent historical studies have tended to show that Fascism in the countryside was the instrument with which the landowners sought to destroy the challenge of rural unrest. It was the north – more 'advanced' than the south in this as in other respects – which set the example. The first paramilitary assaults on centres of agrarian socialism took place around Bologna and Ferrara in 1920, when the Socialist labour leagues in the 'red' provinces of central Italy were routed. The action was condoned, even supported by many respectable Liberals. Similar campaigns in the Lomellina area are described by Francesco Perri in his novel *I conquistatori* (1925). In the 1943 preface to the second edition, Perri blames the proletariat for creating the disturbed conditions which, in his view, had enabled Fascism to come to power. If only to workers had been content with their lot, there would have been no occasion for Fascist violence (Perri 1943, xiv–xv).

These early outbreaks of Fascist *squadrismo* in the countryside were soon imitated in the south. To at least some of Silone's readers, therefore, the first punitive expedition against the village of Fontamara would have about it a familiar ring of truth. The peasant revolt was soon over. Peasants who had reclaimed and started to cultivate previously uncultivated land in accordance with the Visocchi decree were driven from it, often with the connivance, sometimes with the active aid of the local *carabinieri*. The plot of Jovine's *Le terre del Sacramento* hinges on such a situation. Landowners and Fascists combined to force the government to abandon its position of neutrality in land and wage disputes and compelled a return to older and more primitive methods of labour control. Agrarian Socialism had not on the whole been particularly extreme in its demands, and agrarian Fascism was simply a brutal refusal to allow the peasants to make any attempt to improve their living and working conditions.

Mussolini was quick to see that he needed, as previous Italian governments had needed, the support, financial and electoral, of southern landowners. And so, whereas Fascism in the north had proclaimed land to the peasants, in the south its rallying-cry became land to the farmer (Snowden 1985, 180), which was as near as Fascism came to having an agricultural policy in its early days. The shift is clearly reflected in chapter IV of *Fontamara*, in which Berardo and the *fontamaresi* are led to believe that government intervention in the Fucino will result in land for them, only to be told that the slogan now has a meaning different from the one they put on it:

> Fucino a chi lo coltiva. Fucino a chi ha i mezzi per coltivarlo o farlo coltivare. In altre parole, Fucino a chi ha capitali sufficienti. Fucino deve essere liberato dai piccoli fittavoli miserabili e concessi ai contadini ricchi. Quelli che non hanno grandi mezzi di fortuna non hanno diritto di affittare terre a Fucino. Avete altri schiarimenti da chiedere? (Silone 1998, 102)

> Fucino to those who cultivate it. Fucino to those who have the means to cultivate it or have it cultivated. In other words, Fucino to people with sufficient capital. Fucino must be freed from its wretched small tenants and conceded to the rich peasants. Those who don't have large fortunes

have no right to rent land on Fucino. Is there anything else you want clar-
ifying?

Just how closely this cynical statement matches official Fascist policy may be seen
by comparing it with a quotation from the Fascist newspaper *Assalto* of 5 March
1921:

> We must now adopt the other formula: land to those who make it fruit-
> ful and work it most in the general interest of the country [...] The prin-
> ciple of legitimate private property is rescued by the principle that every
> farmer will be able to keep his land if he can make it productive, if he is
> able to make his interests coincide with those of the nation (De Felice,
> 1965, 75–6).

A further inducement for landowners to support Mussolini was his stress on
hierarchy and his promise to restore strong central authority. At the same time,
Mussolini continued to assure his urban supporters that he had not sold out to
the landed classes of the south, for there were, inevitably, tensions between the
different forms of Fascism, tensions so great that in August 1921 Gramsci predicted a split between them (De Felice, 1966, I, 13). But Mussolini displayed skill
and opportunism in holding his movement together, a task in which he was aided
by the ineptitude of the traditional Liberals and divisions among the Socialists
and the Popolari.

Fascism became a Parliamentary party in May 1921, and Mussolini Prime
Minister on 29 October 1922. Since he now included amongst his supporters a
large number of landowners of conservative-reactionary leanings, he quietly
dropped a bill that had been passed in the Lower House early that year allowing
large estates to be redistributed to peasants. There was a sense in which agrarian Fascism was, to use De Felice's phrase, a ball chained to Mussolini's foot, in
the sense that the landowners continued to use Fascism and Fascist violence for
their own ends even when the party wished to present itself as the party of law
and order. *Squadrismo* was officially banned in 1925 but, far from being eliminated, it continued to be used in rural districts (and in some urban working-class
areas) as an instrument of intimidation under their direct or indirect control
(Lyttleton 1973, 279). One of Mussolini's problems was that the *ras*, the local
squad leaders, were out of his control. The circular of 5 January 1927 on the
function of Prefects inveighed against *squadrismo*, asserting that the period of violence and reprisals was over: but in fact it was not. One is irresistibly reminded
of the pompous edicts against the *bravi* which Manzoni cites in the opening
chapter of *I promessi sposi*, the very promulgation of which confirms both the
bravi's continued existence and the impotence of central control. Mussolini clear-

ly needed at this stage both to extend his effective control over the rural areas, bringing his *bravi* to heel, and also to develop an agricultural policy.

The establishment of control over the rural areas was part of the process which led, in the years from 1925 to 1927, to the disappearance of the liberal state. Fascism became the only lawful, permitted channel of political activity for the state and for citizens within that state. One important element in this process was Mussolini's circular of 5 January 1927, which transformed the Prefects from representatives of the state into representatives of the regime, making them the 'secular arm' of Fascism in the provinces. The process of totalitarianization was beginning to take effect.

A second measure to affect the rural areas was the abolition, by the laws of 4 February and 3 September 1926, of local elected councils, headed by a *sindaco*, and their replacement by a *podestà* appointed by Rome on the nomination of the Prefect, and assisted by a small advisory council. Carlo Levi viewed the title of *podestà*, revived from medieval times, as an anachronistic reminder of civil strife (Levi 2001, 80). The principal of nomination from above, while consistent with the heavily centralizing and anti-democratic principles of Fascism, had in many cases the effect of confirming or extending the traditional power of local notables who had gone over to Fascism once they realized it was not simply a transient phenomenon. The ex-*sindaco* of Silone's *Fontamara*, the ironically-named Don Circostanza, is just such a Vicar of Bray type. His nick-name – 'l'Amico del Popolo' – makes one suspect either that he had previously been a member of the Partito Popolare, or that Silone remembered that in Ardengo Soffici's novel *Lemmonio Borreo* (1912) the crooked Socialist Deputy Ghiozzi, who is also a lawyer, like Don Circostanza, is described as 'quel falso amico del popolo'. The irony of Don Circostanza's situation is that he does not become *podestà*, but he attempts to ingratiate himself with the Impresario by siding with him against his former constituents, the peasants. Levi too, in *Cristo si è fermato a Eboli*, similarly depicts a society in which the *signori* had secured their power by becoming Fascists, with Don Luigino successful in becoming *podestà*. But, as Lyttleton points out, some of the students and ex-officers who had taken part in the creation of the first *fasci*, before the movement became generally fashionable in the south, saw their principal enemies in the old clientèles (Lyttleton 1973, 189). Student participation in early Fascism in Jovine's *Le terre del Sacramento* is an accurate reflection of that situation, as is the rise to power of the Impresario in *Fontamara*, a new man who disturbs the traditional power structures he clearly despises.

At the same time as he was extending his control over the rural areas and forming an alliance with the landowners, Mussolini was moving towards the formulation of an agricultural policy which was to bear most harshly on the peasantry and the rural proletariat. The laws of 1924 and 1927 abolishing even more of the remaining *usi civici* were an indication of the way the wind was blowing. The enclosure by the Impresario of the common-land pastures – the *tratturi* – in *Fontamara* is a reference to these measures and to the way in which they could be abused.

Reference has already been made to the political advantages which Mussolini derived from his alliance with the large landowners, but he expected other advantages, too, from his rural policies. He had become convinced that western civilization was in crisis. A tendency to 'supercapitalism' had produced the related phenomena of urbanization and a downward trend in the birthrate. The 'old nations' of Europe – by which he meant chiefly England and France – were decadent. This idea seems to derive mainly from German cultural anthropology, particularly Nietzsche and Spengler, who argued that cultures become sick, weaken and die. The initiative had now passed to the USA and Japan. Mussolini also held that inflation was caused by the excessive rapidity of industrial development and the way in which the cities drew labour from the countryside by internal migration. Italy – confusingly, for those who wish to make some sort of sense out of Mussolini's conflicting attitudes – was both an ancient country, in the sense that it was ancient Rome reincarnated, and a young one, in the sense that it had been united only recently. The object of Mussolini's rural policy was that it should demonstrate Italy's superiority over the old, declining nations, and so lay claim to its right to empire, by overcoming the problems of urbanization and the falling birthrate. Peasants, for their own good as well as Italy's, were to be prevented from seeking work in the cities. They would remain on the land, cultivating their crops and their increasingly large families, living in accordance with what were imagined to be the traditional rural values of hard, healthy physical toil and simple austerity. The 'battle for births' had as its target an increase in the population of Italy of one-third, to sixty million, before 1960 (Mack Smith 1969, 409). Production – of food crops as well as of children – would increase. Italy would become more prosperous as well as economically independent, and Mussolini would have the army of 'eight and a half million bayonets' – as one Fascist slogan put it – with which the empire would be won.

An indication of the way in which the political, economic and 'moral' advantages were expected to flow from Fascist 'ruralism' is to be found in the writings of Arrigo Serpieri (1877–1960), who was Under-Secretary of State for Agriculture from 1923 to 1924 and for Land Reclamation from 1929 to 1935. He wrote in the Fascist review *Gerarchia* in January 1925:

> Se il vecchio ceto medio, che ha fatto la forza dei Fasci, saprà aderire all'anticapitalismo dei ceti rurali e saprà farsi in questi la sua base sociale, spingendoli e guidandoli alla conquista del potere politico, sul quale da decenni essi non hanno quasi alcun peso; allora esso potrà accelerare

l'avvento di una nuova Italia che dai suoi campi fecondi tragga gli elementi non pure di una maggiore ricchezza, ma di una nuova civiltà rurale, più equilibrata, più moralmente sana, solidamente vincolata alla terra e quindi alla Patria (De Felice 1968, 30)

If the old middle class, which has been the strength of the Fasci, can support the anti-capitalism of the rural classes and make them its social base, spurring and guiding them to the conquest of political power, over which for decades they have had almost no control, then that class will be able to hasten the advent of a new Italy which will draw from its fertile fields the elements not only of a new wealth but of a new rural civilization, more balanced, more serene, morally healthier, firmly bound to the land and therefore to the Fatherland.

Passages such as these put into an interesting new perspective Levi's insistence that there already exists a peasant culture which is morally superior to Fascism, but which Fascism can only harm.

The extent to which Serpieri's – and, of course, Mussolini's – vision of rural Italy is based on empty rhetoric, rather than on a shrewd assessment of the real possibilities of Italian agriculture, is revealed when one compares Fascist allusions to Italy's 'fertile fields' to Jacini's sober reminder that nearly two-thirds of Italy's surface area consisted of mountains and hills, which either could not be cultivated or were only marginally usable. But, like Jacini, the Fascists envisaged a development policy which would reinforce existing social structures: if an element of realism is to be found in Serpieri's writings, it is, for example, in his acknowledgement that his policies cannot protect either the landless peasants or those who own little land. In *L'Epoca* of 6 September 1925, on duties on cereals, he wrote firmly that there could be no rewards or prizes for those he described as 'less fortunate producers'. He consistently advocated higher capital investment and greater mechanization, even if this meant lower prices, and therefore posed problems for the poorer peasants whose income would be reduced.

The most striking example of the Fascists' preoccupation with increased production, even if it was inefficient and uneconomic, was the 'battaglia del grano' – the battle for wheat – which Mussolini inaugurated on 14 January 1926.

Jacini's final report had argued that grain was grown in Italy over much too large an area, often in unsuitable conditions. It was in fact unnecessary to grow as much grain as Italy did, since increased mechanization in American farming and the development of rapid transatlantic bulk cargo ships had resulted in the availability in Europe of large quantities of relatively cheap cereals. But 'la battaglia del grano' was intended to make Italy self-sufficient in cereals. It was also intended to secure the support for Fascism of the large producers, who would profit by it, since the methods used to fight it included a protectionist policy to reduce imports and the encouragement of technical improvement in crops and production methods. The policy had a certain limited success, in that by 1939 the production of Italian wheat had doubled, and in the ten years after 1925 imports were cut by 75 per cent: but the cost of Italian wheat was 50 per cent higher that that of American (Mack Smith 1969, 407). The orders to cultivate wheat on totally unsuitable marginal and hill farms inflicted great hardship on the poorer peasants who, as Levi relates, were compelled to shift to forms of agriculture less suited to their immediate purposes. As a modern historian puts it: 'More land for wheat meant less for pasture, olive trees, citrus fruits and vineyards' (Clark 1984, 269). A further consequence of the 'battle for grain', in conjunction with other economic measures, was a fall in land prices of 40–50 per cent within five years.

Other developments were meanwhile also making life difficult for the peasantry. In 1921 and 1924 the American Immigration Acts reduced the number of Italians emigrating to the United States from over three quarters of a million per annum to just four thousand. Further restrictions on emigration were introduced by Mussolini in 1926. Silone's Berardo, in *Fontamara*, is caught in the emigration trap. The effect of these restrictions was to lower the standard of living in emigration areas, to reduce the remittances sent home by Italians working abroad, and to aggravate the problem of rural over-population.

Since many agriculturalists had mechanized in order to cope with a reduced labour supply during the emigration period, there was no way in which they could absorb the labour surplus. A major weapon was thus restored to the landowners: agricultural workers now had to compete more fiercely with one another for jobs, wages were driven down, and any sense of class solidarity which may have been encouraged by incipient unionization was undermined. The number of unemployed young people rose sharply. In these circumstances, the pressure to seek work in the industrial cities of the industrialized north also increased. The 1920s saw a strong drift from the land, but a law of 1928 gave the Prefects power to deport unemployed labourers to their place of origin, while a subsequent law of 1930 forbade agricultural workers to move except with the permission of the Prefect. Even so, the drift continued. The 1921 census had shown three fifths of the population employed in agriculture, that of 1931 less than half (Mack Smith 1969, 405). Many peasants succeeded in emigrating to the north, and Italy became, for the first time, primarily an urban, industrial country. Government statisticians, in this as in other cases, faked their figures to conceal the full truth from Mussolini.

Meanwhile, the international economic crisis of 1926 led to a revaluation of the over-valued *lira* from almost 150 to 90 lire to the pound sterling, in order to curb inflation and stabilize the currency. The new exchange rate benefited those heavy industries that relied on imports of raw materials, but put exporters at a considerable disadvantage. But the consequences of the crisis were more serious for agriculture than for industry. In the autumn of 1927 the government decreed a general wage reduction of 10 per cent. This was an attempt to alleviate a balance of payments crisis by reducing spending on consumer goods: but for the peasants this was only the beginning of a process in which in the same year agricultural wages fell by 40 to 45 per cent compared with the previous year, while the cost of living fell by less than 20 per cent. By 1934, agricultural wages had lost between 50 and 75 per cent of their 1926 value. Overpopulation and underemployment in the rural areas were the price to be paid for the stability of the system as a whole, with the result that ruralism was in reality a policy favouring the north and industry. The point was not lost on the southern peasantry, who left the land in their hundreds of thousands in the Fascist period.

It was in this context of increasing urbanization and worsening rural poverty that Mussolini launched his 'ruralism' campaign in 1927. In a letter of 27 March 1927, he wrote to Giuriati, his Minister of Works: 'Bisogna ruralizzare l'Italia, anche se occorrono miliardi e mezzo secolo' [We must ruralize Italy, even if it takes billions of lire and half a century]. His Ascension Day speech at Palermo, made on 26 May 1927, was his first explicit formulation of his demographic policy. What De Felice calls its ideological manifesto is to be found in Mussolini's preface, entitled 'Il numero come forza', to the Italian edition of Richard Kohrerr's *Regresso delle nascite: morte dei popoli*, published in 1928.

The declared object of ruralism, as adumbrated in Serpieri's previous writings, and merely repeated by Mussolini, was to defend the land and the family and to promote a birth rate that would be an irrefutable proof of the vitality of the Italian nation. Articles on the superior moral health of country-dwellers were common in the Fascist press, and Mussolini himself sought to give further weight to his campaign by having himself photographed, sun-tanned and stripped to the waist, helping with the harvest or guiding the plough, in his role as the 'primo contadino d'Italia' – Italy's leading peasant. He also revealed his fondness for his rural origins in his *Vita di Arnaldo* (1932).

City-dwellers were regularly assured that in the countryside all was for the best in the best of all possible worlds. In 1930 the novelist Grazia Deledda was invited to produce the first of a series of school readers designed to inculcate sound Fascist principles into young school-children. Deledda's *Il libro della terza classe elementare* describes a visit made by the family of a Roman teacher to Mussolini's house at Dovìa, followed by a holiday in Romagna. It makes a crude attack on the communists, explaining that they are people 'che [...] non comprendono i diritti altrui conquistati con il sacrificio' [who fail to understand other people's rights, won by sacrifice]. However, even the communists among the peasantry are not terribly wicked after all since the 'continuo contatto con la natura, con l'alba, con i tramonti e i meriggi assolati [...] li rende buoni come non vogliono a volte sembrare' [continual contact with nature, with the dawn, sunsets and sun-drenched noontides ... makes them good, although they don't at times want to appear so] (Faenza 1975, 19–20).

This type of propaganda was one of Silone's principal targets in the 1933 version of *Fontamara*; many allusions to it were excised from the post-war editions, including the entire Peppino Goriano episode, which began in Chapter VI (now reprinted in Silone 1998, 1488–98). Peppino Goriano had left *Fontamara* for Rome some thirty-five years earlier. After a wretched career as a petty criminal, he had become a professional political demonstrator, hired first by the police and then by the Fascists, in which capacity he had taken part in the sack of the offices of the left-wing newspaper *Avanti!* in 1920 and found his photograph in the newspapers next morning as 'the hero of Porta Pia'. Now, however, the Fascist party is officially the party of law and order, and Goriano, with his long criminal record, has been cast aside. He therefore returns to his native village, where he had always hoped to marry Maria Sorcanera. One is reminded of Vittorini's Alessio Mainardi, in *Il garofano rosso*, who is expelled from his school for taking part in a demonstration celebrating the murder of Matteotti just at the point when the Fascists would prefer to forget it.

One of Goriano's functions had been to provide a satirical attack on urban *squadrismo*, which is presented as professional thuggery, just as the gang that carries out the first attack on *Fontamara* includes in its ranks a number of delinquents and criminals. His second function had been to expose the hypocrisy of Fascism's claim to have restored the law and order which it had itself subverted.

Chapter VII in the first version of *Fontamara* had then gone on to describe how Goriano had been given, at Rome railway station, a Fascist propaganda booklet extolling the virtues of rural life and explaining that, thanks to the new government, peasants worked only an eight-hour day, were insured against accident, illness and unemployment, and paid fewer taxes. This is a clear reference to the Fascist Labour Charter, a highly idealized account of which is also given in Deledda's reader. The bemused peasants assume that this book must be a caricature, written by an enemy of the government, or even by a lunatic, but Goriano tries in his confused way to explain that the Fascist government is a rightwing government that has betrayed the workers, many of whom had helped to bring it to power. All this is omitted from later versions, partly because it marred the unity of the novel, but also, no doubt, because the early history of Fascism was now less relevant to the novel's main theme than it had been in 1933. It was vital in the 1940s to convince readers that the problems depicted in the novel were not simply relics of the past, for which Fascism could conveniently be blamed, but an urgent present issue, in solving which it was essential that modern Italy should not repeat earlier mistakes and injustices. Even so, some telling shafts remain. Consider, for example, Cavalier Pelino's assurances to the *cafoni* that:

> È finito il tempo in cui i cafoni erano ignorati e disprezzati. Ora ci sono delle nuove autorità che hanno un grande rispetto per i cafoni e vogliono conoscere le loro opinioni (Silone 1998, 24).

> The time is over when peasants were ignored and despised. Now there are new authorities, who have great respect for the peasants and want to know their opinions.

Passages such as this could be retained since they had not lost their relevance: in post-war Italy there was once again a new government, and one which claimed, moreover, to be intent on reform with the peasants' interests at heart.

Pelino makes the remarks just quoted during the episode in which he persuades the peasants to sign the blank petition which results in the diversion of their stream to irrigate land recently purchased by the Impresario, thus greatly increasing its value. This can be seen as a piece of land reclamation in miniature, and a reminder that the Fucino plain is itself a striking example of nineteenth-century land reclamation. Another important feature of Fascist agricultural policy was the land reclamation programme directed by Serpieri, which led to the resettlement of thousands of peasants. In 1927, Mussolini said:

> Con questo quinquennio si chiude la politica a favore delle città, che hanno avuto dal Regime tutti i contributi e tutti i concorsi per il loro abellimento e i loro bisogni. Bisogna quindi intensificare da oggi la politica a favore del villaggio [...] Ma per questa politica rurale occorrono maggiori mezzi. Si devono particolarmente tener presenti: primo, la necessità delle sistemazioni forestali ed idrauliche; secondo, l'opportunità di svolgere una politica bonificatrice integrale (De Felice 1974, 142).

> With this quinquennium comes to an end our policy in favour of the cities, which have received from the Regime all the assistance and support they require for their embellishment and their needs. So we must from now on intensify the policy in favour of the villages. [...] But this rural policy will need greater resources. We must particularly bear in mind: firstly, the need for reafforestation and hydraulic programmes, and, secondly, the desirability of developing a total land reclamation programme.

The *Legge Mussolini per la bonifica integrale*, no. 3134 of 24 December 1928, set aside large sums of money for land reclamation schemes. The policy itself was not new: by a law of 1878 the state had accepted responsibility for land development. The first ten years of Mussolini's schemes did produce tangible results, however, particularly in the Agro Pontino, the Tavoliere di Puglia, and the Basso Volturno – the first-named being one of the greatest successes of the regime. As such, it received a good deal of publicity from journalists who were taken on tours to see what the regime had achieved. Corrado Alvaro, anti-Fascist though he was (or became), burnt his pinch of incense at the Duce's rural shrine in a book which his biographers have tended to ignore. His *Terra nuova*, published by the *Istituto nazionale di cultura fascista* in 1935, and illustrated with photographs, describes peasants arriving at Sabaudia and Pontina in the Agro Pontino, being allocated their new homes and land, all being celebrated as 'l'utopia dell'Italia di piccoli proprietari divenuta fatto vivo' [Italy's Utopia for small landowners made real] (Alvaro 1935, 37). The climax to the work is an account of a visit to the new land by Mussolini himself: he is 'tra i pionieri' [one of the pioneers], tirelessly threshing the new harvest, and 'Il popolo italiano ha incarnato in lui un vecchio ideale di giustizia che nella sua storia aveva affidato a personaggi più diversi' [The Italian people has incarnated in him an ancient ideal of justice that, in its history, it has entrusted to the most diverse characters] (ibid., 53–4).

But the draining of the marshes in the plains, and the consequent lowering of the water table, together with the ploughing for cereal crops of what had been hill pasture, had a generally harmful effect on marginal hill farms and on traditional winter grazing lands, thus reproducing in the twentieth century the damage which a nineteenth-century land reclamation scheme had inflicted on Silone's Fontamara. Then, after 1934, money ceased to be available for land reclamation, being diverted instead to fund the imperialistic ventures of which the demographic policy was intended to be the foundation. In the late 1930s the Roman Campagna was still a mixture of swamp and semi-desert. Rossi-Doria's verdict on the policy is that the history of land reclamation in the South is that it was 'una miserabile storia' (Rossi-Doria 1956, 13). And since the new agriculture on what land was reclaimed was more mechanized and used less labour, it replaced a primitive but tested equilibrium with an irreparable imbalance, in which hill and mountain farmers felt all the disadvantages but none of the benefits of reclamation (Rossi-Doria 1956, 15). *Fontamara* could almost have been written as an illustration of this.

The social and moral issues raised by Italy's rural problems had been raised in liberal Italy by Bertani, but then ignored. But whatever the financial and human cost of Fascist agricultural policies and Mussolini's ruralism, there can be no doubt they were extremely popular, and not only with the landowners who had most to gain by them. Large sections of Italian society had been disconcerted by the unsettled conditions of the post-war period and by the rapid social changes that were taking place. De Felice suggests that they expressed their unease by a traditional and conservative criticism of the new society that appeared to be emerging and reacted to it by evoking a return to the cultural and moral values which they attributed in retrospect to the predominantly agricultural society that Italy no longer was. The rural policy was therefore a decisive factor in creating a consensus in favour of the regime that lasted from the late 1920s to the mid-1930s – a symptom of which was the claim that the problem of the south had ceased to exist. If this were indeed the case, one would expect to find the Italian public in the 1930s reading not novels of peasant crisis, but reassuring novels of rural well-being. Some of these will be examined, with the brevity they deserve, in the next chapter.

CHAPTER 4

Literary images of rural contentment

No doubt all urban societies have woven agreeable escapist fantasies around the theme of the essential superiority of life in the country, seen as being healthy and in harmony with nature, far removed from the stresses and strains, the diseases and dangers of life in the city. Italian literature is no exception. Even Verga, in his *Storia di una capinera*, presents the countryside as a place of freedom and happiness and peasant life there as joyful and harmonious, although this is of course rural life seen through the eyes of a young girl who is about to be forced to take the veil. Verga was not so naive as to see rural life in these terms himself, but his heroine could convincingly be described as doing so. Her belief in the rural myth reveals the depth of her longing for freedom and love, and Verga knew that his urban readers would read his novel in this way. In this sense, the rural idyll is a literary device, and Verga's fiction from *Nedda* onwards shows that he was aware of this, for in all the novels and short stories for which he is now most highly esteemed he depicts the peasants' lot as harsh indeed.

What seems surprising to the modern reader, in retrospect, is that critics such as Croce and Russo could manage for so long almost to ignore the poverty and deprivation Verga described and focus instead on the lyrical, on the pathos, and on the strong family ties which Verga attributes to the Malavoglia family. In part, no doubt, they are responding to Verga's own ideology: Crupi makes the point that in Verga people are poor but not exploited ['poveri ma non sfruttati'], (Crupi 1977, 17), and in part Croce's aesthetic would have led him and his followers to concentrate on the more conventionally 'poetic' qualities of the works they discussed.

But it may well be, in addition, that the binary oppositions of the urban versus the rural, the sick versus the healthy, the corrupt versus the pure, develop most rapidly under the stress of the rapid development of industrialization, which attracts large numbers of workers and their dependants to the cities before the infrastructures that are needed to support them can be put in place. Thus Wordsworth inveighed against 'the increasing accumulation of men in cities' in the preface to his *Lyrical Ballads*, while Thomas Hardy complained of 'the modern vice of unrest' in *Jude the Obscure*.

In the case of Italy there was in addition the urbanization that was a result of the centralizing tendencies of the united state. The binary oppositions can be seen perhaps as being most developed in societies that have in fact ceased or are on the point of ceasing to be predominantly rural. Australia is a case in point: most Australians now live in cities, but their mythology resides in the bush, so much so that a recent Minister for Primary Industries frequently asserted that the rural community was vital to the country's national identity. Mussolini's ruralism policy saw Italy become less rural than ever before.

In Italy, the Milanese *scapigliati* lamented the building boom that was transforming Milan:

> Zappe, scuri, scalpelli,
> Arïeti, martelli,
> Istrumenti di strage e ruina,
> L'impero è vostro!
> O tempi irrequïeti!

> Spades, axes, drills,
> Rams, hammers
> Instruments of destruction and ruin,
> The empire is yours!
> Oh unquiet times!

These lines are from Emilio Praga's 'Case nuove' in *Il libro dei versi* (1877), but similar sentiments are to be found in Tarchetti's novel *Paolina* (1865) and in the *Note azzurre* (1870–1907) in which Carlo Dossi delights in reflecting, as in a distorting mirror, the seamy side of Italy at its most 'Victorian'. The sordid qualities of city life are stressed in a number of works of the period: the titles of Serao's *Il ventre di Napoli* (1884) and Arrighi's *Il ventre di Milano* (1888) are indicative of the tendency. Even in the works of the *scapigliati*, which tend to have urban settings, one can find, by way of contrast, occasional celebrations of the contrasting purity of nature.

The end-of-century crisis then gave greater prominence to the cult of the rural, which may in part account for the popularity in the early decades of the twentieth century of the novels and short stories of Grazia Deledda (1871–1936) in the *Biblioteca romantica Speirani*, set in a Sardinia which few of her urban mainland readers knew, but which, as it is presented in her works, timeless and untroubled by industrialization, they clearly loved. Tuscany, however, was less remote and therefore better known than Sardinia, and it was here that Ardengo Soffici chose to set his novel, *Lemmonio Borreo* (1912).

Lemmonio Borreo is a man who, at the age of thirty, nauseated by the corruption of the cities he has seen, returns to his Tuscan village to discover his roots and his identity. The fertility of Tuscan soil and the moral and physical health of the men who work it convince him that here is the secret of Italy's future welfare. Here lies the secret of Tuscany's production, over the centuries, of great men and great artists. A pedant might object that neither Dante nor Michelangelo tilled the fields, as far as we know, but Soffici does not entertain doubts of this mundane kind. His solution for Italy's present woes is that Lemmonio Borreo, a stout stick in his hand, and accompanied by a pair of like-minded supporters, should sally forth conducting a campaign of physical violence and of cunning to right the wrongs he encounters. In moments of doubt or discouragement it is nature herself, with her miraculous beauty and fertility, that renews his courage and hope. More than a quixotic enterprise is at stake when a strong individual can decide what is best for others, and engage even in crime for what he perceives to be the other's 'good'. It is significant that this essentially conservative 'revolution' begins in the countryside and is based on 'rural' values (which include the dignified but inevitable poverty of the peasants) before moving to the city, which is seen as a new and greater challenge, but not as a source of positive values.

Soffici's novel sounds remarkably Fascist. Indeed, Borreo's reactionary revolution seems to prefigure Fascism. Not surprisingly, it was republished in the Fascist period in a revised and enlarged version, but its most 'Fascist' passages are to be found in the first edition. Asor Rosa, writing on the influence of Fascism on literature, states that:

> saremmo tentati, come tutti del resto, di definire la presenza del fascismo nel campo delle lettere e delle arti come l'espressione di quella dialettica fra modernità, arieggiante all'industrialismo, e tradizione, imperniata essenzialmente sul ruralismo, in cui mi sembrerebbe consistere l'elemento vitale della spiritualità fascista. Ma è questa dialettica veramente peculiare del regime fascista? (Asor Rosa 1975, 1500).

> We would be tempted, like everyone else after all, to define the presence of Fascism in the field of literature and the arts as the expression of that dialectic between modernity, imitating industrialism, and tradition, based essentially on ruralism, in which the vital element of Fascist spirituality seems to me to consist. But is this dialectic really peculiar to the Fascist period?

To pose the question in these terms is, of course, to imply a negative answer: the city-country dialectic predates Fascism, as we have seen. From our present point of view, however, there can be no doubt that the first world war gave particular impetus to the idealization of rural life. The Italian army, which had displayed great heroism and fortitude and sustained heavy losses, was for the most part a peasant army; and the supposedly rural virtues of that army are so frequently contrasted with the supposed corruption, vice and disease of factory workers that Bevilacqua has written of an 'unadulterated rural romanticism' (cit. in Asor Rosa 1975, 1364). Salvemini, for instance, writing of the problem of unemployment in war industries in the post-war period, clearly sees the loss of factory jobs as no great disaster and contrasts life in industry with 'the much healthier life of the fields'. Asor Rosa comments that Salvemini's views imply a complete lack of mobility for the peasants (Asor Rosa 1975, 1365). One could perhaps go further: in so far as he seems to imply that the peasants ought to remain on the land for their own good, the Socialist Salvemini's position is an essentially conservative one, not as far removed as one might expect from Fascist policies, although inspired no doubt by very different motives.

One may wonder, then, whether post-war writers were doing much more than continue the tendency of much nineteenth-century literature to describe rural life in idealized terms, according to which purity and sound moral values are to be found only in the countryside. The Father in Pirandello's *Sei personaggi in cerca d'autore* (1921) takes his son away from his mother so that, by being brought up in the country, in contact with nature, he might grow up strong and healthy. The father seems to equate this with a 'certain moral health'. The works of Piero Jahier (1884–1966) were particularly influential in this regard.

Jahier was an interventionist, and volunteered for the army in 1915, serving as an officer with the *Alpini*, who specialized in mountain fighting. He published *Con me e con gli Alpini* in the review *Riviera Ligure* in January 1917 and subsequently republished it in book form in 1919. Jahier describes his peasant soldiers with evident admiration and sympathy. He admires their patience and their courage, their tenacious struggle against poverty and hardship. Death is mentioned, but almost in the abstract: Jahier conveys none of the brutal physical details of dying which one finds in most other accounts of the war. Among the consolations the army offers are health, equality, obedience, discipline, comradeship, and a tranquil conscience. Peasants are superior precisely because they are accustomed to endure poverty and deprivation, which enable them to appreciate the small things of life, and are therefore an excellent training for war. In this view of peasant virtues, patience becomes a positive quality, rather than a purely defensive reaction to deprivation, while poverty is elevated to a spiritual condition: in his 'Arte poetica' of 1915, he states quite clearly:

> Non dico la ricchezza bene, né la povertà male. Dico che è una qualità profonda la miseria; dico che è una qualità irreparabile; dico che è una qualità eterna. Rassegnati, perché tu 'sei povero in eterno, secondo l'ordine della miseria' (Jahier 1983, 8).

I don't say wealth is good, or poverty bad. I say wretchedness is a deep quality; I say it is an irreparable quality; I say it is an eternal quality. Resign yourself, for you 'are poor for eternity, after the order of wretchedness'.

It was surely not possible for Jahier, the son of a Waldensian pastor, to write those words without having in mind Psalm 110: 4:

You are a priest forever,
in the order of Melchizedek.

Poverty and patience in Jahier are pseudo-values, quite different from the same qualities as described by Silone, Levi, Jovine and Pavese.

It was perhaps not surprising that in 1918 General Caviglia, charged with the difficult task of raising the First Army's morale after the disastrous route of Caporetto, should ask Jahier to edit a trench newspaper. The result was *L'Astico*, which was the only newspaper to be edited and printed in the fighting zone. In the immediate post-war period, Jahier went on to edit another journal, *Il nuovo contadino*, which was intended to assist the peasants in settling down again after the war. It depicts peasant life as based on the same pseudo-values as those applauded in his previous works, but now a dissenting voice can be heard. Jahier advocates reconciliation and harmony between the various social classes for the sake of the general good. He admits that peasants are exploited, but is convinced that all problems can be resolved by the exercise of mutual good will. He rejects the slogan of 'land to the peasants', however, because, he asserts, the peasants themselves recognise that this would make them the slaves of the land, not free men. All forms of violence are to be rejected, since they cannot create a social order. If workers controlled the factories and peasants the land, the result – as everyone knows – would be poverty and hunger.

One of his peasant correspondents put an alternative point of view, arguing the necessity of the class struggle and the assertion of the peasants' rights. Jahier rejected this view until he discovered that his 'peasant' newspaper was financed by the Associazione Agraria Toscana (Genovesi 1986, 16), consisting mainly of landowners, presumably because his peaceful, interclass approach was considered one that would help to preserve the status quo. Given Jahier's intense moral concern, which sought constantly to strip away hypocrisy and arrive at the truth, it is at least likely that it was the realization of his own naivety, and of the way in which it had been exploited by a power group interested in defending their own privileges, that led to his total silence during the Fascist period.

There is, then, nothing peculiarly Fascist about the exaltation of rural 'values' which turn out on closer examination to be pseudo-values attributed to the peasantry or to the 'people' in general by writers who are distant from the people. Gramsci makes the point that in Italy the intellectuals are distant from the people, that is, from the 'nation'. They are tied instead to a caste tradition that has never been broken by a strong popular or national political movement from below. This tradition, according to Gramsci, is abstract and 'bookish', and the typical modern intellectual feels closer to literary figures such as Annibale Caro (1507–66) or Ippolito Pindemonte (1743–1828) than to an Apulian or Sicilian peasant (Pertile 1986, 162).

Commenting on this point, Lino Pertile argues that this attitude saved Italian literature from ever becoming too involved with Fascism, and that it is therefore impossible to speak of Fascist poetry or Fascist prose fiction in the way that we can speak of Fascist politics. In general, one could also argue that the very incoherence and inconsistency of Fascism made it impossible to write Fascist literature. It has been argued that the ideological failure of Fascism was in fact particularly serious for literature, and that not even those writers who were Fascist supporters could go on to express their convictions artistically (Guarnieri 1976, 17). The rural novel, however, provides exceptions to this general rule. There has been a tendency of late in both France and Germany to see the rural novel as symptomatic of bourgeois mystification and of dangerous social and ideological currents (Hongre and Lidsky 1970; Zimmermann 1975; Schweizer 1976). The *Bauernroman* in Germany was an expression of the *Heimat* movement and linked to National Socialism. In Italy, a number of rural novels written in the 1920s and 30s express an implicit or explicit Fascist ideology advocating the preservation of national traditions and forestalling any attempts at social emancipation. One of the more successful of these is Delfino Cinelli's *Castiglion che Dio sol sa* (1928; revised ed. 1931).

Castiglion che Dio sol sa is set in Tuscany, near Siena and the Val d'Elsa, which is also the region favoured by the *Strapaese* group. It tells the story of Gherardo Anguillesi, whose forebears had also been farmers but whose father had left the land to engage in a career in commerce. Anguillesi himself is an art connoisseur. Now, having reached maturity – he is almost forty – he buys an estate in the country. He finds that it has been completely neglected for years. The peasants, who are *mezzadri* or share-croppers, are ignorant and inefficient, set in their outdated ways, cheating their landlord when they can and perpetually finding excuses for postponing essential tasks until it is too late to do them properly, remind one irresistibly of those on Levin's estate in Tolstoy's *Anna Karenina*, two Italian versions of which had appeared by this date. Anguillesi sacks his manager, who turns out to be ineffectual, assumes direct control of the estate, manages his farms efficiently, getting rid of unsuitable tenants and, with the help of his bank, modernizes his equipment and methods, finally producing a profit which is modest but satisfying. It is difficult not to see the estate as an Italy in miniature, with Anguillesi as an energetic and reforming Duce. The alliance between Anguillesi and his bank even mirrors the modernizing tendencies of Serpieri's agricultural policies. Not that the novel was merely a prudent ritual gesture in Fascism's direction on the part of its author; in 1925 Cinelli had retired from industry in order to farm near Siena, and the novel probably incorporates some of his personal experiences, but set in an implicitly Fascist ideological framework.

The young Elio Vittorini's 'Ritratto di Re Giampiero' (1927) is also an example of an allegory of contemporary Italy which 'should, like Mussolini, have taken Italians back to their real identity based on rural wisdom, healthy violence and instinctive parochialism' (Bonsaver 2000, 13).

Lucio d'Ambra's *Il guscio e il mondo* (1931) is a more explicitly Fascist rural novel. Gerolamo Buonconvento, the head of a large family and owner of a large estate near Viterbo, squanders his patrimony and commits suicide. His son, Ludovico, faced with debts of six million lire, sells the estate to a Jewish moneylender. (The novel has a marked anti-Semitic streak.) He then makes a successful career for himself in Rome as a banker, and returns with his seven children to the family estate, which the repentant moneylender leaves to him in his will. All his children are brilliantly successful in their various careers, and his sons are convinced Fascists, burning with zeal to contribute to Italy's rebirth. Ludovico appeals to them to join him in managing the estate:

> Qui c'è per tutti lavoro, e il più nobile, il più fecondo lavoro umano, quello che è più vicino alla natura e a Dio, alle due verità fondamentali dell'essere umano. Badare alle terre nostre [...] (d'Ambra 1931, 312).

> There is work for all here, the most noble, free and fertile human work of all, which is nearest to nature and to God, the two basic truths of human existence. Caring for the land, our land [...].

His sons can see what is needed if agriculture is to flourish:

> Rinascita? Bene. E prima di tutto bisogna far rinascere la terra e un'aristocrazia dei campi capace di servirla non con la gretta indifferenza dei mezzadri, ma con la passione eroica dei proprietarii, dei gran signori terrieri per cui più splende il casato quanto più la terra è vasta e feconda.

> Rebirth? Agreed. And first of all we need the land to be reborn, and an aristocracy of the fields capable of serving it not with the mean indifference of the share-croppers, but with the heroic passion of the landowners, the great landowners, for whom the extent and fertility of their land is an index of the glory of their family.

In the end one of his sons, Geppi, gives up a promising career in Mussolini's air force in order to take over the family estate.

Peasants necessarily figure in novels such as these, since the land can hardly be worked without them, but they figure only in one or two stock roles, either as family retainers, staunchly loyal to the existing social order, or as ignorant obstacles to progress. One might expect them to figure more prominently in a novel about land reclamation, since they are being re-settled in large numbers in the new towns and villages, but such is not the case in Francesco Sapori's *Sotto il sole* (1935), which is set in Littoria both before and during the reclamation programme, so that we witness the transformation of the area from malarial swamp to fertile fields.

The novel begins, somewhat implausibly, with a group of children near Fogliano who decide that they have had enough of playing at being soldiers and decide instead to play at land reclamation, since that is a game in which they can all cover themselves with glory. One might rather have expected them to cover themselves with mud, but the narrator assures us that these children, who belong to a poor fisherman's family, are preoccupied by thoughts of glory. No doubt Sapori felt this to be more appropriate in Mussolini's Italy, where the concept of *bonifica* had become 'central to many discourses of fascist modernity' (Ben-Ghiat 2001, 4), a handy metaphor for Fascism's social engineering project.

The central character of the novel is the engineer Stacchini, who is in post as engineer in charge of reclamation works both before and during the Fascist period. He is therefore able to comment on the weakness of government in liberal Italy and on the total transformation brought about by Mussolini. Parts of the novel read like a propaganda tract; others, because of the difficulty of constructing a plot based on land reclamation, read like episodes from a rural soap opera. The highlight of the novel is clearly intended to be the visit of the Duce himself to the completed commune of Sabaudia. Mussolini helps with the harvest, threshing for three hours and receiving the same pay as the others. A peasant exclaims: 'Fa come noi. Lavora a nostro modo' [He does it like us. He works the same as us] (Sapori 1935, 402). There is an interesting parallel here with Alvaro's *Terra Nuova* (Chapter 3).

It is not difficult to see that rural literature of this kind was an important factor in the literary environment, which had to be taken into account by novelists wishing, even in the post-Fascist period, to present an alternative view of rural life. This is particularly true if they wish to interpret peasant society as offering authentic alternative values that do not coincide with those of Fascist ruralist literature. All the novelists with whom we are concerned distance themselves, implicitly or explicitly, from the kind of ruralism which falsified rural life.

Silone tackles the problem – characteristically – head-on, by prefacing *Fontamara* with a lengthy introduction in which he describes the village of Fontamara and the conditions in which the peasants live and work. One important function of the introduction, then, is that it supplies insights and information not readily available to his readers in 1930. He concludes that his novel presents to the reader an image of southern Italy that is in strident contrast to that which is often found in literature. In literature, as is well known, says Silone:

> l'Italia meridionale è una terra lieta e bellissima, in cui i contadini vanno al lavoro cantando cori di gioia, cui rispondono cori di villanelle abbigliate nei tradizionali bellissimi costumi, mentre nel bosco vicino gorgheggiano gli usignuoli (Silone 1933, vi).

> southern Italy is a happy and extremely beautiful land, where peasants go to work singing joyful choruses, answered by choruses from peasant lasses dressed in very beautiful traditional costumes, while nightingales warble in the nearby wood.

But literature, claims Silone, has not given a true picture of peasant life. There is, he says, no folklore in his novel, and nothing about dress. There is no local dialect word for nightingale and, he adds, peasants do not sing, least of all on their way to work. It is difficult to reconcile this with what other sources say, however: E. Canziani's *Through the Appenines & the Land of the Abruzzi* (1928) has chapters on folk song and peasant costume. But Levi also notes that the peasants of Gagliano tramp to work in silence, and that song is not an important feature of their lives.

Another important function of the preface to *Fontamara*, therefore, is to counter, in advance of the narrative, what Silone reasonably and naturally considers to be the ill-informed prejudices of his Italian readers about peasant life, subjected as they were to Fascist propaganda and ruralist literature. There is no indication in the 1933 version that Silone envisaged the foreign readers he mentions in the post-war editions, in which his emphasis changes. In the 1940s, with the southern problem once more the subject of open debate and with the neorealist novel flourishing, he can assume that many of his Italian readers' illusions have been dispelled, but they might still be held by foreigners:

> Questo racconto apparirà al lettore straniero, che lo leggerà per primo, in stridente contrasto con la immagine pittoresca che dell'Italia meridionale egli troverà frequentemente nella letteratura per turisti. In certi libri, com'è noto, l'Italia meridionale è una terra bellissima [...] (Silone 1998, 14).

> This tale will seem to the foreign reader, who will be the first to read it, to be in strident contrast with the picturesque image of southern Italy

which he will often find in literature for tourists. In certain books, as we know, southern Italy is a most beautiful land [...].

The revision is a strange one since, although by 1945 Silone had acquired an extensive non-Italian readership, the revised novel (as we shall see in chapter 6) clearly envisaged an Italian readership and had certain very specific local aims.

It might be objected that Silone's use of a preface points to a certain limitation in his narrative techniques or to a lack of confidence in them. *Fontamara* was, after all, his first novel, and Verga had not felt the need to write that kind of preface to *I Malavoglia* in 1881. But Verga's situation was very different from Silone's. When Verga was writing, the problem of the south had become a matter of open and increasingly urgent debate, and Sicily's social and agricultural problems were being described and analysed in print in considerable detail, while the events to which the inhabitants of Aci Trezza refer – albeit uncomprehendingly, for example, the battles of Lissa and Custozza – were part of an unsatisfactorily completed process of unification with which a novelist could reasonably assume his mainly northern, urban readers to be familiar. Silone, like Verga, wishes to describe events not directly but through their effects on the very limited awareness of his characters: but unlike his Sicilian predecessor he cannot, in the Fascist era, or even in the immediate post-war period, assume that his readers are familiar with the events to which he is referring. In Verga's Italy, the names of Lissa and Custozza needed no authorial gloss; they were national humiliations, and by contrasting their own (probably patriotic) reactions to those disasters with those of Verga's characters, nineteenth-century readers could begin to understand the world of Aci Trezza, in which taxes on salt and pitch were of more consequence than distant wars, and at the same time measure their distance from it. Silone's preface therefore asserts the accuracy and realism of the text; or one could say that it effectively relates the text to the extratext, revealing to urban readers, to whom the name of Torlonia might suggest wealth and culture, the squalid source of that wealth. Even so, while granting that some of the information conveyed in the preface is certainly the result of Silone's awareness of the ignorance of his reading public, the fact does remain that a number of the points made in the preface are repeated and amplified in the narrative.

Levi sees the problem of his relationship with ruralism and falsifying literature on the south in different terms. In his eyes, it is Gabriele D'Annunzio who represents the patronizing, aulic tradition at its most false. Some critics have seen Levi himself as a 'decadent', cast in the Dannunzian mold (Muscetta 1953), but others correctly point out that Levi is careful to distance himself from the great 'image-maker' (De Donato 1974, 83; Carducci 1983 (2), 36). But why should Levi single out D'Annunzio rather than, say, Deledda, who has often been accused of setting her fiction in a mythical, ahistorical world, and not noticing the significant social changes going on under her very eyes?

I believe that Levi was aware that he might be accused of being Dannunzian because some of his themes and the very language he uses to state them could make it appear to the hasty reader that he shared the Abbruzese writer's vision of the south. His constant use of words and phrases such as 'due civiltà', 'due tempi', 'barbaro', 'animalesco', 'primitivo', 'misterioso', 'arcano', would inevitably have brought to mind, in a literary culture in which D'Annunzio was an unavoidable presence, the language of *Le novelle della Pescara*, *Terra Vergine* and *Il trionfo della morte*. Levi's account of sexual mores in Gagliano would inevitably have suggested similar associations. 'La veglia funebre' in *Le novelle della Pescara* comes instantly to mind when one reads in *Cristo si è fermato a Eboli*:

> L'amore, o l'attrattiva sessuale, è considerato dai contadini come una forza della natura, potentissima, e tale che nessuna volontà è in grado di opporvisi. Se un uomo e una donna si trovano insieme al riparo e senza testimoni, nulla può impedire che essi si abbraccino [...] (Levi 1965, 121).

> Love, or sexual attraction, is regarded by the peasants as an extremely powerful force of nature, such that no will is capable of opposing it. If a man and a woman find themselves together, under cover and without witnesses, nothing can prevent them from embracing each other [...].

In addition, his painter's eye and his sensitivity to form and colour, which make him respond to the beauty of these 'terre malariche' [malarial lands] and their undernourished children leave him open to the charge of Dannunzian aestheticism.

Levi was aware of these possibilities. His vocabulary in fact owes more to Jung than to D'Annunzio (on which subject see chapter 10), and his response to beauty never masks the indignation and compassion which the spectacle of poverty provokes. Even though Levi is prepared to recognize the validity of D'Annunzio's view of the peasant world as 'timeless' (in a sense to be discussed in chapter 9), he takes care to distance himself from D'Annunzio. He refers scornfully to 'letterati paganeggianti' [paganizing men of letters] who imagine that happiness can be found in such a life as the peasants lead, and describes modern Matera, with its pretentious new Fascist-style public buildings as being like an open-air stage-setting in bad taste for a Dannunzian tragedy (Levi 1965, 107). This reference to Dannunzian tragedy prepares us for an account of a performance at Grassano, by a troop of wandering players, of D'Annunzio's *La fiaccola sotto il moggio*, a tale of murder and revenge in a now impoverished family of landowners. Levi is impressed by the performance, and by the peasant audience's reaction to it, but he nevertheless comments sharply that D'Annunzio, as a 'letterato italiano' was bound to betray the peasants, thus effectively distinguishing between his own (authentic) view of peasant life, not bookish but based on experience, and that presented in the play, making the point that he is not a man of letters and that he is distancing himself from the aulic tradition.

Jovine also attacked D'Annunzio and his aestheticism (Procaccini 1986, 61), accusing the Abruzzese poet of despising the working classes (Jovine 1945, 112), but his problem was that the conclusion to his first novel, *Un uomo provvisorio* (1934) had a remarkably ruralistic ring about it.

Un uomo provvisorio is the story of a young doctor, Giulio Sabò, who leaves his native Molise and goes to Rome, to specialize in neurology. There, his introspection and his scepticism reduce him almost to suicide. In this respect, Sabò resembles one of Svevo's early characters, but unlike Alfonso Nitti, Sabò is saved – saved by a return to his native province, by the resumed practice of his profession, forced on him in an emergency, and by the love of a good woman, all of which bring him an involvement in life which he had never known before. Sabò returns to his roots in the spring, a choice of season that is heavily symbolic. The narrator's account of healthy peasants working the land is highly idealized, as they are seen essentially as working in harmony with nature and enjoying a physical and psychological health which Sabò has lost and which prompts in him a desire to go 'in cerca di un immane contatto con la terra' [in search of an enormous contact with the land] (Jovine 1934, 213). Having rediscovered his roots and decided to marry Iolanda, Sabò can face the future with a new confidence which sounds almost like an endorsement of Mussolini's demographic policy:

> 'Noi due – pensava Giulio; – da noi due verranno dei figli, tanti figli'. Con un volo rapidissimo della fantasia li vide crescere, farsi adulti e andarsene a dorso nudo, con una muscolatura michelangiolesca, vanga in ispalla e testa al vento. Sudare e cantare, violare la terra con gesti potenti.
>
> Ma la riflessione gli diede una fitta nel cranio. Si svincolò dall'abraccio e affondò la testa tra le spighe come se avesse voluto restituire il suo cervello alla terra (Jovine 1934, 236).

> 'We two', thought Giulio, 'will have children, lots of children'. In a rapid flight of the imagination he saw them grow up, become adults and go off, stripped to the waist, with Michelangiolesque musculatures, with spades on their shoulders and the wind in their faces. To sweat and sing, to violate the earth with powerful gestures.
>
> But the thought gave him a sudden headache. He slid out of her arms and sank his head in the corn as if he wanted to give his brain back to the earth.

Jovine need not have been a Fascist to write in these ruralistic terms, but Fascist sympathies would undoubtedly have made him more inclined to do so. In the short novel *Ragazza sola*, published in *I diritti della scuola* in 1936-37, Livia goes from Rome to teach in a village school in order to recover her mental and physical health, but then returns to Rome and the man she loves. That Jovine at one stage of his development had Fascist leanings need not surprise us; he was probably no different in this respect from many idealistic young people who could see that Italian society was in need of reform and took at face value Fascism's promise to carry out that reform. As a primary school teacher he seems to have been dissatisfied with the state of the Italian educational system and greeted Gentile's reform of 1923 with considerable enthusiasm. He may have made no real distinction between Gentile's idealism and Fascism (Lalli 1981, 21). But how far did his Fascism take him? In 1925 he signed an appeal in support of Gentile's reforms which was published in *Il Matese* (Lalli 1981, 22). The British Library catalogue also attributes to Jovine co-authorship (with Lino Domenighini) of a very Fascist children's history of Italy, *La patria fascista. Storia di ieri e di oggi.* The volume itself gives only the surnames of the authors, without initials or first names. None of the recent monographs on Jovine even mention it (Carducci 1977: Lalli 1981: Procaccini 1986). The British Library catalogue gives its date of publication as 'ca 1930'. The Keeper of Italian Books at the British Library informs me that he is '60 per cent sure' of the attribution. Since Jovine was still expressing some support for Fascism, albeit unorthodox, in 1929, the attribution may well be correct.

In 1937, increasingly out of sympathy with the regime, Jovine went to work in North Africa. By the time he returned in 1939, he had lost all sympathy for Fascism, and the series of articles which he wrote in 1941 for the *Giornale d'Italia*, republished in book form as *Viaggio nel Molise*, is remarkable for its almost ostentatious abstention from ruralist rhetoric. Indeed, his comments on the 'asprezza della lotta per vivere' [harshness of the struggle for life] (Jovine 1976, 86) could be read as an ironic comment on the Fascist cliché of Molise as the 'provincia ruralissima'. Some comments, apparently bland if considered out of the context of Fascist policies, imply criticism of Fascist agricultural policy. These articles are inspired by a constant awareness of the poverty and hardship of peasant life, especially in the mountain areas, and by a keen sense of the social and political history of the region. Here we have traces of that historical material which is imaginatively transformed into the De Risio household in *Signora Ava* (1942). This awareness of the history of Molise, combined with an attention to present reality and a choice of more congenial literary models, emancipated Jovine from the ruralism which had vitiated *Un uomo provvisorio.*

There is a sense in which the problems of association with ruralism and ruralistic literature, which Levi and Jovine had to address, did not exist for Pavese.

He was proud of the fact that the poetry which he wrote between 1930 and 1935 was basically naturalistic, contrasting both with Fascist rhetoric and hermetic abstractions. In narrative fiction, his models were American rather than Italian. Pavese claimed – with considerable justification – to have discovered Italy by turning to America (Pavese 1962, 247).

It is now time for us to turn our attention to more authentic novels of peasant life.

CHAPTER 5

Fontamara: the novelist and the text

Fontamara is a remarkable first novel that is now more familiar to readers in the much revised versions which Silone published in the 1940s than it is in the original version which was written in 1930–1 and published in 1933. (Some monographs still give 1934 as the date of publication, but the text itself bears the date of 1 November 1933.) It is also the first Italian novel by a writer who feels himself able to identify with the peasantry: it is, therefore, one of the very few examples of national-popular literature in the Gramscian sense (Virdia 1979, 41). Since it is my contention that the revision process is the result both of greater artistic maturity on Silone's part and the changed social and political situation in Italy in the period immediately following the second world war, this chapter will discuss Silone's political formation and the publishing history of the successive versions of the novel. Other aspects of the novel and its revision will be dealt with in chapters 6, 7 and 8.

THE AUTHOR

Fontamara is the expression and result of a national and a personal crisis. The national crisis was that provoked by the agricultural recession which began around 1926 and was exacerbated by the great depression of 1929, while Silone's personal crisis stemmed from his experience and observation of Stalinism at work in Soviet Russia and his consequent break with the Communist Party. This break took him out of active politics and led him to turn to writing, which became not just a substitute for action, a way of appealing directly to the people, but also a way of meditating on politics.

Ignazio Silone is the pseudonym of Secondino Tranquilli, who was born in 1900 in Pescina de' Marsi, a small town in the Abruzzo region, and died in Geneva in 1978. One of the purposes of a pseudonym may be to conceal 'legal' identity and thus, in Silone's case, to spare his family some political embarrassment, but the alternative name used may also reveal important personality traits or tell us something significant about the writer's view of himself and his purposes. That of Silone is a case in point. His pseudonym is particularly helpful, since Silone has written about himself so movingly and powerfully – in the essays in

Uscita di sicurezza, for example – that he often seems to insert his mature self as autobiographer into the space between his readers and the young man he once was. Indeed, one sometimes wonders whether the younger Silone we know from the mature man's autobiographical writings is not to some extent an invention, as it were, of the older Silone. In fact, his novels have recently been read in terms of a 're-invention' of himself (Leake 2003).

This view might at first appear to lend some weight to recent charges that Silone was a Fascist police informer in the 1920s, in addition to being a leading organizer of the outlawed Italian Communist Party. After all, if that were the case, would he not have had cause to reinvent his youthful self? Especially if the complicated double game he was playing led to a nervous breakdown. Even if we do decide that Silone may have engaged in the process of myth-making in which all autobiographers to some extent indulge, his youthful pseudonym enables us to discover something of what the young Secondino Tranquilli was like and to conclude that he was a very remarkable person.

Silone's father was a once modestly prosperous farmer at Pescina de' Marsi, on the north-eastern edge of the Fucino plain, who came down in the world and at one point emigrated to South America. His mother was a weaver and a dyer. The former seems to have exerted a strong influence on his son's development: it was certainly through his father's perceptions and reactions that Silone first became aware of the appalling conditions in which the peasants of Abruzzo lived and worked. In *Uscita di sicurezza*, Silone relates a story of the first elections he could remember, probably those of 1907. Almost all workers in the area depended for their livelihood on the local landowner, Prince Giovanni Torlonia, whose property the fertile Fucino plain then was. Silone's father and uncles were no exception, for although they owned some land, presumably fairly marginal, in the hills to the north of the plain, they also leased some more fertile land on the Torlonia estate. Since the conditions under which the land was leased and labourers employed were stringent, to say the least, the Prince was very unpopular, and his decision to stand as a candidate in the elections came as a surprise. But, as his bailiffs explained, this was the age of democracy, and the people were free not to vote for the Prince who, by the same token, was free to prevent those who voted against him from working on his land. Since the area was still suffering from the over-population and surplus of labour which was a direct consequence of the draining of the former lake between 1852 and 1876, and since there was no alternative employment in the area, and no social services to support the unemployed, this was a serious threat. Even so, Silone's father apparently took the view that since he intended not to vote for the Prince he was bound, in all honesty, to declare his intention, if asked to do so, thereby running the risk of losing his – and his brothers' – tenancy. Only with great difficulty did friends and relatives persuade him to maintain an ambiguous silence. A certain rugged honesty and independence of mind, and a sense of social justice, seem to have been among the qualities which the young Silone inherited or learned from his father.

Silone also became aware at a very early age that the values on which people based their public lives were very different from those which shaped their private morality. This, too, is the subject of a very revealing episode in *Uscita di sicurezza*. Silone relates that one of the local gentry set his dog on a seamstress, who took him to court but could find neither witnesses prepared to give evidence on her behalf nor even a lawyer prepared to conduct her case. Bribed witnesses testified that she had provoked the dog, and she had to pay costs. The magistrate, a friend of the Tranquilli family, explained that, although he knew the facts of the case, he was bound by the evidence produced in court to reach the verdict he had presented.

Silone tells us that he thus came early in life to the conclusion that, for most people, however honest and just they might be in the confines of their private lives, justice and truth were abstract concepts which had nothing to do with everyday life in public. Lenin's biographers tell us that although he was a decent man in his personal relations, he was ruthless and intolerant in political life. Again, Silone could possibly be projecting back into his earlier life perceptions formed later. But even his mother, he tells us, a woman of apparently exemplary piety, reacted to the magistrate's story by reflecting that his was an 'orribile mestiere' [awful job], and that it was 'meglio badare ai fatti nostri in casa nostra' [better to stay at home and mind our own business] (Silone 1999, 805). This attitude is the one normally adopted by the inhabitants of Fontamara when faced with difficult situations. Silone's perception was reinforced by the exploitation and corruption which flourished on a massive scale in the chaos which followed the 1915 earthquake, in which his mother was killed. His father had died a year earlier, and Silone's education in boarding schools was the result of the charitable educational work of Don Orione, whom Silone describes with gratitude and affection in 'Incontro con uno strano prete' in *Uscita di sicurezza*.

In this social jungle, where was integrity to be found? Silone tells us that a local anarchist, a doctor in a nearby village, used to say that one had to become either a rebel or an accomplice – an anarchist or a conformist, in other words. But anarchism, in spite of its relatively strong Italian tradition, would have represented a lone battle, or a personal skirmish against authority, with no hope of victory: Silone records that this particular anarchist in fact lost his practice and literally starved to death.

Inevitably, then, it was the Socialist Party that attracted Silone's allegiance in his desire to work for social justice. He rose with remarkable rapidity in the party's hierarchy. He worked first as secretary of the Socialist agricultural workers' union, and then as a youth organizer. In 1921 he was one of the leading founder members of the Italian Communist Party, taking with him into the new formation a large part of the Socialist youth movement. It was shortly after this, in 1923, when writing articles from a Barcelona prison for the Spanish trade-union newspaper, *La Battailla*, that he started to use the pen name Silone, after the Abruzzese Quintus Pompaedius Silo, who led the Marsican rebels against Rome in the Social War of 90 BC. Since one of the aims of that war was to claim for all Italians the rights and privileges of Roman citizenship, the name express-es rebellion against excessively strong and oppressive central government, as well as identification with the underprivileged. A series of laws, beginning with the Lex Julia of 90 BC, duly extended the franchise: but it would not have escaped Silone's attention that in their struggle the Marsi suffered heavy losses. The inhabitants of Fontamara are similarly claiming no more than the rights of full citizenship from an oppressive central government, and they too pay heavily for their temerity.

Silone chose the first part of his pseudonym, Ignazio, when he published *Fontamara* in 1933. As he explains in *Uscita di sicurezza*, his use of the Christian name of Ignatius Loyola, the founder of the Jesuit order, was intended to express his feeling that the discipline involved in working for the Communist Party was very like that which was implied in accepting the rule and sense of purpose of a religious order that was organized on military lines. Gramsci also made frequent use of military metaphors to indicate that the revolutionary movement was to be an austerely dedicated and hierarchical force. In 1927 Harold Laski, wrote of the Bolsheviks that:

> They are, as a party, comparable to nothing so much as the Society of Jesus. There is, in both, the same rigorous and unyielding set of dogmas, the same iron rigour of discipline, the same passionate loyalty capable of unlimited self-confidence. [...] Like the Jesuit, the Russian Communist [...] feels himself essentially the servant of a great idea (Laski 1927, 51–2).

In Silone's case, however, an additional factor prompting his choice of pseudo-nym may have been the very prominent association of the Torlonia family with the main Jesuit church in Rome, the Gesù, an association prominently pro-claimed in marble lettering (see chapters 6 and 7).

But meanwhile, in 1926, a crucial year in the history of Fascism, a series of unsuccessful attempts on the life of Mussolini had provided the pretext for the so-called 'special laws' under which all opposition parties were suppressed. Of the anti-Fascists, the Communists were at that time the most determined and the best organized. In addition, they represented in Italy the 'red menace', fear of which had helped to bring Mussolini to power. It was therefore against them that Fascist repression was chiefly directed. Gramsci was arrested and condemned to twenty years in prison, in the course of which he died. Many others were incarcerated or sent in *confino*, to enforced residence in some remote place. Others chose to go abroad rather than conform and, like Turati and Salvemini, proudly referred to themselves by the ancient term of *fuorusciti*, indicating that they had deliberately chosen exile in order to continue a resistance which had become impossible at home. The party was then reorganized under two centres or headquarters. One was abroad, under Palmiro Togliatti, who went to Moscow, survived the Stalinist purges, and became the party's post-war leader. The clandestine Italian centre was directed by Silone, who remained in Italy for a time, distributing illegal newspapers and pamphlets, and organizing an internal underground network. It was during this period that he studied with particular care the social composition of Fascist support, publishing in *Stato Operaio* a number of articles whose conclusions have been endorsed by recent historians. The social analysis of Fascism which Silone offers in *Fontamara* is firmly grounded in observation and experience.

Clear references can be found in Silone's novels to his origins and his political activities. The title of his first novel derives from the Via di Fontamara in Pescina where the Tranquilli family lived until 1915, and the 'solito sconosciuto' [the usual unknown person] of that novel owes much to the author's own experience. The central character of *Il seme sotto la neve*, Pietro Spina, hiding from the Fascist police, finds that his memories of travelling all over Italy on behalf of the Peasant Leagues are particularly precious to him. It is one of Silone's strengths as a novelist that he never lost touch with his roots – or what he described as his 'subsoil' – in Abruzzo (Silone 1999, 1369-80).

Eventually, Silone too had to leave Italy. Arrested in and expelled from various countries, he finally settled in Switzerland in 1930, by which time he was seriously ill with tuberculosis. He was also on the point of leaving the Communist Party, with which he had become seriously disillusioned. Since the causes of Silone's disillusionment and the development of his political ideas are relevant to any interpretation of *Fontamara*, this is the appropriate point at which to outline his political position at the time of writing that novel. It was not easy, of course, for Silone to break with the Communist Party, given the intense nature of his commitment to it and to his companions: but his reasons for doing so are perfectly consistent with those which compelled him to join it in the first place. It was not Silone that had changed, but the party: or perhaps it would be more accurate to say that he had come to understand it more clearly.

Between 1921 and 1927 Silone visited Moscow several times as a member of the Italian Communist delegation. In Soviet Russia, he soon became aware that the Communist Third International, on which he had pinned his hopes for a truly democratic society, had degenerated into a bureaucracy and a tyranny. A crisis was provoked in 1927 when Stalin, as part of his manoeuvring to have

Trotsky expelled, attempted to impose a rigid party discipline on delegates, requiring them to condemn documents they had not even been allowed to read. Silone refused, regarding Stalin as demanding a sacrifice of honesty and integrity he was not prepared to make. Technically he could not resign: formally he had to be expelled. In 1929, the year in which the action of *Fontamara* is set, he was given sick leave. The definitive break came in 1931, when he was formally expelled. Officially at any rate he was still a member, albeit a disillusioned member on his way out of the party, when he wrote *Fontamara*, and one would therefore expect his analysis of the plight of the *fontamaresi* to be a marxian one in its general outlines: the possibility that the Socialism of the novel may not be entirely orthodox will be considered in chapter 8.

A number of factors led Silone to turn to writing in his Swiss exile. His isolation effectively cut him off from political action from 1927 onwards: indeed, abstention from political activity was a condition of asylum imposed on refugees by a Swiss government which valued its neutrality highly and was determined that it should not be compromised. Silone was, moreover, seriously ill, and thought himself likely to die. Writing was a means of continuing his struggle and of appealing directly to the people. But why a novel, rather than an autobiography, or a piece of political analysis, such as Salvemini and Borgese were writing? One possible answer to that question is that autobiography was out of the question for Silone for the time being, since coming to terms with his still developing experience was as yet too painful to be dealt with – it was only later, after the break with the party had become definitive, that he felt able to depict his own dilemmas in *Pane e vino* and *Il seme sotto la neve*. And in any case, his most urgent concern seems to have been to write not about himself but about the effects of Fascism on rural Italy. He did indeed also write a political analysis of Fascism – *Der Faschismus – seine Entstehung und seine Entwicklung* (Zürich 1934) – but, as Silone explained to his fellow-exile Carlo Rosselli, who had invited him to contribute to the periodical *Giustizia e Libertà*, there was a sound common-sense reason for opting for the novel form:

> Non è per caso che la forma prevalente della mia attività, qui, sia letteraria. Anzitutto, non tutti si lasciano sermoneggiare, ma tutti si lasciano raccontare: *Fontamara* è stato letto da alcune centinaia di migliaia di stranieri, che non avrebbero mai letto un opuscolo o un libro sistematico. Inoltre c'è una larga parte della realtà che vive in noi, la quale non può estrinsecarsi che in forma fantastica [...] (Bagnoli 1984, 245–6).

> It is not an accident that the main form of my activity here is literary. First of all, not everyone will let you sermonize at them, but everyone will let you tell them a story: *Fontamara* has been read by hundreds of thousands

of foreigners who would never read a systematic pamphlet or book. And then, there is a great deal of reality alive inside us that can only be expressed in imaginative form.

A further reason for writing a novel may be that a work of narrative fiction can deal with both the particular and the universal, although Silone perhaps only gradually became aware of this, with the result that there is more emphasis in later versions of the novel than in the first on the story's wider implications (see chapter 8).

THE NOVEL

Fontamara was written in 1930–1. An Italian edition, in the Fascist period, was out of the question, and it did not appear at all until the spring of 1933, when it came out in a German translation, with the help of 800 subscribers. The Italian version came out in Paris in November of the same year. Its international success was remarkable, and no doubt came quickly because it could be used as anti-Fascist propaganda, although that fact alone is clearly not enough to explain the spell the novel continues to cast over successive generations of readers. It is true that the way in which the novel was used for propaganda purposes, particularly during the second world war, when thousands of copies were distributed to Italian prisoners of war, has led some critics to regard Silone only as an anti-Fascist writer with no message of more general significance. It was not uncommon in the post-war period, when he began to publish in Italy, to find reviewers who affected compassion for a writer they regarded as linked exclusively to one period in Italy's history, describing him as a novelist without a cause, as though oppression of the poor and underprivileged had, in a newly enlightened world, suddenly ceased to exist. Others, appalled by what they saw as Silone's anti-literary style, dismissed him as one who had won a reputation abroad for reasons which had nothing to do with art or literature (Russo 1951, 378). It can be shown, however, that the post-war versions of *Fontamara* were directly relevant to the situation in Italy in the 1940s. This theme will be developed in chapter 7, while chapter 8 will examine the more general implications of the presence in the novel of a Christ-figure.

But since there is still considerable confusion in Silone criticism about the post-war revisions of the text, it may be helpful to outline at this point the history of the text.

The 1933 Italian text was republished in some time in the 1940s, most probably in 1945 according to British Library staff, by Jonathan Cape of London. It was this version which was used for propaganda purposes and which was first read by many Italians. This was unfortunate for Silone's reputation, since the text was badly printed and full of errors. In 1945, Ernesto Buonaiuti began to publish it for the first time in Italy in his review *Il Risveglio*. Buonaiuti had much in common with Silone; he had been a Roman Catholic priest, but had been unfrocked because of his modernist views. Subsequently he had lost his university teaching position since he had refused to sign the required declaration of loyalty to the Fascist regime. He also shared Silone's admiration for Mazzini. The remarkable affinity of thought and culture between Silone and Buonaiuti, which has never been studied as it should be, helps to explain Silone's choice of review. Unfortunately, however, the review collapsed later in the same year.

At the time of writing, it has not been possible to locate a complete run of *Il Risveglio*, but the impression given by critics that the 1933 and 1945 texts are identical, is mistaken. The 1945 version is considerably revised (Moloney 1996). With the collapse of the review, a further revised edition was published in 1947 by Casa Editrice Faro, which had already brought out the first edition in Italy of *Il seme sotto la neve* (1945). The 1949 Mondadori edition also contains further revisions, and can be regarded as the definitive edition, since the changes made for the 1953 edition were minor. Silone's successive revisions enable us to study in some detail the evolution of his thought and the way in which he changed the text to suit the changing circumstances in which it was republished.

But since it was as an anti-Fascist writer that Silone first presented himself to the reading public, the next chapter will be devoted to an analysis of his depiction of rural society in the Fascist period.

CHAPTER 6

Fontamara and rural society in crisis

Fontamara accurately depicts the extension of Fascist power into the country-side, but it also shows it as disturbing traditional power structures, which the gentry seek to preserve as far as they can by transferring their allegiance to Fascism, while the peasants lose faith in them and, reduced to new depths of despair, are made ready for radical change.

THE PEASANTRY

Fontamara consists of ten chapters, which are narrated in the first person singular by three narrators in turn. They are the members of a peasant family, Giuvà, his wife Matalè, and their unnamed son, who have escaped to Switzerland from a village in Abruzzo, which has been subjected to a particularly brutal attack by Fascist *squadristi*. The choice of narrative method is bold, and seems to indicate remarkable confidence on Silone's part that he can so identify with peasant characters and peasant mentality that, when they speak in their own voice, his own more sophisticated and educated voice will not be heard. It is one of the criticisms that can be made of Pavese's *Paesi tuoi* and Moravia's *La romana*, for example, that the narrator's perceptions are not those of the Turinese mechanic and Roman prostitute in whose voices they are expressed. Silone is thus able to present himself in his preface in the fairly traditional role of transcriber and editor; but he is not content simply to adopt a passive role, and he prefaces the narrative with an introduction in which he gives the reader a short description of Fontamara and its way of life, an account of the draining of Lake Fucino and of the arrival of his unexpected visitors, and discusses briefly the problem which has faced those Italian novelists, from Manzoni onwards, who have wished to depict in their fictions lower-class characters whose native language is not standard Italian but a dialect which would be more or less incomprehensible to their mainly urban and middle-class readers.

Within certain limits, Silone's choice of narrative technique is successful. His-torical and contextual information of a kind which might not crop up naturally in a conversation between peasants is conveyed in the preface, leaving the three narrators free to concentrate on their experiences. It is true that it is not easy to distinguish between them on the basis of character or speech; one has to rely instead on an awareness of the gender of the speaker or of where the action is taking place – on the Fucino plain women were generally not employed on the land as day-labourers, and so Matalè relates what takes place in the village while the men are at work, and the son gives an account of his attempts, with Berardo, to find work in Rome. At times, however, the narrators seem to speak with Silone's voice, as when they explain local customs or circumstances.

One may feel, too, that Silone has not so much resolved the dialect problem as evaded it, by merely warning his readers that the *fontamaresi* do not speak Italian, which is for them a foreign language, but their very limited dialect. He has translated their narrative, he tells us, as best he can, into the language learnt at school (Silone 1998, 15). One wonders, after Verga, whether such a warning is necessary. But although the language is 'borrowed', as Silone puts it, he insists that the way in which the story is told is authentic. And this is where Silone, technically, has been most successful. His narrators use a rambling, anecdotal method, full of listings and repetitions, which is the product of that long tradition of story-telling to which he refers in the preface, as does Jovine in his presentation of *Signora Ava*, and which ethnologists such as G.B. Bronzini and R. Cianferoni have in recent years begun to study systematically. Silone also succeeds in creating characters who speak out of a remarkable but totally convincing ignorance of the specific political events taking part in the world beyond the mountains which are the limits of both their physical and intellectual and cultural horizons. But at the same time they combine this ignorance with a natural shrewdness and a perception of the way in which social structures work to their disadvantage. Their naivety may tempt sophisticated urban readers to look down on them and to criticize their behaviour and reactions as inadequate or inappropriate. But at the same time that very naivety is often the expression of qualities which the novelist regards as admirable – honesty, openness and spontaneity – as well as of a basic humanity which exposes the oppression under which the peasants suffer, so that the reader's final reaction is one of sympathy and respect. And although their ignorance and ineptitude in some situations may seem comic, they are capable of slyly laughing back at 'clever' outsiders and making readers question the validity of conventional values.

The primary extra-text to which the novel points is the social reality of the village of Fontamara in the year 1929. Silone implies that the village is fictitious, when he points out that it does not figure on any map. But it is, he asserts, typical or symbolic not only of the backward area of Marsica, but also of much of southern Italy (Silone 1933, v). The village is small and remote, little more than a hamlet, and consists of about one hundred houses. It is what in the Italian system of local government is designated a *frazione*, like Levi's Gaglianello; that is to say, it has no Town Hall or municipal offices and is part of the municipality of Avezzano. Its name has the same function as the symbolic names which George Eliot uses in *Adam Bede*, like 'Hayslopes' in 'Loamshire', which borders on 'Strongshire'. It differs from the convincing imitations of real names used by Thomas Hardy, such as 'Egdon' or 'Casterbridge'. Fontamara's name refers to the 'bitter spring' which is the source of controversy, while juxtaposition of the bleak hills on which Fontamara is situated with the fertile Fucino plain aims at the same sort of symbolic effect which is achieved by Scott's border country in *Old Mortality* or D.H. Lawrence's juxtaposition of rural and industrial landscapes in *Lady Chatterley's Lover*, in that it offers a landscape which is both real and symbolic, both an historical and social entity and a realm of the imagination.

The village is situated in the hills to the north of the Fucino plain, but although the professional middle classes – priests, doctors, lawyers, as well as the larger landowners – all live in or near the 'capoluogo', it is far from being a one-class, still less a classless society. Most of the houses are little more than hovels ('casucce', 'catapecchie'), single-room dwellings with one opening which functions as door, window and chimney, exactly like those described by Levi in *Cristo si è fermato a Eboli*, surviving examples of which, some still inhabited, are still to be seen in the south. Parents, children and animals live, sleep and procreate in that one room. It has been estimated that in the 1930s between 300,000 and 400,000 Italians were living in hovels made of no more than earth and sticks; many others, as Levi shows, were living in caves. The statement that most houses in Fontamara are of this kind implies of course that there are exceptions, and in the definitive version Silone makes it clear what these are; there are about ten larger houses and an ancient *palazzo*, no longer lived in and almost falling down (Silone 1998, 8). The word *palazzo* in this context denotes no more than a large house; its empty state may be a result of the 1915 earthquake, which devastated the region and figures prominently in Silone's other accounts of the area, or it may be a convenient symbol of the village's economic decline; Silone does not tell us. What he does make clear is that the larger houses belong to the small landowners and that on Fontamara's social scale there are two rungs only. On the lower are the 'cafoni', a disparaging term used for landless peasants and labourers; on the upper are the 'piccoli proprietari'. Members of a third category, consisting of Baldissera the cobbler, Elvira the dyer, and probably a barber and a carpenter, but perhaps not the local prostitute, ironically named Marietta but vulgarly known as Sorcanera or 'Black Fanny', are to be found on both rungs. As Caroline White has pointed out, 'incidental and allusory evidence [...] suggests that most Mediterranean villages are highly stratified' (White 1980, 3), and Fontamara is no exception to the general rule. N.T. Colclough, describing peasant society in a village he calls Pertosa, writes:

> The peasant hierarchy could be thought of as a continuum; at the bottom
> were the dishonoured and the landless, at the top families whose honour

was unimpinged and who had sufficient land to meet their needs. The position of individual families on this scale was fluctuating and precarious; the misconduct of a daughter, the death of a household head, a bad harvest and a score of other factors of this sort could lead to a rapid descent (Colclough 1971, 214; cf. Rossi-Doria 1956, 21).

Silone also makes it clearer in the later versions that the society he is describing is stratified but not static. The *braccianti* aspire to land ownership – although they rarely achieve it – either through a judicious marriage alliance or by dint of hard work and sacrifice. It is much easier for small farmers to sink to the level of landless labourers; Giuvà relates in chapter 3 that almost all the men of the village are compelled by poverty to conform to what was once the practice of the poorer *braccianti*, namely to get up before dawn in order to walk to Fossa and stand around in a humiliating human cattle-market, waiting to be hired by the wealthier landowners. This means trudging up to nineteen kilometres a day before starting work and, of course, reversing the journey, this time uphill, at the end of the day. There was nothing unusual about this; peasants working on the Paestum plain used to get up at between one and two a.m. for a ten-hour working day. We also know from other sources that the increased supply of labour which resulted from the ban on emigration led at this time to a depression in wages, and some *cafoni* were so desperate for work that they once again accepted the custom, common in southern Italy before the first world war, whereby employers fixed wages only after the work was done. Few peasants own no land whatever, and the 'cafone senza terra' [landless peasant] is generally despised by his fellow-villagers. Giuvà is aware that this moral condemnation of the landless peasant as a weak, stupid and passive person is based on the low price of land in former days and no longer relates to the current situation; but the peasants are presented as being conservative in their attitudes, and even Berardo, who refuses for as long as he can to conform, sees the acquistion of land as the essential prerequisite for marriage to Elvira. Giuvà clearly regards the need to stand in the market place and offer himself for hire as humiliating, and the system reinforces the landowners' contempt for the *cafoni*.

Silone is describing in *Fontamara*, from the point of view of the peasants, a process of proletarianization which began with the draining of Lake Fucino and was accentuated by the agricultural crisis of 1926 and its consequences. As one might expect, it is consistent with Marxist-Leninist theory. In *The Eighteenth Brumaire* Marx described a peasantry being gripped ever more tightly by capital and subject to increasingly onerous taxation. Assuming that contemporary France was representative of wider historical processes, he predicted the disappearance of the European peasant, who would join the ranks of the proletariat. The earlier disappearance of the English peasantry seemed to Marx to confirm that this was the inevitable course of history. Marx's views were substantially repeated by Engels in *The Peasant Question in France and Germany*, according to which the peasant is a survival of a past mode of production, doomed to become a rural proletarian unless rescued by Socialist co-operation (Marx-Engels 27, 1990, 486). The peasant family, unable to produce even its own means of subsistence, falls further into debt – as do, in Silone's account, the peasants of Fontamara. Goodman and Redclift comment:

> It is a measure, perhaps, of their confidence in the correctness of their analysis that Marx and Engels did not need to take account, theoretically, of situations in which the peasantry would survive (Goodman and Redclift 1981, 5).

But Silone, far from being convinced of the inevitability of the disappearance of the peasant class, sees its survival as desirable, and in this respect he is not at all Marxian.

The peasants are trapped by their poverty and ignorance in a harsh routine of toil which seems unchanging and unchangeable. Since the novel's action takes place in 1929, the traditional escape route of emigration to the USA has now been closed. In addition, Silone fictionally anticipates the application of a ban on internal migration that was enacted only in 1931 at the height of the depression. He thus distorts or telescopes the historical facts in order to make the mountains surrounding Fontamara and the plain take on the aspect of a prison wall:

> serrano il feudo come una barriera senza uscita. [...] La vita degli uomini, delle bestie e della terra sembrava cosí racchiusa in un cerchio immobile saldato dalla chiusa morsa delle montagne e dalle vicende del tempo. Saldato in un cerchio naturale, immutabile, come in una specie di ergastolo (Silone 1998, 8-9).

> they shut off the Feud like a wall with no way out. [...] The life of men, animals and land thus seemed enclosed in a motionless circle welded together by the closed vice of the mountains and by the rotation of the seasons. Welded into a natural, unchangeable circle, as though in some kind of prison.

And with their intellectual horizons as limited as their physical, Silone shows the peasants as having a clear view of their place in the social hierarchy. In chapter I, Michele Zompa gives an account of local social structures which is naive only in appearance. He is speaking to Cavalier Pelino, who has come to collect signatures for the petition which, although they do not know it at this stage, will deprive them of their water:

'In capo a tutti, c'è Dio, padrone del cielo. Questo ognuno lo sa. Poi viene
il principe Torlonia, padrone della terra.'
'Poi vengono le guardie del principe.
'Poi vengono i cani delle guardie del principe.
'Poi nulla.
'Poi ancora nulla.
'Poi ancora nulla.
'Poi vengono i cafoni.
'E si può dire ch'è finito'.
'Ma le autorità dove le metti?' chiese ancora più irritato il forestiero.
'Le autorità' intervenne a spiegare Ponzio Pilato 'si dividono tra il quar-
to e il quinto posto. Secondo la paga. Il quarto posto (quello dei cani) è
immenso. Questo ognuno lo sa' (Silone 1998, 29).

'Above everybody there's God, the lord of heaven. Everybody knows
that.
'Then comes Prince Torlonia, lord of the earth.
'Then come the Prince's guards.
'Then come the Prince's guards' dogs.
'Then nothing.
'Then nothing again.
'Then nothing again.
'Then come the *cafoni*.
'And that's it, you might say'.
'But where do you put the authorities?' asked the stranger, growing even
angrier.
    'The authorities', put in Pontius Pilate, by way of explanation, 'are in
the third and fourth categories. According to their pay. The fourth cate-
gory (the dogs') is enormous. Everybody knows that'.

Called 'cafoni' by the rest of society, they have come to accept the disparaging implications of the term; one is reminded of the American James Baldwin's
bitter injunction to his nephew to remember that to be born black in a world of
white supremacy was to be born 'a worthless human being'. The peasants
assume, moreover, that the social order is as immutable as the round of the seasons. Confronted by the news that the stream is to be diverted, the villagers cannot believe it:

Perciò noi pensammo che la deviazione del ruscello probabilmente fosse
una nuova beffa. Infatti, sarebbe proprio la fine di tutto, se il capriccio
degli uomini cominciasse a influire perfino sugli elementi creati da Dio,
cominciasse a deviare il corso del sole, dell'acqua stabiliti da Dio. Sarebbe

come se ci avessero raccontato che gli asini stavano per volare; o che il Principe Torlonia stava per cessare di essere un Principe; o che i cafoni stavano per cessare di patire la fame; in una parola, che le eterne leggi di Dio stavano per cessare di essere le leggi di Dio (Silone 1998, 32).

So we thought the diversion of the stream was probably another practical joke. In fact, it really would be the end of everything if men's whims began to influence even the elements created by God, began to deviate the course of the sun, the course of the water, all ordained by God. It would be as if they had told us that asses were going to fly; or that Prince Torlonia was going to stop being a Prince; or that peasants were going to stop suffering hunger; in a word, that the eternal laws of God were going to stop being the eternal laws of God.

The concept of eternity must in the minds of the peasants be somewhat flexible, since they know that Lake Fucino, which was the third largest lake in Italy after Lakes Garda and Maggiore, was drained in the previous century. Each generation of peasants assumes that the way they remember things is the way things have 'always' been: in an illiterate society with no photographs or written records, 'always' means 'within living memory'. On another level, Silone is pointing out that his peasants have a false consciousness which accepts the present social order as inevitable and which will be broken down by the pressure of events.

In such adverse circumstances one might expect the peasants to cooperate to alleviate common hardships; but such is not the case. This small society is rent by bitter divisions. In his preface, Silone tells us that when the harvest is unusually good, the unexpected profit is usually spent on lawsuits:

Perché bisogna sapere che a Fontamara non vi sono due famiglie che non siano parenti; nei villaggi di montagna, in genere, tutti finiscono con l'essere parenti; tutte le famiglie, anche le più povere, hanno interessi da spartire tra di loro, e in mancanza di beni hanno da spartire la miseria; a Fontamara perciò non c'è famiglia che non abbia qualche lite pendente. La lite sonnecchia negli anni magri, ma s'inasprisce di repente appena c'è qualche soldo da dare all'avvocato. E sono sempre le stesse liti, interminabili liti, che si tramandano di generazione in generazione in processi interminabili, in spese interminabili, in rancori sordi, inestinguibili, per stabilire a chi appartiene un cespuglio di spine. Il cespuglio si brucia, ma si continua a litigare, con livore più acceso (Silone 1998, 10).

Because you need to know that in Fontamara there are no two families that are not related; in mountain villages, generally speaking, everyone is related to everyone else; all the families, even the poorest, have interests in common, and in the absence of wealth, they have their poverty to share out; and so in Fontamara there is not a family without a lawsuit pending. The case, we know, may lie dormant in the lean years, but it becomes bitter again as soon as there is a bit of money to give the lawyer. And the cases are always the same interminable cases, handed down from generation to generation in never-ending actions, in never-ending expense, in half-hidden, never-ending grudges, to establish the ownership of a clump of thorn-bushes. The clump burns down, but the litigation smoulders on, with more venom than ever.

The novel describes a year in which the harvest is far from good, and the behaviour patterns of the peasants are, as a result, perhaps even worse than those described in the preface. When the workmen arrive to divert the stream, the women are alerted, but at first they all find some pretext to avoid going to the town to protest: 'Come al solito, nessuno "poteva" andare. Ognuna insomma voleva fare i fatti suoi' [As usual no-one "could" go. They all wanted to mind their own business.] (Silone 1998, 33). And when the stream is diverted, each villager seeks to secure his own water supply at the expense of the others. Pilato tells the workmen: 'Vedete, l'importante è che voi lasciate l'acqua per i miei fagioli [...] gli altri crepino' [Look, the important thing is for you to leave enough water for my beans [...] The others can peg out.] (Silone 1998, 67). Jovine's short story 'La diga' is also about a peasant who tries to monopolize the water of a stream (Jovine 1960, 207–13). Although Giuvà sees Pilato as an egoist, he is doing no more than articulate what the others feel. It is difficult to accept at face value the view of those who argue, as Whyte does, that Silone's peasants 'have a certain cohesion and act together instinctively in certain matters' (Whyte 1970, 51). One of the points the novel makes is that they have to learn, with some difficulty, to act together.

Doubts have been expressed about the accuracy of Silone's depiction of this aspect of peasant life, since it conflicts with many observations and assumptions made about peasant communities, even by experts in the field. Robert Redfield, for example, writes that: 'We may summarize the economic character of the peasant village by saying that it combines the primitive brotherhood of the pre-civilized folk community with the economic nexus of civilized society', and that 'the peasant village maintains its local solidarity' (Redfield 1965, 33). The concept of local solidarity in fact underpins the first chapter of Redfield's book, and assumptions such as these have led writers such as Maraspini to comment: 'Without wishing to impugn the sincerity of the authors who have described the south in their novels, one cannot avoid noticing that to achieve the desired effect of stagnation and gloom, they have tended to excessively darken the picture' (Maraspini 1968, 257).

The implication of comments such as this seems to be either that Silone has described Fontamara in terms of its failure to conform to his preconceived (Marxian) norms of class solidarity, or else that he has polemically exaggerated the divisive consequences of poverty in order to throw into greater relief the villagers' achievement in winning through to a form of associationism. That Levi, in *Cristo si è fermato a Eboli*, describes the village of Gagliano in terms of an already well established sense of community and brotherhood, is likely to puzzle readers still further; can both accounts of peasant society be accurate and reliable? Salvemini, who knew the south well, found Silone's peasants 'at times too stupid or insufficiently human' (Origo 1984, 215). Comments such as these seem to reveal a profound misunderstanding of the novel – a point to which I shall return in chapter 8 – and Silone's characteristic response was to set his peasants' poverty and ignorance into even greater relief in the later versions, filling out the details of their daily trudge to work, for example, and adding a comment on their weariness, as well as inserting references to their pursuit of their own interests (Silone 1998, 30, 33, 62, 66, 108).

That Silone polemically stresses the naivety and ignorance of his peasants seems undeniable, but one must not exaggerate the degree to which he exaggerates. A work of art does not function in the same way as a sociological treatise, after all. There are a number of possible reasons why Silone stresses certain aspects, although he certainly is not concerned merely to demonstrate 'the idiocies of rural life', to use Marx's phrase from the *Communist Manifesto* 'that Western political scientists drag out whenever Communist "manipulation of the peasantry" is discussed' (Tarrow 1967, 10). Silone explained to Salvemini that in his view peasant morals and character had been corrupted by changes (Origo 1984, 214) – in other words, that they had been brutalized. This process of brutalization may no doubt be an aspect of the process of proletarianization which Marx had described. But, paradoxically, it is this factor that enables Silone to assert the inherent superiority of the peasantry over the gentry. The latter oppress the former in order to preserve or improve their already relatively high standard of living, whereas the peasants seek no more than their right to a human dignity which the gentry, by their unscrupulous self-seeking, have lost.

Studies of peasant life in Italy, however, provide ample evidence that Silone's account of village life – allowing for a certain heightening of the colours – is substantially accurate. E.C. Banfield, in a controversial account of the values on which the inhabitants of a southern village base their lives, argued that the unit on which social values are based is the nuclear family; everyone else – especially other members of the family – is looked upon as a potential rival or enemy. Everyone, according to this account, pursues only the interests of his own family unit and acts on the assumption that everyone else will do likewise. For this pattern of behaviour, Banfield coined the term 'amoral familism' (Banfield 1958,

10). It is doubtful, however, whether the value-judgement implied in the epithet 'amoral' is appropriate, and more recent monographs have tended to prefer the noun 'familism' without the adjective, thus recognizing that a moral code does indeed exist in such societies. It is also a matter of dispute as to whether – or to what extent – support or cooperation is expected from or given by other members of the family. White surveys the literature on the subject and concludes that her own observation 'accords with other studies which suggest that close kin are expected to cooperate, and do feel a mutual obligation to help in crises' (White 1980, 69–70).

At first, no clear-cut pattern of relationships seems to emerge from the behaviour of the 'cafoni' of Fontamara. The preface suggests that an extreme form of familism is the norm; but Giuvà and Matalè do what they can to help their niece Elvira, and also Berardo, who wishes to marry her. On the other hand, Giuvà is on very bad terms with his brother-in-law, Ponzio Pilato, 'in quanto nessuno di noi era disposto a sacrificarsi per l'altro' [in so far as neither of us was inclined to sacrifice himself for the other] (Silone 1998, 66), even attacking him with a pruning-hook when he discovers him urging the workmen diverting the stream to leave enough water to irrigate his own land without regard for the welfare of others. Berardo reciprocates Giuvà's friendship by accompanying him to work, thus preventing him from engaging in further conflict with Pilato. Giuvà, however, is well aware that Berardo has no land; he cannot therefore be considered a rival as far as the water is concerned, as Pilato is. Support may therefore be seen as being given to friends and relatives only in situations in which their vital interests do not clash with those of the nuclear family, and Giuvà's observation that 'Quando c'è la fame i cafoni hanno sempre avuto un solo scampo: divorarsi tra di loro' [When there is hunger about, peasants have always had only one means of survival: devouring each other] (Silone 1998, 140) is not invalidated, merely modified.

The general accuracy of Silone's observation of peasant life in the region – which, after all, he knew well – has been confirmed by recent field work, which suggests that a number of factors may influence the degree of cooperation and mutual support which obtains within a given community. These factors include the prevailing system of land tenure; shared perceptions of the community's history; competition for scarce resources – obviously a dominant factor in Fontamara – and shared attitudes towards external hostile forces.

THE GALANTUOMINI

Don Abbacchio

Chief amongst the external forces operating to the detriment of the peasants is, of course, Fascism; and, in 1929, Fascism has through the Lateran treaty allied itself with the church. Ironic reference is made to the Concordat in chapter I, with an account of a sermon preached by the time-serving priest Don Abbacchio, who had informed his congregation that with the Concordat 'cominciava anche per i cafoni una nuova epoca' [a new era was beginning for the peasants too] (Silone 1998, 26). In fact, it seems that the only tangible benefit to come their way is a new species of flea, a favour granted to them by Jesus at the request of the Pope – rather than the Fucino land, or exemption from taxes, or a good harvest, which were the gifts Jesus had wanted to bestow. The fleas have the merit of distracting the peasants from thoughts of sin without harming the financial interests of the church or of the so-called 'good Christians' further up in the social hierarchy. In retrospect, we see that the preface's image of the village houses clustered around the church bell-tower like a flock of sheep around the shepherd is fiercely ironical.

Silone thus comments on what he sees as the true nature of the Lateran treaty, and he reinforces his criticism of it in chapter VI, when Don Abbacchio concludes his sermon on the charming peasant-saint Giuseppe da Copertino, who performed cartwheels for the delight of the Virgin Mary, by criticizing the villagers for their lack of discipline – a favourite Fascist slogan-word – and for their non-payment of taxes. Here, Silone presents the priest as the worthy representative of a church which has allied itself with a repressive government. Since the worldly-wise and grasping priest's name is derived from the regional term for the succulent roast lamb which was traditionally – in the age before the freezer – eaten at Easter, he is sharply contrasted with the Lamb of God whose sacrificial example he so conspicuously fails to imitate, and we usually encounter him in situations in which he is attempting to squeeze a few more *lire* out of the peasants in return for his inadequate pastoral ministrations, or in alliance with the wealthy, as when, in a drunken state, he concludes the banquet in chapter II with the final words of the Latin Mass, 'Ite missa est', and leads the guests out into the garden to urinate, or when, in chapter III, he comes to warn the villagers not to oppose the Impresario, arriving to do so in the Impresario's horse-drawn trap.

A comparison of the sermon episode in chapter VI of the final version and chapter VII of the 1933 version shows that interesting and important changes have taken place. In the first edition, Don Abbacchio does not mention his flock's failure to pay their taxes; instead, he exhorts them to pay about fifty *lire* for a priest – presumably himself – to reside in the village for special devotions lasting nine days. The only point at issue is his greed, a point which had in any case already been made in the same chapter by his raising the price of a mass from ten to twenty *lire* (at a time when agricultural wages are falling). The revision gives additional sharpness to Silone's criticism of the church's compromise with the state. A second improvement lies in the identity of the saint about whom Don Abbacchio preaches; the choice in the original version of San Berardo, the patron saint of the Marsica and protector of the peasants, was a clumsy way of signalling the way in which Berardo's role was to change as a result of his encounter with the Solito Sconosciuto. The revision introduces a welcome note of humour as well as removing a certain ponderousness, while Don Abbacchio becomes more clearly emblematic of the church's failure, by its tolerance and even encouragement of Fascism, to defend authentic Christian values. Silone's view of the Concordat as an unholy alliance between church and state would have been reinforced by Pope Pius XI's notorious description of Mussolini as 'the man sent by providence'. His account of his own development in *Uscita di sicurezza* also suggests that the Concordat would merely have confirmed a view of the church which he had formed at a relatively early age, and that Don Abbacchio, while owing something to Manzoni's cowardly Don Abbondio, is also modelled in part on the priest who taught him the catechism at Pescina. Both priests disclaim any interest in what happens outside the church. Neither preaches a social gospel.

Indeed, one could hardly expect Don Abbacchio to start putting the world to rights – not simply out of cowardice, but out of self-interest. Remote southern hill and mountain parishes were not likely to attract the best men, and priests in the south were in any case traditionally part of the local ruling oligarchy, often owning land (like Verga's Reverendo, in the story of that title in the *Novelle rusticane*), and sometimes related to a local landowner. Fontamara's priest is not so related; but he is closely associated, as we see in chapter II when the women of the village go to Avezzano to protest when work starts on the deviation of the stream.

As is often the case in Silone's novels, this episode is characterized by a certain robust, sardonic humour, even by elements of farce, as the superior townspeople play cruel jokes on the ignorant villagers who do not even know that the *sindaco* has been replaced by a *podestà* (see chapter 3). But, as always, the humour reveals, not conceals, the solid bedrock of seriousness on which the episode is based. For the women are taken, much to their surprise, to the house of the new mayor, who turns out to be a relative newcomer, known only as the Impresario (or entrepreneur). A banquet is being held at his home to celebrate his appointment, attended by all the local notables, including Don Abbacchio, and Don Circostanza, the former *sindaco*. Since the women also call on another local landowner, Don Carlo Magna, this second chapter constitutes an effective introduction to local power structures at a moment when they are being subjected to new pressures as a direct result of the extension of Fascist control over the countryside.

Clientelism

By presenting us with a peasant's-eye view of Fontamara, Silone enables us to see rural society as highly stratified. Chapter I introduces us to the peasants and rural artisans; chapter II introduces us to the gentry and to the patronage system, or clientelism, on which the peasants are dependent. The *galantuomini* are at the top of the very localized society hierarchy; Prince Torlonia, since he has massive wealth and lives in Rome, is seen in both a broader context and as part of a national hierarchy. (A lengthy passage in the 1933 version (Silone 1933, 142–3), describing the workings of clientelism from local to national level, was subsequently omitted, probably because it was incompatible with the peasant's-eye view of the situation.)

The local gentry owe their power and position in part to their control of land and therefore of employment possibilities, in part to their monopoly of scarce skills, since they are the only class which has received any education above the primary level. Local professionals, teachers, lawyers, doctors and the more important local government officials are recruited from their ranks. They therefore dominate the patronage system, which is present throughout southern Italy. Clientelism is often described by its participants as an exchange of favours – 'uno scambio di favori' – in which the patron gives, or sometimes only promises to give jobs, loans, letters of introduction to influential people in exchange for political support, gifts in kind, or money. That 'gifts' are sometimes handed over by the client has also led to the system being described in terms of friendship ('l'amicizia'), which adds another dimension of meaning both to Don Circostanza's nickname and Berardo's willingness to die for the sake of a friend.

The peasant's illiteracy, or near-illiteracy, and his occupational insecurity make him dependent on the system, even though it demonstrably operates to his disadvantage in that it keeps the rich rich and the poor poor. Tarrow makes the valid point that clientelism is quite different from feudalism, in that in feudal society social relationships were formalized, hierarchical and legally sanctioned, and obligations were mutual. Clientelism, on the other hand, is informal, shifting, and is not recognized by the existence of formal institutions (Tarrow 1967, 69). Nor are its obligations mutual, since only the peasants are bound by them. This is the point Levi makes when, in *Cristo si è fermato a Eboli*, he describes the two doctors of Gagliano as exercising a bastardized version of feudalism over the peasants.

Since Silone gives to one of his characters a 'feudal' name, it is not immediately clear that he is aware of the distinction, but in fact the peasants themselves see clientelism as a consequence of the influx of lawyers and administrators – described by Sonnino as 'a southern plague' – brought in by the process of unification (Silone 1998, 150). Another effect of clientelistic relationships of which Silone is well aware is that they are independent and vertical, and therefore discourage horizontal or class loyalties. Clientelism and familism are therefore mutually reinforcing. Hence the 'cafoni' are in no position to make common cause against either their patrons or Fascism. One of the problems which concerns Silone is that of finding a way of breaking through this vicious circle.

Don Carlo Magna

The two key figures in the previously well established but now threatened local patronage system are Don Carlo Magna and Don Circostanza. The former's name seems at first to link him with a feudal aristocracy, but we learn that his wealth dates only to the post-unification period when one of his ancestors purchased former church lands which 'i buoni cristiani non osavano ricomperare' [good Christians did not dare to buy back] (Silone 1998, 47). The disparity between the exotic overtones of the Carolingian emperor's name and its real origin in his servant's refusal to let callers see him on the grounds that he is eating – 'Don Carlo? Magna' (Silone 1933, 28) – makes it clear that Silone's irony is at work again, suggesting perhaps that the descendants of the landowning middle class which came to the fore in the nineteenth century were inclined to squander their patrimony in imitating the behaviour and life-style of the older aristocracy rather than imitating the energy of their parents or a later generation of capitalistic investors; clogs to clogs in three generations, in the English north-country saying, or 'la ricchezza c'è chi la fa e chi la gode' in Italian.

Don Carlo's wife, Donna Clorinda, owes her name in the 1940s versions to the warrior heroine of Tasso's chivalrous romance, the *Gerusalemme liberata*. This is another happy revision, since in the 1933 version she was called Donna Zizzola, which can mean either – vulgarly – tits, making her a counterpart to Maria Sorcanera, or a trifle or a bagatelle, when she is in fact a formidable lady indeed, remorselessly exacting gifts in kind from the peasants who come to see her and fighting unscrupulously to defend the interests of her family against the newcomer, the Impresario.

When the peasants first learn of the diversion of the stream, they assume that Don Carlo Magna must be responsible for this abuse of power, but they are surprised – even maliciously pleased – to learn that Don Carlo has sold the land on to which their water is now being diverted to the Impresario for a low price. The Impresario plans to irrigate the previously dry land and thereby increase its value. This small piece of 'bonifica integrale' naturally operates to the detriment of the peasants. We need not take at face value the view of the women of Fontamara that Don Carlo's fortunes have declined because he has been a gambler and a womanizer: these are probably the symptom, rather than the cause of his decline, as seen by the peasants. Once again, Silone is depicting, in fictional terms, what sociologists report in their studies. Colclough, for example, records that one family in Pertosa, which was very wealthy early in this century, was bankrupt by 1919. There were objective reasons for this – fluctuations in the share market, the devaluation of the *lira* in world war I – but the peasants saw it as the result of the reckless gambling and gullibility of the head of the family (Colclough 1971, 222). One needs always to remember that Silone is offering, without interpretative comment or explanation – in which respect he differs significantly from Levi – a naive peasant's-eye view of the situation.

Don Circostanza

Don Carlo Magna's declining fortune and his lack of business sense when confronted by a modern entrepreneur mean that he has become less important and influential as far as the peasants are concerned, although they are apparently slow to realize this. The same is true of Don Circostanza, whose name is as revealing as that of the landowner. In 'Liberal Italy' he was elected *sindaco* of the area and, when suffrage came to depend on a literacy test, he had ensured his regular re-election by teaching the *fontamaresi* to write only his name so that they could vote only for him. Indeed, even their dead were temporarily resurrected on polling-days to ensure his majority, and at five *lire* per vote the elections had represented a modest but useful source of income for them.

Virdia makes the valid point that through Don Circostanza Silone is criticizing not only Fascism but also pre-Fascist political parties and social structures (Virdia 1979, 55). In the 1933 version of the novel, in fact, he is explicitly described as having been the local 'capo del partito del popolo' (Silone 1933, 146) in order to increase his influence with the peasants, which suggests that he had at one time been a member of the Partito popolare, which in 1920 had won nearly a quarter of the municipal councils, mainly in the rural areas. His former theme of 'Fucino deve appartenere a chi lo coltiva' [Fucino must belong to those who cultivate it] reinforces this suggestion, since the Partito popolare was proposing land reform in the post-war period. He is therefore seen by the peasants as the natural defender of the region against outsiders (Silone 1933, 146).

The *fontamaresi* are dependent on Don Circostanza even for the most ordinary transactions of life. They would not at one time even have contemplated embarking on so weighty a transaction as the purchase of a railway ticket without a 'lettera di raccomandazione' from him. He conducts all their lawsuits. In consequence, whereas they see Don Carlo Magna simply as an exploiter, since he only hires their labour, they are conditioned to see Don Circostanza as their benefactor; he is invariably referred to as 'the friend of the people'. In return, Don Circostanza exploits them, using to the full his superior knowledge of current events and the law in order to do so. When Berardo had wished to emigrate, for example, Don Circostanza had, 'as a favour', bought his land from him, certainly knowing that emigration restrictions were about to be introduced, so that Berardo would not be able to leave anyway. But he wanted the land, not to farm it, but to extract pozzolana from it.

This detail is one of those added in 1947 to make Don Circostanza a more rounded character and to fill out the picture of clientelism as a very one-sided 'exchange of favours'.

The advent of Fascism, however, has reduced the extent of Don Circostanza's patronage. The first indication we have of this is the reference in chapter II to the abolition of voting, which is clarified by the information given later that the office of *sindaco* has been abolished. The peasants react to this news with characteristic incredulity; what they regard as the 'natural' order of things has been disturbed. But Don Circostanza, unlike Don Carlo Magna, is a Vicar of Bray type and, as his name suggests, is quick to adapt to changed circumstances, and he sees that there may be an advantage to be gained by using his reputation as 'l'amico del popolo' to become an intermediary between the Impresario and the *fontamaresi*, aiding the former by hoodwinking the latter. We see him in this role in chapter II, when he uses his eloquence to persuade the peasants that the water can be divided on the basis of equal shares consisting of three quarters of the water to the Impresario and three quarters of the rest to the villagers, and again in chapter VI, when he persuades the only apparently reluctant Impresario to agree that the stream should flow on to his land not for the fifty years which the latter had proposed, but only for ten lustres. The 'cafoni' are so accustomed to being treated with contempt that Don Circostanza is able, by his use of seeming sympathy and flattering eloquence, to put across the grossest deceptions. Don Abbacchio, as we have seen, plays a similar role, and it is significant that we meet them both for the first time at the banquet for the new *podestà* – who treats his sycophantic guests with a contempt which suggests that he has already seen through them. Donna Clorinda, by contrast, attempts to incite the villagers to start an insurrection in which the Impresario would be killed, thereby getting them to do her dirty work for her.

Now it was a declared part of Fascist policy to renew the structures of southern society. Steinberg quotes Michele Branchi, the Calabrian general secretary of the Fascist party in 1922, as saying that the government intended to

> renew, rejuvenate and purify political life, scraping off the ancient parasitic incrustations, destroying the little electoral conventicles, uprooting the little cliques, which have survived for decades with the complacent protection of the authorities to the great detriment of free, healthy and civil assistance to the people (Steinberg 1986, 96).

This was Fascism in its revolutionary pose. Steinberg comments:

> The arrival of the Fascists in the seat of power alarmed these 'parasitic incrustations' and their wealthy paymasters, their mafiosi supporters who acted as electoral agents and poll-watchers, their cousins, friends' friends, clients, dependents and hangers-on.

Il Popolo warned, shortly after the Fascists took power, that the clientèles were ready to adhere to any movement capable of looking after their interests (Steinberg, ibid.), and this is the process that Silone depicts in *Fontamara*. Gramsci, writing in 1927, also identified such types as Don Circostanza:

> Nei paesi invece dove l'agricoltura esercita un ruolo ancora notevole o addirittura preponderante, è rimasto in prevalenza il vecchio tipo, che dà la massima parte del personale statale e che ancora, localmente, nel villaggio e nel luogo rurale, esercita la funzione di intermediario tra il contadino e l'amministrazione in generale. Nell'Italia meridionale predomina questo tipo, con tutte le sue caratteristiche: democratico nella faccia contadina, reazionario nella faccia rivolta verso il grande proprietario e il governo, politicante, corotto, sleale; non si comprenderebbe la figura tradizionale dei partiti politici meridionali, se non si tenesse conto di questo strato sociale (Gramsci 1974, 150).

On the other hand, in places where agriculture still plays a notable or even a dominant role, the old type has remained prevalent, which provides most of the government service staff, and which locally, in villages and rural areas, still functions as an intermediary between the peasant and the Administration in general. This type is predominant in southern Italy, with all his characteristics: democratic when dealing with the peasants, reactionary when dealing with the big landowners and the government, scheming, corrupt, treacherous; one could not understand the traditional shape of southern political parties if one did not take account of this social stratum.

The peasants come to see, however, that Don Circostanza is betraying them and is intent only on safeguarding his own position. The disadvantages of clientelism were considerable, but the system had the apparent merit of appearing to offer a form of security; the peasants at least knew where they stood. Now, with Don Circostanza's public betrayal, they are ready to consider the possibility of further change in a world they had previously thought of as immutable.

Don Circostanza's nickname has rich literary overtones. In Manzoni's *I promessi sposi*, the cynical Ferrer calms the rioting Milanese by reminding them that he is 'l'amico del popolo', while in Soffici's *Lemmonio Borreo*, a corrupt Socialist Deputy, also a lawyer, is presented as a 'false friend of the people'. In addition, Silone would surely have had in mind one of Lenin's major early works, namely his 1894 essay *What the 'Friends of the People' are and How They Fight the Social Democrats* (Lenin 1963). The 'Friends of the People' whom Lenin caustically attacks are Russian liberals, who had launched a series of attacks on the Marxists. In his view, they tended dishonestly to gloss over class antagonism and the exploitation of the workers: 'Scratch the "friends of the peo-

ple'", wrote Lenin, 'and you will find a bourgeois' (Lenin 1963, 153). Don Circostanza is a false friend of the people, concerned only to further the interests of
his class at the expense of the peasants.

The Impresario

A number of images in the preface to *Fontamara* suggest that the peasants' world
is unchanging: and in the sense that theirs is a life of unending toil and exploitation, so it is. Yet they themselves perceive that changes which take place at
national level usually have a deleterious effect on their standard of living. Giuvà
is aware that unification brought with it both increased taxation and an influx of
new bosses. The novel therefore manages to convey the peasants' view of their
own lot as unchanging and at the same time to convey a sense of history as
dynamic, rather than static. The most prominent representative in the novel of
change brought about by national politics is the Impresario.

Names are significant in Silone's fiction, and that this character lacks a name is
particularly significant. For the Impresario has no individual, personal identity; he
is an entrepreneur and is described in terms which remind one of Gramsci's
account of the 'imprenditore capitalistico' (Gramsci 1974, 13–4). He has no clientelistic or kinship relationship to those he exploits and abuses. He represents at
one and the same time Fascism and its control over the rural areas and a new corruption which replaces the old – new in both its extent and its relative efficiency.

When the Impresario first arrives, he is despised by the local gentry as an outsider, an upstart; but he has the backing of a Roman bank. In the context of the
latifondi he would not have been an entirely new figure: for decades the lease-
holder had not been a man with experience of farming and local roots, but a
businessman with savings or access to credit. What is new about the Impresario
is his security, his permanence and his political power. On the *latifondi* the *mas-
saro*, or farm manager, normally had only a short-term contract.

Since the story is narrated by peasants, we have no means of knowing how he
acquired his political power-base, although we do see how he uses it to full
advantage. His purchase of Don Carlo Magna's land, which will now greatly
increase in value, echoes Don Circostanza's earlier acquisition of Berardo's, suggesting that he is exploiting the ignorance and lack of initiative of the gentry just
as they had previously exploited the peasantry, which is a nice irony. But it is
important to see also that what the Impresario is doing is, ostensibly, to imple-
ment Fascist agricultural policy, to which the language of the novel unmistak-
ably points. When the peasants complain about the diversion of their stream,
they are brusquely informed that they themselves have requested it in the interests of higher production, for the benefit of landowners with greater capital to
invest in agriculture. The language of the fake petition would have delighted
Serpieri's heart (see chapter 3), echoing as it does his views. What that fake peti-

tion does not mention, of course, is that the Impresario is the sole beneficiary of this particular piece of land reclamation. Similarly, a law of 6 June 1927 ordered that communal lands suitable for cultivation should be divided among peasant proprietors (Lyttleton 1973, 352). When the Fontamara sheep-runs are enclosed, the only 'peasant' proprietor to benefit is the Impresario. Numerous references to his abuse of power are scattered throughout the novel.

Corruption of this kind was not new, although it was no doubt encouraged by the fact that the *podestà* was an unpaid official, appointed, and not answerable to an electorate. After unification, much common land had been enclosed as private property, often simply through control of local government. This became part of the pattern of southern life; a survey of Calabria in 1910 found in one commune alone eighty-three usurpations of common land, twenty-one by members of the mayor's family, and a further dozen or more by communal councillors and their friends (Mack Smith 1969, 237). Mack Smith even records the case of a Sicilian Marchese who diverted a river to power his mills and compensated his people for their loss by having Mass said for them on feast days in his private chapel (ibid.). Modern historians are justified in stressing the continuities of Italian history. What is new in the case of the Impresario is that he is the officially appointed representative of central government who can justify his actions in terms of that government's agricultural policy, and can use to enforce his authority squadrist methods which, although used by southern landowners before Fascism, were nevertheless particularly associated with Fascism and were new in the experience of the peasants described by Silone.

Prince Torlonia

Silone's decision to set *Fontamara* in the hills to the north of the Fucino plain had a number of advantages, one of which was that the setting juxtaposed marginal hill farming and a wealthy *latifondo* which had been brought into being by a large-scale land reclamation operation with the backing of a big bank; and so, although the lake had been drained in the nineteenth century, the novel is able to make an oblique comment on Fascist land reclamation policy.

The region of Abruzzo consists mostly of hills and mountains, suitable mainly for extensive or semi-extensive methods of agricultural production. The most significant exception to this is the fertile Fucino plain. The lake which formerly covered it was drained between 1852 and 1876 by a company in which Duke Alessandro Torlonia (1800–86) had bought up all the shares in 1854. For draining the lake, Duke Alessandro was rewarded by a grateful government not only with the title of Prince but also with the outright ownership of the 37,050 acres (15,000 hectares) of land now available for cultivation.

The reclamation of the land was an impressive feat of civil engineering; attempts had been made at it since Roman times. The basic problem was that streams, rain and melting snow drained into a broad, shallow basin with no natural outlet. Two French engineers, Brisse and Rotrou, constructed an outlet into the Liri valley to the west which followed the course of one begun by the Emperor Claudius, and ensured that the plain would remain immune to flooding by a system of drainage channels which are still in use today.

Brisse and Rotrou wrote a full account of their work in which, although they state that Torlonia's intention was 'to make a vast private estate' (Brisse & Rotrou 1876, 27), they maintain that 'his work had no political character, and the population of the country knew that it was undertaken only for their benefit (ibid., 121). According to them, 'thousands of families were called, thanks to him, to take their share of that prosperity' (ibid., 73). Their share, however, was a small one. Silone's statement, in the preface to the novel, that the average temperature of the zone fell notably as a result of the loss of the water, is correct. The average fall was one degree centigrade, which of course conceals greater falls in the cold seasons. Oddly enough, Silone made the mistake of writing in the preface to the first edition that the temperature rose after the water disappeared, perhaps thinking only of the increased temperatures which resulted in the summer months. He could also have added that the water-table in the hills fell, which was also one of the side-effects of some of Mussolini's reclamation schemes, and explains why the stream was so precious to the *fontamaresi*. It became difficult to grow vines, and the olive-trees which had once covered the south-facing slopes disappeared. Nor were the hill villagers allowed to lease land on the plain; that was to be a privilege reserved for the inhabitants of the villages which had bordered on the former lake.

Although some land on the plain was farmed directly by the Torlonia estate, an attempt was made to lease some of the remainder to local peasants, but it is doubtful whether this could have been more than a public relations gesture. Few peasants could afford to invest money in land which would not yield a crop for several years. In any case, the doctors, lawyers, teachers and wealthier farmers to whom the land was mainly leased had the advantage for Torlonia of constituting a class of *galantuomini* whose interests coincided largely with his own and who were therefore committed to the preservation of the existing social order. The increasing poverty of the hill villagers resulting from the deterioration of their land, together with the general surplus of labour in the area, made this an easy task. The area illustrates a general point about the southern economy in a way which *Cristo si è fermato a Eboli* does not:

> The most basic factor in the economic, social and political setting of the South was the co-existence in the same area of minuscule private property and the sprawling latifundia. The instability of the former, the availability of cheap labour for the latter, the fragmentation of occupational

roles, and the political dependence of the peasant on the landowner were all poised between these two axes (Tarrow 1967, 292).

Silone describes the Torlonia estate as operating a colonial regime. He gives few details of what he means by this, but we know from other sources (Grieco 1953, Liberale 1977 (1) and (2)) that tenants and workers on the estate were allowed to use the private estate roads (which are now public) only for access to work, and not for journeys between villages. They were not allowed to take water for irrigation from the drainage canals, which in any case were not properly maintained, so that certain areas were still subject to flooding. They were not allowed to construct on the estate any kind of shelter, either for their own use during bad weather or for storage purposes. Part of their rent had to be paid in a compulsory crop, namely sugar beet.

There is an episode in *Il seme sotto la neve* in which the central character, Pietro Spina, sees in a mountain village the bust of some local worthy, possibly the Prince himself. It is covered with snow and therefore unrecognizable, and Pietro ironically hails it as a statue erected to the sugar beet. What sounds like a piece of whimsy has a cutting edge which will escape us unless we know that Torlonia was a sugar-beet baron and therefore one of the richest men in Italy. The domestic production of sugar beet rose from 6,000 tons in 1898 to over 300,000 tons in 1913 as the result of a tariff which quadrupled the price of imported sugar (Seton-Watson 1967, 288–9). The Torlonia estate built its own refinery on the west of the plain, and the beet with which the rents were paid had to be delivered there, where it was priced at an artificially low level by the Torlonia management. Estate guards in the blue Torlonia livery, armed with shotguns, enforced the estate regulations and kept the intimidated work force in its place. Recent studies of the *latifondo* stress its capitalist nature and nineteenth-century origins. The Torlonia estate combined intensive production of high value cash-added crops with old-fashioned subjection of the labour force.

It is not surprising that the Torlonia estate was the scene of struggles over land tenure in 1919 (Sabbatucci 1974, 190, 241); and it was the scene of further disputes in 1929, the year in which the action of *Fontamara* is set. The Torlonia tenants frequently sub-let their land, not wishing to farm it themselves. Increases in rent were naturally passed on, and at the end of the financial chain were the labourers who worked the land. In 1929, in a period in which, as we have seen (chapter 3), agricultural wages were falling much more quickly than the cost of living, tenancy contracts on the Fucino plain became due for renewal. Prince Torlonia sought rent increases of 50 per cent. The increases were naturally approved by the *Associazione nazionale fascista degli agricoltori* of the Province of L'Aquila, of which Torlonia was president. Disputes between the estate and the tenants reached such a pitch that Giuseppe Bottai, the minister for agriculture, was called in to arbitrate. It may or may not have been coincidence that in the same year Torlonia agreed to let his splendid villa in Rome's then fashionable Via Nomentana district to Mussolini for the symbolic rent of one *lira* per annum; at all events the Duce's family moved in in November. In June, the Bottai arbitration gave Torlonia a 20 per cent rent increase and reinforced his beet monopoly, as well as his financial monopoly through the Banca del Fucino, which he controlled, and from which tenants in debt were required to take loans. Bank, beet and land together constituted what came to be known locally as the 'three-jawed vice' which held the peasants in a remorseless grip.

Chapter IV of *Fontamara* must therefore be read as a peasant's-eye view of the Bottai settlement, in which the peasants are treated merely as so many extras, required to stand up, cheer and shout slogans they do not understand in a carefully orchestrated demonstration of Fascist 'solidarity'. Silone's claim, in the preface, that the strange facts that he is about to relate actually took place, needs to be taken seriously. In the first version of the novel Silone gives details of the proposed rent increases which are suppressed in later revisions, presumably because his peasants' main concern is with the possibility that they might at last be allowed to lease land. The Fucino plain is compared to the Promised Land, and Berardo by implication to Moses; now they learn that they are to be excluded from it in the name of productivity (see chapter 3).

The visitor to Avezzano cannot help being impressed by the sheer extent and obvious fertility of the plain, as well as by the complexity of the work required to drain it and channel the water through the mountains to the Liri valley. The town of Avezzano itself was almost entirely destroyed during the 1915 earthquake and was hastily rebuilt in undistinguished style. Palazzo Torlonia, on the corner of Via Anna Maria Torlonia, overlooks Piazza Torlonia, whose fountain not surprisingly bears the Torlonia coat of arms. It is a two-storey brick building which is unimpressive until one compares it with the sordid squalor of the near-by villages. The most impressive signs of Torlonia opulence, however, are to be found in Rome. Visitors to the Church of the Gesù see Alessandro Torlonia's name repeated four times in large block capitals in the nave, since he paid for its sumptuous marble cladding. It would not have escaped the ironic eye of the author whose novels always included a Christ-figure that one repetition occurs over the entrance to the Crucifix Chapel, next to the chapel dedicated to Ignatius Loyola, the saint from whom Silone took part of his pseudonym. The Torlonia family church, however, was San Giovanni in Laterano, and it is here that they have a coldly neo-classical funerary chapel, one of the last to be permitted in Rome. The laudatory epitaphs on the tombs remind one that in Michele Zompa's dream, the Pope explains to Jesus that he cannot distribute Fucino land to the *fontamaresi* because that would upset the Prince, and the Prince is a 'good Christian'. Not far away from San Giovanni was one of the family's city residences, a Renaissance palace which was one of the few allowed to remain standing when Mussolini cleared the area to make way for the vulgar Via della Conciliazione. There was another elegant Torlonia residence in central Rome, in Via Bocca di Leone. Nor should one forget the villa and park at Frascati which, like the Via Nomentana residence, is now the property of the commune in which it stands. Silone could hardly have chosen a wealthier or a more powerful opponent. The change of ownership of the plain and of various other Torlonia properties is an indication of the change in the family's power and status, which were not seriously challenged until the post-war period. The way in which *Fontamara* reflects and even contributed to that challenge is the subject of the next chapter.

CHAPTER 7

Fontamara and 'la lotta del Fucino'

THE REVISION PROCESS

Silone returned to Italy from his Swiss exile in October 1944. He had by that time written two novels in addition to *Fontamara*, namely *Pane e vino* (Bread and Wine, 1937) and *Il seme sotto la neve* (The Seed under the Snow, 1942), both of which deal with his personal struggle on leaving the Communist party as well as with the peasantry of Abruzzo. It was natural that Silone should wish to bring to the notice of the Italian reading public novels which had achieved a certain success abroad, especially as he was about to resume political activity once more, seeking to found a *Partito socialista unitario* which would be a broad Left coalition party. He therefore started to publish *Fontamara* in a very much revised form in weekly episodes in Ernesto Buonaiuti's review *Il Risveglio* in 1945, but the review was short-lived and the full text of the novel had not appeared by the time it collapsed (Moloney 1996). It was then published in book form in 1947, with further revisions, by the relatively obscure Faro publishing house, which was also publishing Gramsci. Then, in 1949, the much better known publishers Mondadori brought out another edition with further changes, on which Silone must have worked in 1948, and possibly even in late 1947.

Silone's comments on the re-writing, and on the motives which led him to undertake it give the impression that he was in pursuit of greater understanding on his part and a greater degree of communication with his readers. In 'A Note on Revision' which was written for the first American translation of this edition, Silone wrote: 'I agree entirely with what Hugo von Hofmannstal said about writers: that they are the sort of men for whom writing is more difficult than for others'. He went on: 'Therefore, because I feel myself bound up in a most intricate way with the story, it happens that I continue to think and dream about it, and in this way the book continues to live, grow and change within me even when it is already in a bookseller's window' (Silone 1977, 14). Since in the same 'Note' Silone also says that he could easily spin out his existence writing and re-writing the same story, it seems to me that insufficient attention has been paid to the way the novel has changed in the light of the author's statement in this 'Note on Revision' that his concern when he came to re-read his text was 'not due at all to the contrast between my book and the natural reality I had before my eyes, but to the contrast between the story of 1930 and its development in me since then during all those years in which I had continued to live it'.

This statement is potentially misleading since it seems to imply that the revisions of *Fontamara* are the result solely of greater artistic maturity, or else of changes in Silone's philosophy and not of changes in the extratextual reality of Abruzzo.

The attention of critics has for the most part been focussed on the structural and stylistic changes Silone made in the post-war versions of the novel. Many critics, however, seem unaware of the fact that many changes which they attribute to the 1949 version appeared for the first time in either 1945 or 1947. The omission of most of chapter VI of the 1933 text, dealing with the 'eroe di Porta Pia' and the rise of Fascism in Rome, certainly sharpens the focus and increases the coherence of the later version, which now deals almost exclusively with rural society. The language and imagery of the 1945–9 texts are also much more homogenous, and the contrast between the violence of the Berardo of the early chapters and the self-sacrificing Christ-figure of the later chapters is considerably toned down (McLaughlin 1986). But it will be my contention in this chapter that some important changes which Silone made to his text can certainly be attributed to the author's reactions to circumstances prevailing in Abruzzo in the 1940s, while others, to be discussed in the following chapter, can be attributed to Silone's personal development and to developments in his ideology.

EVENTS IN THE FUCINO PLAIN

In June 1944 the last German troops retreated from the Fucino plain to take up defensive positions further north. With the arrival of the Allies, freedom returned to Fucino. But what kind of freedom? The Allies did not bring with them any greater social justice, and the immediate effect of their policies 'was to consecrate the social status quo, based […] on the most ruthless exploitation of the rural poor' (Ginsborg 1990, 36). 1944 saw the beginning of a wave of peasant protest all over southern Italy. In the autumn of that year, the Torlonia management decided not to hire labour from nearby villages to plough and sow winter wheat on one of the farms, which soon became notorious as the 'azienda di strada trenta', from the number of the road leading to it. The reason for the decision may simply have been economic: the times were still uncertain, and why sow wheat on what might yet become once more a battlefield? But the reason may equally well have been political, based on a desire to remind the peasants that whatever expectations they may have had in the heady excitement of post-war freedom, they were still dependent for work on the Torlonia estate. Whatever the motive behind it, the decision came as a severe blow to the peasants of Ortucchio, in the south-west of the plain, and on 16 October they marched to the farm in question to begin a work-in, which they called 'a strike in reverse' – 'uno sciopero a rovescio'. They do not seem to have envisaged forming a cooperative to occupy the land in the terms envisaged by Gullo's decrees. The episode took place in what, in Cinanni's analysis, was still part of a wave of spontaneous occupations, organized locally (Cinanni 1979, 15).

It is difficult to say precisely what were the aims of the peasants at this stage. They certainly intended to work on the land and sow wheat. Liberale, writing some years after the event, states that they also wanted to assert their right to ownership of the land. It is difficult on the basis of the fragmentary and often very biased evidence available to deduce exactly what happened next: but to put it in reasonably detached terms, the peasants – who no one suggests were armed, although police evidence described their attitude as 'threatening' (Liberale 1977 (2), 43) – came into conflict with what might be described as the forces of law and order, namely a group consisting of seven *carabinieri* and five Torlonia estate guards, all armed, led by the commander of the *carabinieri* station at Gioia de' Marsi. The forces of law and order opened fire. One peasant was killed and five were wounded. Here as elsewhere, the landowners showed that they were pre-pared to fight at all costs. It is not unreasonable to ask whose law and whose order were being enforced, but since *carabinieri* High Command had given orders that occupations were absolutely and unhesitatingly to be prevented, a policy not entirely consistent with that of the Government, it would seem that the forces of law and order were committed to the maintenance of the *status quo ante bellum*.

This episode provoked a wave of strikes and occupations of the land directed at the Torlonia management. The immediate and probably natural reaction of the Government was to send in detachments of the *Celere*, the police Flying Squad, and *carabinieri* reinforcements, which turned out to be unnecessary since the peasants, organised and peaceful in their methods as never before, were not engaged in insurrection but in a generally peaceful campaign of civil protest (Liberale 1977 (2), 43, 54–5). If the unrest of the post-world war I period had been characterised by the ability of the landowners to organise, the post-world war II period was characterised by the peasants' ability to organise. The Torlonia show of force on 16th October looks in retrospect to have been an attempt to demonstrate that in spite of the fall of Fascism nothing, fundamentally, had changed, but it was an anachronistic gesture, reminiscent of those which had taken place, and had indeed been effective, earlier in the century, such as the episode at Candela in 1902, when eight workers were killed when *carabinieri* opened fire on unarmed pickets during a strike of agricultural labourers. The officer in charge on that occasion was subsequently decorated for bravery and promoted (Snowden 1985, 133). The pattern of collusion between landowners and police which had characterized the repression of the peasant movement in the first post-war period was certainly being reproduced in the second. This was not surprising, since the Abruzzo Prefect warned the Government that Fucino was 'still in the hands of the old element' (Liberale 1977 (1), 26). It is also probable that the wave of land occupations that were sweeping Italy as the Germans retreated in 1944 generated a degree of panic and over-reaction. Peasants at nearby Magliano de' Marsi had already occupied land belonging to Baron Masciarelli. With a growing number of peasant deaths, *Fontamara* acquired a new resonance.

When Fascism collapsed in 1943, the problem of the south was even further from a solution than it had been when Mussolini came to power. The ban on emigration and the stimulation of the birthrate had exacerbated the problem of surplus labour, and class divisions had widened. The gap between north and south had also widened. It was not only on the Fucino plain that the landowners had forgotten nothing and learned nothing. The peasants, on the other hand, had learned a good deal. In the first place, the resistance movement had done much to change peasants' attitudes. True, the resistance had not been a peasant movement: but peasants had sons who took to the mountains to avoid the Fascist call-up, peasants handed over food supplies to the partisans, who gave them certificates which often over-stated the amount they had requisitioned so that the peasants were able to withhold some of their produce from the authorities. They also sheltered escaping prisoners-of-war and aircrew who had been brought down over German-held territory. Thus they were able to cheat and deceive officialdom on a scale that was new to them. Another factor whose influence is difficult to assess was the black market, which reversed the traditional relationship between townspeople, now at best respectful customers, at worst supplicants for food, and peasants, whose income increased considerably as a result. And when the Allies arrived, the sheer material wealth they brought with them radically altered the peasants' view of what they, too, might expect to achieve. In these circumstances, the peasants of the Fucino plain were no longer prepared to accept the hunger, humiliation and increased indebtedness that the suspension of work traditionally brought with it. It is also quite possible that they were prepared now to assert their right to the ownership of land. The text of Silone's novel unambiguously attributes to the peasants of Fontamara the view that it is work, not purchase, that gives a man a right to own land – a sentiment voiced most expressively by Berardo in Chapter IV.

As was the case in the years after the first world war, there were numerous occupations and work-ins all over Italy in a wave which more or less followed the perimeter of the territory liberated by the Allies as they advanced northwards. The peasants were clearly motivated by their enhanced consciousness of the possibilities of land ownership. For one crucial difference between the two post-war periods was that in the 1940s Italy was being liberated, an oppressive regime had been overthrown, with all the promise of change which that entailed. Another was that because the newly active Communist party saw the *latifondi* as lands usurped by the bourgeoisie, the Fucino basin was one of the areas where the PCI's organisations were strongest (Tarrow 1967, 283). It was in fact the Communists who led and coordinated what became known as the 'lotta del Fucino'. The peasants of the area, between late 1944 and late 1949, have been described as permanently mobilized against the 'Eccellentisima Casa Torlonia' (Liberale 1977 (2), 49).

The conflict reached its peak between December 1947 and January 1948. Brutal repression was no longer an option open to landowners now, given that Communist newspapers and Communist Deputies could give unwelcome publicity to their every move, but between December 1947 and January 1948 the Torlonia management took out injunctions against 3,000 tenants who had fallen into debt, threatening eviction if the debts were not settled within a prescribed period. Liberale (1977 (2), 49) states that the aim was, as in 1929, to create much larger farming units. But in 1949 the peasants won a partial victory, and the Bottai settlement of 1929, which in Chapter IV of *Fontamara* is described from a peasant's point of view, was finally revised in their favour. Rents were reduced, the right to construct shelters and to circulate freely on estate roads was granted, checks were introduced on the handling of beet at the estate sugar refinery, and the estate agreed to renew the drainage system.

The campaign was resumed, however, and with fresh intensity, when in February 1950 peasant organisations took the view that the estate had not kept its side of the bargain. Over 4,000 tenants and *braccianti* began another strike in reverse, this time by maintaining the long-neglected drainage channels and estate roads. The aim of the campaign was now explicitly to drive Torlonia out and to expropriate the Fucino estate, an objective finally achieved in March 1951, when the *Gazzetta Ufficiale* published the decree expropriating the estate. But even this victory was marked by murder: on 30 April 1950, *braccianti* waiting to be hired were fired on, and two were killed.

There was of course a national dimension to the 'lotta del Fucino' such as there had not been to earlier struggles, particularly during the Fascist period. Occupations took place in many parts of Italy, but the Communists, through their Deputies in Parliament and through the media, gave special prominence to the Fucino campaign. This may have been one of the factors which made possible the more prestigious 1949 Mondadori edition of *Fontamara* so soon after the modest edition with the more obscure Faro press.

As we have seen, the southern question was once again a topic for free and open debate. And with Communist and Socialist deputies in Parliament – even, for a time, Communist ministers in the cabinet – and with government policies apparently favouring regionalism and decentralisation, the prospects for land reform looked favourable. A. Rossi-Doria divides the years 1944–9 into two periods. In the first, from summer 1944 to summer 1946, the Communist Minister Gullo was able to take the initiative in matters of agricultural reform. He was less free, however, in the second Bonomi government and in the Parri government. In the first De Gasperi government, one of his decrees was annulled, after which he lost the agriculture portfolio.

The Christian Democrats, until 1947, presented themselves as a party leaning to the left, and allied themselves with the other two main parties, the Communists and the Socialists. They even asked landowners to be prepared to make sacrifices for the sake of a fairer distribution of land. But in 1946 the Roman Catholic Church made it clear to both the Christian Democrats and to the United States that it was implacably opposed to the continuation of the alliance with the Communists. The Christian Democrats wanted American aid to continue, and could not afford to alienate their right-wing support in the south. In 1947 the Socialist party split, and in May of that year Prime Minister De Gasperi, under pressure from both the Americans and his own right wing, excluded the Communists from his government. Meanwhile, constitutional reform was proceeding in confused fashion: article 40 of the new constitution protected trade union activity and the right to strike, 'within the framework of the laws that regulate it'; but the existing laws were mainly those of Rocco's penal code and the public security code of 1931, which had not been repealed (Clark 1984, 320–1). It seemed to many Italians that Italy's post-war freedom was going to be very limited indeed and that the country was slipping towards the right. In fact, in the 1948 elections, the PCI and PSI lost ground, slipping from 219 seats in parliament to 103, while the DC gained, advancing from 207 in 1946 to 306 in 1958, in both cases out of 574. In this context, the wave of occupations in autumn 1949 was an expression of increasing frustration.

TEXT AND EXTRATEXT

All these considerations suggest that one of Silone's aims in revising and re-publishing *Fontamara* in the 1940s was to remind and to warn: to remind Italians how Fascism had dealt with the problem of the south, and to warn that the clock could not be put back. The revised version of the novel was Silone's contribution to the 'lotta contadina', and as a part of that contribution he removed over-specific references to wages and conditions of work, which he described as relics of a 'vulgar Marxism', and stressed the importance to the peasants of land ownership and of their right to ownership, a right earned by toil: 'Non basta comprarla, perché una terra sia tua. Diventa tua con gli anni, con la fatica, col sudore, con le lacrime, con i sospiri' [It's not enough to buy it, for land to become yours. It becomes yours with the years, through your work, through your sweat, through your tears, through your sighs] (Silone 1998, 68). This is the view which the peasants of Jovine's *Le terre del Sacramento* also achieve as a result of their occupation and the deaths of Luca and his companions.

The validity of this suggested reading of the novel is confirmed by Silone's tendency to omit from the post-war versions of the novel the adjective 'fascista' and phrases which include it. For example, Berardo, when arrested in Rome, and thinking that the police suspect him of theft, cries 'Noi ladri? ... Ladri sono i sindicati fascisti che ci han rubato trentacinque lire' [Thieves, us? ... The Fascist unions are thieves, they stole thirty-five lire from us] (Silone 1933, 174). This reference to the cost of a work permit which does not provide them with work is retained in the final version (Silone 1998, 177), but with the omission of the epithet. Similarly, the phrase 'dei capi fascisti' [Fascist bosses] (Silone 1933, 180) is omitted, leaving only the words 'alti funzionari dello stato' [high civil servants] (Silone 1998, 183). It could be argued that the adjective was in any case redundant: in Italy in 1929 unions and important state officials could not be other than Fascist. But, on the other hand, the use of the adjective tied the action of the novel and therefore the attention of the reader too specifically to Fascist Italy and detracted from its current relevance. The enemy, in the 1940s, is no longer Fascism *tout court* but what Carlo Levi calls in *Cristo si è fermato a Eboli* 'l'eterno fascismo italiano' (Levi 1965, 251), the centralizing alliance between right-wing government and southern landowners which was not peculiar to Mussolini's Italy. A reference to Mussolini, in the ironic form of 'Musolino', is also omitted in 1947, perhaps because Silone was not certain how many of his readers would catch the allusion to the middle-class revolutionary Benedetto Musolino junior (1809–85), who, as Hearder rightly says, 'should not be confused with a much smaller and more miserable figure – Benedetto Mussolini'. Musolino had attempted to provide the peasantry with leadership (Hearder 1983, 147). When Don Circostanza, in accordance with new government regulations, makes deductions from the wages of peasants who have been working for him, Giuvà says: 'La legge di Mosè dice: non rubare' [The law of Moses says: Thou shalt not steal], to which the Friend of the People replies in 1933: 'Adesso non c'è Mosè, ma Musolino' [It's not Moses now, but Musolino] (Silone 1933, 127), which is both witty and alliterative. But in the final version he answers: 'La legge di Mosè serve per il tribunale di Dio [...] Quaggiú comanda la legge del Governo' [The law of Moses is valid for the court of God [...] On earth, the government's law rules] (Silone 1998, 131), which is in keeping with his character, as he shelters behind the excuse of government legislation, but has an effect similar to that of the omission of the adjective 'Fascist'. It is worth noting that as early (or as late) as 1945 those who argued against the cession of land to the peasants were reported in the pages of the Communist *Rinascita* as doing so in defence of the 'higher interests of national production' (Gullo 1945, 175), in a phrase which interestingly echoes Fascist rural policy.

A further series of revisions relates to what I would see as the relatively greater optimism of the final version of the novel. It is often assumed that *Fontamara* is a tragedy: Aliberti goes so far as to compare it to a classical tragedy, in which the protagonist, Berardo, is overcome by an external force, which in this case is economic and social oppression (Aliberti 1977, 62–3). Others have seen it in more optimistic terms. Irving Howe, for example, maintains that it ends with a defeat but nevertheless exudes revolutionary hope (Howe 1961, 126). The problem is to demonstrate that hope in the words or situations described in the text. In both versions of the novel Berardo dies in a Fascist jail: in both versions the village is subjected to a second and much more savage punitive expedition as a result of which its inhabitants are either killed or scattered. One could hardly level at Silone the charge often made against Vasco Pratolini, namely that of setting his characters in a world of hope and certainty which is unreal. The bleak ending of the first version of *Fontamara* certainly shows a community which has learned for the first time in its history to cooperate – in order to produce its newspaper, *Che fare?* – and to question, rather than patiently to accept: but that, in the light of the community's destruction, is of limited value. The most one can say is that three of their number have escaped and told their tale to the author, who has in turn ensured its transmission to a wider audience. But in 1930, when Silone wrote his novel, Mussolini was firmly in control; the consensus on which his power was based may have been artificial but it appeared to be holding, and there was more cause for compassion than for hope.

By the mid and late 1940s, however, the political situation in Italy was very different. The dark night of Fascism was over, and even though the Christian Democrats had moved to the right they had nevertheless in 1947 set up a Permanent Committee for the South and put themselves forward as a reforming party (Capo 1984, 34–5). Silone's problem, in revising his novel, was to convey the degree of optimism which was appropriate to the post-war situation but which would not seem gratuitous or artificial in the light of the 1929 setting of *Fontamara*. Jovine faced a similar problem when writing *Le terre del Sacramento*.

In all versions of the novel, Silone presents his peasants as inherently conservative. Their view of the social order is that, like the round of the seasons and the work that goes with it, it is immutable. Ernest Gellner argues that agrarian society 'values stability, and generally conceives the world and its own social order as basically stable. Some agrarian social forms at least seem to be deliberately organized so as to avoid the dangers of possibly disruptive innovations' (Gellner 1988, 17). This immutability does not bring security, however: on the contrary, it implies a life of more or less permanent insecurity. The notion that 'both in the material and the psychological sense, peasant life means security' (Bailey 1971, 27–8) most certainly did not apply to peasants in Mussolini's Italy, particularly if they were landless. Such structure and continuity as the *fontamaresi* have is provided by the system of clientelism, which comes under threat from the Impresario as former patrons lose their power: '... anche per i vecchi proprietari è arrivato il giorno della penitenza' [... the day of penitence has come for the old landowners too] (Silone 1998, 49). More importantly, from our present point of view, they regard all innovations with suspicion, on the understandable grounds that changes are more likely than not to operate to their disadvantage. We see this very clearly in chapter I, when they assume that Pelino's invitation to sign the petition will have as its consequence the inevitable tax. And we see it, too, in the very words the peasant narrators use to describe changes or innovations – 'novità' (Silone 1998, 191), as one might expect, but also 'stranezza' (Silone 1998, 41, 193), and even 'disgrazia', in the sense that an innovation is necessarily a misfortune (Silone 1998, 62). Uniformed *squadrismo* is 'una novità di pochi anni' [a innovation of the last few years] (Silone 1998, 117).

It is interesting to see the sequence in which these words occur, since they only occasionally used in this way in Silone's other novels, although dialect speakers tell me that 'novità' and 'stranezza' are used in this way in Abruzzese. There is, in addition, an interesting literary precedent in Verga's tale 'Nedda', in which, when the landowner's son tells the 'fattore' to pay Nedda her full week's wage even though working hours have been reduced by bad weather, the 'fattore' replies: 'Tutti i proprietari del vicinato farrebbero la guerra a voi e a me se facessimo delle novità' [All the landowners in the district would be up in arms against us both if we introduced innovations] (Verga 1969, I, 44).

In his preface Silone refers to the 'strani fatti' (Silone 1998, 7) which he is about to relate, strange events in the sense that they contrast with all that in the following paragraph is described as 'solito' or customary: the latter adjective is used nine times to describe the round of toil and poverty. The Impresario's rapid acquisition of wealth, on the other hand, is seen by the peasants as 'insolito' (Silone 1998, 42), and it is when they hear of his appointment as *podestà* that Matalè comments: 'Quando le stranezze cominciano, chi le ferma più?' [When novelties start, who can stop them?] (Silone 1998, 41). The question expresses not only bewilderment but also a certain gloom, for the Impresario, by reason of his capitalistic methods, is perceived by the peasants – and rightly so – as a threat. Greater despondency is expressed in chapter III, when the peasants wonder how much of their water they will lose and for how long: 'Quando le disgrazie cominciano, chi le ferma più?' [When misfortunes start, who can stop them?] (Silone 1998, 62). The first punitive expedition to the village provokes the use of an even stronger verb: 'Quando le stranezze si scatenano, chi le ferma piú?' [When novelties break out, who can stop them?] (Silone 1998, 116).

The dénouement of the novel brings a further group of similar questions and comments. When Berardo's mother reflects on his fate, she concludes that Elvira's death has perhaps 'saved' him. Another of the women comments – twice, and therefore very pointedly – 'strana salvezza morire in carcere' [Strange salvation to die in prison] (Silone 1998, 191), a phrase which emphasises Berardo's Christ-likeness. And the suggestion that the inhabitants of the village should compose their own lithographed newspaper is also hailed as 'una nuova stranezza' (Silone 1998, 191). Matalè muses, in words identical to those she had used earlier, 'Quando le stranezze cominciano, chi le ferma più?' (Silone 1998, 191). The newspaper is not so obviously a misfortune, but it is still an innovation, and so to be regarded with suspicion. Peasant cooperation, in the divided world of familism, is also an innovation, as Giuvà realises with hindsight: 'Era una stranezza e non ci rendevamo conto' [It was a novelty, and we didn't realise it] (Silone 1998, 191). Giuvà is aware, however, that much of what is happening is new: 'Strano, pensavo tra me, strano quante novità in una volta' [Strange, I thought to myself, strange how many new things are happening at once] (Silone 1998, 193). And when Giuvà persuades his initially reluctant wife to help distribute the newspapers, she comments: 'Quando le stranezze cominciano [...] nessuno le ferma più' [When novelties start ... no one can stop them] (Silone 1998, 194). Not only has the traditional mentality of 'minding one's own business' been broken down, and cooperation become acceptable, but there has been a shift from the interrogative ('chi le ferma più?') to the affirmative ('nessuno le ferma più'), and, I would suggest, there has also been a shift from the despondency expressed when the question was first being put to an optimism which is now – in the 1940s – being expressed by the author, if not by his cautious characters. Now that the peasant movement has learned co-operation at the grassroots level, it cannot be stopped. To be sure, the optimism is cautious and tempered: the second punitive expedition takes place, the community is scattered, its survivors will probably die in exile. The price to be paid is high, but the cause will ultimately triumph. In this way, Silone manages to balance the bleakness appropriate to an account of peasant crisis in 1929 with the cautious optimism appropriate to the 1940s.

PEASANTS AND PARTY

Fontamara also makes an important contribution to the discussion about the methods which the peasant movement should use. We have already seen that in Marxist-Leninist thought, the deteriorating working conditions of the peasantry were expected to turn them into a rural proletariat. This, in turn, was expected to produce a new class consciousness. Lenin, in *The Development of Capitalism in*

Russia (1899), went on to consider the feasibility of a political alliance between peasant groups and the industrial proletariat. This idea was taken up by Italian Marxists: Amendola wrote in 1931 of the need for a 'proletarian-peasant front' against Fascism (De Felice 1974, I, 99), and Gramsci in his *Questione meridionale* advocated 'a general revolutionary action of the two classes in alliance'. Gramsci indeed regarded the peasantry as potentially the most revolutionary force in Italian society: it was therefore important to impose on their spontaneous rebellion the Marxist consciousness of the party and the leadership and direction of the industrial proletariat. It was as though the peasants were to be an insurrectionary force in the countryside, while the 'real' revolution took place in the factories (Tarrow 1967, 249). The idea that the southern peasants, left to themselves, could do nothing, because theirs was a tradition of primitive rebellion, and that they needed the direction of the northern working class goes back in Italy at least to Salvemini's *La questione meridionale* of 1898–9. Once universal suffrage was obtained, Salvemini modified his views, taking the line that henceforth southern Socialists would have to fend for themselves, with no benevolent alms from northern Socialists (Salvemini 1963, 71–89). But the more orthodox Marxist view was that the peasant movement could not simply be left to grassroots initiatives.

Salvemini himself, however, assumed that *Fontamara* merely repeated this by now orthodox view of the subordinate role of the peasantry, 'as befits', he wrote, 'a Communist by whom the peasantry need to be rescued by Marxist industrial workers, the chosen people of the new era' (cit. in Origo 1984, 215). But if by 'Communist' Salvemini meant a faithful and orthodox member of the party, it is as well to remember that Silone in 1930 did not so regard himself: in his *Memoriale dal carcere* of 1942 he described himself as having just left the party in 1930. (Offically, he did not leave until 1931, but we may take him here as referring to a psychological rather than a formal break with the party.) In any case, after his visit to Moscow in 1927 and the disillusionment he experienced at that time, it was hardly to be expected that his views would remain orthodox, and certainly by the 1940s he was pursuing a very independent line of thought. Yet it is often assumed that the unnamed political agitator of Fontamara, il Solito Sconosciuto, is an autobiographical figure, and that he must therefore be a Communist. The first of these assumptions seems to me to be very reasonable, since as an underground worker Silone had been responsible for the publication and distribution of party newspapers and propaganda (Scurani 1969, 10). But the second assumption seems to me to be contradicted by the very text of the novel, which undermines the conventional Marxian view of the relationship between the peasants and the Communist movement in order to stress the autonomy of the former.

The Solito Sconosciuto makes his first appearance in the novel in chapter IV, after the meeting at Avezzano to 'discuss' the future of the Fucino lands. In both versions of the novel he warns the *fontamaresi* to be on their guard against an agent provocateur; but when, in later versions, he tries to engage them in further conversation, they find his remarks incomprehensible and Berardo, after twice warning him to 'mind his own business', throws him into a ditch. The episode was perhaps amplified in the later versions in order to make more convincing his later recognition of Berardo in Rome. The way in which this first encounter ends reflects the difficulty urban intellectuals have in establishing contact with the peasants and suggests that they are by no means their natural and inevitable leaders.

The second encounter between the Solito Sconosciuto and Berardo, in Rome, is a convenient but rather far-fetched coincidence, characteristic of the way in which Silone in his first novel manipulates events and his characters for the sake of the plot. But he needs to convert Berardo to the agitator's point of view, and has to find some means of bringing the two men together in a situation in which Berardo cannot abruptly terminate the conversation by throwing his interlocutor into another ditch. Even before they are arrested, the Solito Sconosciuto gives Berardo an interesting account of his activity. He prints and distributes clandestine newspapers, denouncing scandals and injustices, and urging workers to strike. Initially, he confined his activities to certain factories, but then extended them to the suburban areas and army barracks, and has recently been in Abruzzo. His accounts of himself do not differ significantly in this respect in the various versions of the novel, except in one important respect: in 1933 he is made to say: 'Dovunque lui arriva, i cafoni si rivoltano. Dovunque i cafoni si rivoltano arriva lui' [Wherever he turns up, the peasants rebel. Wherever the peasants rebel, he turns up] (Silone 1933, 173). In the later versions, however, the first of these two sentences is omitted: he no longer foments revolt, he merely responds to it and assists it. Similarly, when he is released from prison and makes his way to *Fontamara*, he limits his participation, firstly, to printing a pamphlet about Berardo and his village, and, secondly, to handing over to the villagers a simple lithographic press to enable them to write, print and distribute their own newspaper, *Che fare?*

Silone clearly sees intellectuals like himself as having a vital part to play in the peasant movement, and in so far as the Solito Sconosciuto puts forward ideas and convinces Berardo of their validity he seems to be acting in accordance with a Marxian view: Gramsci, for example, was quite clear that the peasant movement must begin with the intellectuals. But in that the Solito Sconosciuto thereafter leaves the peasants to their own devices, he departs from orthodox Marxian practice.

Judy Rawson has shown that the title of the *Fontamara* newspaper has a long history in religious, revolutionary and literary contexts (Rawson 1981). The religious context need not concern us for the moment, although we shall need to return to it later; but in the revolutionary and literary contexts the title *What is to be done?* (Chto Delat?) was used by Nicolai Chernyshevsky for the novel he wrote while in prison in 1863. It was greatly admired by successive generations of young revolutionaries, including Lenin, who used its title for a tract of 1902 in which he dealt with a plan of action for the formation of a network of agents to assist the workers' movement (Lenin 1961). Vittorio Foa has written that Lenin's tract was a classic 'reference point' for young Communists of his generation (Foa 1991, 245). The first step to be taken is the establishment of a newspaper. But Lenin advocates the creation of a national, not a local, newspaper, regarding a local journal as too easily suppressed by the authorities and not raising matters of national interest. One of the functions of a national newspaper, in Lenin's thought, is to impose the party's policy on all its members and supporters, since the masses are incapable of formulating an ideology for themselves. The spontaneity of the workers needs always to be guided. One could perhaps compare this to the way in which, in the 1940s, the Italian Communist Party dispatched its intellectuals into the countryside in an attempt to direct and control a movement which had already begun spontaneously. Their behaviour was in striking contrast to that of the Solito Sconosciuto, and it seems likely that his almost ostentatious abstention from interference in the peasants' affairs and the creation of a strictly local newspaper must indicate Silone's dissent from the Marxist-Leninist line on which current Communist Party activity was based, a dissent which he makes a shade more marked in revising the novel in the context of the PCI's attempt to take over the peasant movement in the 1940s.

It may be possible to see *Che fare?* in Gramscian terms as an example of 'integral journalism'. Writing on 'Giornalismo' in his *Prison Notebooks*, the Sardinian specified: 'The type of journalism which will be considered in these notes is that which could be called "integral" ... that is, which not only aims at satisfying all the needs (of a certain category) of its public, but aims at creating and developing those needs and thus, in a sense, at stimulating its public and progressively extending its area' (Gramsci 1966, 131). At all events, *Che fare?* is precisely the kind of local journal that Lenin roundly condemns (Lenin 1961, 486).

In 1927, the Communists had argued that the agrarian crisis revealed the essential weakness of the Italian economy and created a basis for the peasants to intervene alongside the workers in the struggle against Fascism (De Felice 1968, II, 467).

The presumption is that the workers are already fighting Fascism and that the peasants are to be their latest recruits. But Silone's peasants are not recruited to the urban workers' army. In the 1933 version Berardo appeals for unity between workers and peasants in words which sound uncomfortably like a party slogan:

'L'Unità... Hai mai sentito questa parola?... Bisogna portare a Fontamara questa parola... Basta con gli odî tra cafoni. Basta con gli odî tra cafoni e operai. Una cosa sola ci manca: L'Unità... Tutto il resto verrà da sé'

Unity... Have you ever heard that word?... You must take that word to Fontamara... Enough of hatred between peasants and workers. Unity is the one thing we lack... Everything else will follow (Silone 1933, 184–5).

These words are subsequently omitted from the novel, which focusses instead on co-operation within the local community. Nor do the peasants fight: they merely, for the first time in their lives, begin to question the validity of the social order and ask what can be done to right their wrongs. If theirs is a revolution, it is one of a most unusual kind. Of what kind it is, and on what ideology it is based, will be the subject of the next chapter.

In the present context, it is enough to emphasize the extent to which Silone's view of the role of the peasantry and the urban working class differs from that which was being put forward by the Communist Party in Italy in the 1940s. Luigi Cacciatore's claim, at the Eboli conference on the land question in December 1947, that the alliance between peasants and workers was 'an indestructible reality' (Capo 1984, 78) has all the air of being a triumph of rhetoric over reality. Capo, on the other hand, sees the occupation movements as a spontaneous popular movement which was 'not at all disposed to allow itself to be utilized or instrumentalized by political parties for aims other than the conquest of the land' (ibid., 192). Capo also argues that land reform was not in fact a priority for the Communist Party, which merely wanted to use peasant unrest for its own purposes, while power would be won by its élite, the urban working class (ibid., 48, 82). If that is the case, one has to reject any interpretation of the novel, such as Virdia's, which sees the peasants as achieving an awareness of solidarity with the working class (Virdia 1979, 56), not on the grounds that the text of the novel does not support it, but that it specifically rejects it.

History, meanwhile has added a wry footnote to the text. By the late nineteenth century, most of the Torlonia land was let or sub-let to peasants from the surrounding villages. Continuous population increases produced progressive fragmentation of the holdings. In 1910 there had been 1,600 registered tenants. By 1914, these had become 4,800. By the end of the second world war, 9,000 tenants rented 29,000 parcels of land. Of the 16,000 hectares expropriated, 13,000 were assigned in 9,000 lots. Tenants simply became owners. King comments: 'The great failure from the social point of view was that no land was available for the 2,000–3,000 braccianti who had in fact been the foremost agitators in the struggle for expropriation' (King 1973, 101). Asked in 1969, 'Ma l'Abruzzo di *Fontamara*, 1930, esiste ancora?', Silone replied:

'Ci sono i residui di quel *Fontamara* d'una volta. Non nel piano del Fucino, evidentemente, che [...] è oggi una delle regioni più progredite d'Italia, ma nelle valli, per esempio, nelle alte valli che circondano il Fucino ci sono ancora paesi in condizioni forse peggiori di Fontamara, villaggi senza luce, senz'acqua [...]'.

There are remains of that Fontamara of once upon a time. Obviously not on the Fucino plain, which is […] today one of the most advanced regions of Italy, but in the valleys, for example the high valleys around the plain, there are still villages in conditions perhaps worse than *Fontamara*, villages without light, without water […] (Rosato 1969, 23).

The peasant movement was defeated after all, albeit not in the bloody manner Silone had anticipated.

CHAPTER 8

Ignazio Silone and Comrade Jesus

Christ-figures play a vital part in Silone's fiction. For the sake of his new-found friend, the Solito Sconosciuto, Berardo allows himself to be killed in a Fascist jail. The death of Luigi Murica in *Pane e vino* is patterned on that of Jesus, while the title of the novel points to a commemorative 'last supper' held after his death. Pietro Spina in *Il seme sotto la neve* confesses to a murder he has not committed in order to save the deaf and dumb Infante. Both these novels were written before the 1947 version of *Fontamara* and show the extent to which Silone had in the intervening years become increasingly preoccupied with the person of Jesus. Nor did that preoccupation diminish in later years. Lazzaro in *Una manciata di more* (1952) is a 'red Christ'. Luca sacrifices himself, willingly suffering imprisonment, in *Il segreto di Luca* (1956), for the sake of a woman's honour. In *La volpe e le camelie* (1960) a Fascist spy commits suicide rather than ruin the life of a refugee's daughter, whom he loves. They all make their sacrifice not so much on account of unorthodox but dearly-held principles or ideologies as for the sake of people they hold dear, in accordance with Silone's reading of the gospel according to St John 15:13: 'Greater love has no man than this, that a man lay down his life for his friends'. Inevitably, and appropriately, studies such as Edwin M. Moseley's *Pseudonyms of Christ in the Modern Novel* (1962) and Theodor Ziolkowsky's *Fictional Transfigurations of Jesus* (1972) all have an obligatory reference to Silone or a chapter on him. Nor is it even regarded as surprising that an author who was at one time a member of the Communist Party and was certainly never a member in his mature years of any church should so consistently express so deep an admiration for Jesus. It is not necessary to go as far as José Miranda, who has argued that Karl Marx, at the height of his maturity, was a Christian (Miranda 1977); one need only remember *Jésus* (1927), by Henri Barbusse, a friend of Silone, which interpreted the life and teachings of Jesus as anticipating communism, or Milan Machovec's *A Marxist Looks at Jesus* (1976), in which, while arguing that the Christian tradition has distorted and betrayed the image of its founder, he also maintains that Jesus is the man who did more than anyone else before him to introduce into human history the idea of love for one's fellow human beings. Jesus represents for Silone the unconditional, loving acceptance of one's fellow human beings: an acceptance which, if necessary, can be carried to the limits of self-sacrifice.

Silone has chosen to set his novels in an area of Italy associated with Franciscan spirituality and in which there survived amongst the peasants a piety which had its roots deep in the past. He wrote in *Uscita di sicurezza* that:

> Presso i più sofferenti, sotto la cenere dello scetticismo, non s'è mai spenta l'antica speranza del Regno, l'antica attesa della carità che sostituisca la legge, l'antico sogno di Gioachino da Fiore, degli Spirituali, dei Celestini. E questo è un fatto d'importanza enorme, fondamentale, sul quale nessuno ha mai riflettuto abbastanza. In un paese deluso esaurito stanco come il nostro, questa mi è sempre apparsa una richezza autentica, una miracolosa riserva (Silone 1998, 823).

> Amongst those who suffer most, under the ashes of scepticism, the ancient hope in the Kingdom, the ancient expectation of that Love which will replace the law, the ancient dream of Joachim of Fiore, the Spirituals, of men like Celestino, has never died out. This is a fact of enormous, fundamental importance, on which no one has reflected sufficiently. In a country as disappointed, tired and exhausted as ours, this has always seemed to me to be authentic riches, a miraculous reserve.

Or, to use the terms which Hobsbawm uses in his *Primitive Rebels* (1963), primitive rebellion and messianic religion are never far apart. This applies not only to *L'avventura di un povero cristiano*, which deals with the hermit who became Pope Celestino V, but to all Silone's major works: the implied Utopia of *Fontamara* and the Pietro Spina novels is more redolent of Franciscanism than of Marxism. Silone recorded in *Uscita di Sicurezza* his belief that the peasants were more open to Joachim than to Gramsci, and in the Pietro Spina novels he expresses the view that not only were the peasants not open to politics but that it was understandable that they should not be. Giuseppe Gangale, who wrote on the south for Gobetti's review, *Rivoluzione liberale*, states that this peasant mentality predates the heresies of the twelfth century (Basso 1961, 454). It is interesting that Silone denied that his novels were political novels. They were, he said, anti-political, in that they represented the condition of man caught up in the mechanism of politics, and that it was obvious that their author was on the side of man, not of the mechanism (Virdia 1979, 4). Silone goes on to say in his autobiographical essay that the peasants' piety may by now be diluted by superstition or overlaid by scepticism, or by the encroaching ethic of the consumer society, but it seems foolish to deny its reality. Salvemini used to tell his Harvard students that superficial observers do not register the existence of this mystic Italy. Writing about Abruzzo and Molise in 1948, Silone insisted that it was still Italy's most Christian region (Silone 1948, 9)

The significance of a Christ-figure in a work of fiction, however, will vary greatly according to the historical circumstances in which the action is set and those in which the author is writing. In *Fontamara*, Silone is careful to remind us that the events he relates take place in 1929. The prestige of the Fascist government was then at its height, and one important factor contributing to this situation was undoubtedly the signing of the Lateran Treaty in February of that year. The Roman Catholic Church officially recognised the regime and introduced the teaching of religion into state schools. The state, for its part, recognised papal sovereignty over the territory of the Vatican and revived and strengthened that article of Carlo Alberto's *Statuto* of 1848, which had declared the Roman Catholic faith to be the national religion. Although the election of 1929 was on a single-list basis, it seems reasonable to suppose that many – perhaps most – of the votes cast in favour of Fascist candidates were a genuine expression of support for the government. In *Fontamara*, it is Michele Zompa who reminds us of the reconciliation of Church recalling that 'Dopo la pace tra il papa e il governo, come ricordate, il curato ci spiegò dall'altare che cominciava anche per i cafoni una nuova epoca' [After the peace between the pope and the government, you remember that the priest explained to us from the altar that a new era was beginning for us peasants as well] (Silone 1998, 26).

Silone's use of Christ-figures, and the religious dimension of his work, are almost invariably explained in terms of his upbringing, his mother's undoubted piety, and the place that Christianity, and the Franciscan tradition in particular, occupy in Abruzzese peasant culture. Another factor, however, may well be the tendency of the Fascist state to usurp the language and imagery of religious discourse. Historically, this tendency can be traced back in Italy to the Risorgimento; Alberto Banti, for example, argues that the emotional appeal of much nationalist discourse owed much to the story of Christ (Banti 2000, 123). Silone can be seen as reacting to Fascism's use of religious vocabulary, as well as the involvement of the Roman Catholic Church, by depicting Christ-figures who make their appearance as misfits, outcasts or fugitives in a state which officially professes the religion of 'peace on earth, good will to men' at the same time as it fosters aggressive nationalism and militarism. The ethic which the state practises exposes the falsity of its official policies: it is difficult to see the peace-makers of the Beatitudes in those who were intended to wield what Mussolini referred to as his 'eight and a half million bayonets' in colonial conquests. It goes without saying that Silone's Christ-figures are challengingly polemical in intention, since they, like the original on which they are based, are despised and rejected by a materialistic society. Equally, it becomes difficult to see as the body of Christ a worldly-wise Church that endorses Fascism. In this respect, Silone's attitude towards Christianity differed significantly from that of Mazzini, who in other respects exerted a strong influence over him. Silone's reverence for Jesus has much in common with Mazzini's but, as Silone notes, Mazzini thought that the 'revolutionary energies' of Christianity were exhausted (Silone 1939, 15). Silone, however, is careful to draw a distinction between what he sees as the undiminished subversive potential of Christianity and the time-serving conformism of the church and its worldly hierarchy.

The priests whom we meet in Silone's novels fall into two categories. Don Abbacchio, in *Fontamara*, is a grasping and materialistic member of the local power structure, attempting to use his spiritual authority and influence to further the Impresario's purposes. In other novels, however, we come across unorthodox priests who challenge the status quo. Don Benedetto, in *Pane e vino*, will not bless the national flag, seeing such an act as a sin of idolatry: and when the younger time-serving conformist, Don Picirilli, says that he has written an article for the diocesan magazine on 'the scourge of our times', Don Benedetto enquires with deceptive mildness whether his subject is war or unemployment. Don Picirilli has, of course, written about modesty in dress, and he explains that the diocesan magazine deals only with spiritual, not political matters. The notion that subjects like war or unemployment have no moral or spiritual dimension and are therefore no concern of the church could be put forward only by a moral moron, and Don Benedetto naturally rejects it. There is surely an echo here of the priest who in *Uscita di sicurezza* tells the young and enquiring Silone that he is there to teach Christian doctrine and that what happens outside the church is no concern of his. Don Benedetto eventually pays for his unorthodoxy with his life.

Silone, then, sees the church as an establishment which is part of society's power-structures, siding with the powers of oppression and therefore morally bankrupt, within which it is difficult and dangerous to attempt to put into practice the precepts of the gospels. It is however noticeable that the attack on the church and its alliance with the state is sharper in the 1933 version of *Fontamara* than it is the post-war versions, which may be one factor contributing to the assumption by some critics that Silone must have retreated from his early Marxism to more conservative positions (Annoni 1974, 35; Padovani 1982, 103).

Michele Zompa's dream describes how Jesus's desire to grant a special favour to the peasants to mark the signing of the Lateran Treaty is frustrated by the Pope. In the first version, Jesus wants to distribute the Fucino land to the peasants: but the Pope objects that Prince Torlonia would not agree, and that he contributes to St Peter's coffers. Jesus then proposes exempting the peasants from paying their taxes: but the Pope replies that the government will not agree, and that the government contributes to St Peter's coffers. Jesus, still eager to relieve the peasants' misery, suggests allowing them a bumper harvest: but the Pope reminds him that the prices of agricultural produce would fall as a result, and he must remember that bishops and cardinals are big land-owners. In the course of revision, these exchanges are toned down. The Prince must now not be deprived of his land because he is 'a good Christian', as are members of the government, and the fall of agricultural prices would distress not prelates but merchants, who are also described as 'good Christians'. The references to St Peter's coffers disappear, as do the financial benefits to the church of its alliance with the state. In part these changes are no doubt an effect of the general toning-down of the cruder aspects of Silone's irony from the first to the final version: but in part they must also be a reflection of the fact that Italy is no longer ruled by a dictator who was hailed by Pope Pius XI as a 'man sent by providence'.

In *Il seme sotto la neve*, Don Severino, a priest who still has a conscience, poses the question of whether we would recognize Christ if he were to return today. Could we tell the difference between Christ and Barabbas, if the latter were in uniform, on horse-back, his chest covered with medals, and if he were followed by armed men, and acclaimed by crowds of servants, scribes and priests, while Jesus on the other hand was escorted by two policemen, like a common refugee or outlaw? In that novel, the final description of Pietro Spina being led off to prison for a crime he did not commit, handcuffed between two policemen, more than adequately answers the question, while the description of Barabbas could be read as an ironic account of Mussolini.

It is however clear that Berardo Viola, who is the only peasant character in *Fontamara* to be strongly individualised, is not a Christ-figure in the opening chapters. When we first meet him, he is a wild young man who stands out by virtue of his great strength, his violent temper and his destructive tendencies. He smashes the street-lamps on the grounds that since the village's electricity supply has been cut off they serve no useful purpose. (One wonders whether Silone knew that the drunken Karl Marx, after a London pub-crawl of epic proportions, had also smashed street lamps.) Berardo's 'bitter doctrine' is that 'Non si discute con le autorità' [You don't argue with the authorities] (Silone 1998, 73). His instinctive reaction is to meet oppression and injustice with violence: 'Egli non lasciava impunita nessuna ingiustizia che ci venisse dal capoluogo' [He left unpunished no injustice meted out to us from the local town] (Silone 1998, 72) His proposed method for dealing with the Impresario is simple:

> Mettetegli fuoco alla conceria e vi restituirà l'acqua senza discutere. E se non capisce l'argomento, mettetegli fuoco al deposito dei legnami. E se non gli basta, con una mina fategli saltare la fornace dei mattoni. E se è un idiota e continua a non capire, bruciategli la villa, di notte, quando è a letto con donna Rosalia. Solo così riavrete l'acqua (Silone 1998, 74).

Set fire to his tannery and he'll give you back your water without quibbling. And if he doesn't understand that argument, set fire to his timberyard. And if that's not enough for him, blow up his brick-kiln with a bomb. And if he's an idiot and still doesn't understand, set fire to his house one night when he's in bed with Donna Rosalia. That's the only way you'll get your water back.

At this stage, neither loving his neighbour nor turning the other cheek, Berardo has more in common with his bandit-ancestors than with the Jesus of the gospels. If, in this first part of the novel, there is an implicit comparison with a biblical figure it is with Moses when, in chapter IV, Berardo leads the villagers to the 'promised land' of the Fucino plain, lured by the slogan of 'Fucino a chi lo coltiva'.

In Silone's use of this slogan at that point in the novel, there is perhaps a clue to the way in which we might interpret Berardo's actions. 'Land to those who cultivate it', in the sense of 'Land to the peasants', had been used by Mussolini in the early days of Fascism, and only when he realized his need of the support of the southern landowners was it given the meaning it acquires in chapter IV of *Fontamara* of 'Land to those who have the capital with which to cultivate it'. But the slogan also has anarchist associations. Michael Bakunin (1814–76), who had been very influential in Italy, had used it in its primary meaning of 'Land to the peasants'. It could well be that we are intended to see the Berardo of the early chapters as a violent anarchist.

The anarchist movement was, by and large, a product of the eighteenth and nineteenth centuries and was a reaction against the increasingly powerful centralized and industrialized state which more and more seemed to be the model to which most developed countries were conforming. Starting from the premise that people are inherently good and reasonable, anarchists believe that it is possible for all organs of the state to be abolished, to be replaced by free association and the voluntary cooperation of individuals and groups. Anarchism has always been a significant presence in Italian political life since the mid-nineteenth century. Bakunin, who has been described as the father of modern anarchism, came to Italy in 1864 convinced that it was the weakest link in the chain of reactionary Europe. The continual violent mass protests of the period were the grounds for his belief and led him to describe the Italian peasantry as 'naturally revolutionary' (Bogliari 1980, 38). This view is supported by Tarrow, who argues that:

> the southern Italian peasant was an anarchist extraordinary, not only by virtue of his poverty and ignorance, but because of his social instability. Bakunin's concept of spontaneous and continual revolution was as appealing in the south of Italy as it was among the anarchic peasant masses of southern Spain (Tarrow 1967, 277).

The activities of Bakunin and the Italian anarchists in 1873–4 are the subject of Bacchelli's novel *Il diavolo al Pontelungo* (1927). It is also worth remembering Bakunin's dictum that revolutions are made by those who have nothing to lose (Joll 1980, 41), as well as Giuvà's comment that Berardo 'ragionava come uno che non ha nulla da perdere' [talked like somebody with nothing to lose] (Silone 1998, 74).

Italy is one of the countries in which anarchism has always been strong. It had been at the centre of the waves of protest that unsettled Italy up to the first world war, and the movement continued to be a vital part of the Italian Socialist movement until the 1920s. In 1929, the year in which the action of the novel is set, Errico Malatesta, the most consistent of Italian anarchists, was living in Rome. Kropotkin's *Paroles d'un révolté* had earlier been translated into Italian as *Parole d'un ribelle* (1904) by an obscure young Socialist school-master named Benito Mussolini, who found the book overflowing with a great love of oppressed humanity and infinite kindness. Silone – who had at one stage worked in Spain and may also have come across anarchism there too – was naturally well aware of the anarchist presence and influence in Italy, and he had read such anarchist writers as Proudhon (1809–65), Blanqui (1805–81) and probably Kropotkin (1842–1921), as well as Bakunin. Carl Levy has shown that two generations of socialists, Turati's and Gramsci's, could not avoid the anarchist tendency (Levy 1999, 2); certainly no one as involved in left-wing politics as Silone could have been unaware of the need to define his position with regard to anarchism, the correct tactics for a revolutionary party and the relationship between intellectuals and the revolutionary movement. In *Uscita di sicurezza* he links anarchism and Franciscanism, arguing that Franciscanism and anarchism have always been the most accessible forms of rebellion to lively spirits in the Marsica region: but in that same essay anarchism is represented as a lonely struggle against authority, doomed to failure. Can Silone reasonably be described as an anarchist, then? The description of the kingdom of God in *L'avventura di un povero cristiano* as the age of the Spirit, with neither Church nor State has both Joachimite and anarchistic overtones, and towards the end of his life Silone argued that institutions tended to become ends in themselves, forgetting the purpose for which they were originally created (Gurgo & Core 1998, 425–6).

It is noteworthy that when he was arrested in Switzerland in 1942 on charges of communist and anarchist plotting, Silone rejected the charge of communism with some feeling – as well he might, given that he had broken with the party – but he did not comment on the charge of anarchism. It is however the case that anarchists have tended to regard Silone as one of their number: Herbert Read, for example, listed him among the thinkers who have most contributed to strengthen anarchist thought in recent decades and Colin Ward alludes to him in *Anarchy in Action* (1973). But just as he described himself as being a Christian 'in his own way' (Gurgo & Core 1998, 388), Silone's response to such tributes was to say that he could not be defined as an anarchist in 'the historically determined meaning of the term' (D'Eramo 1971, 547) – which is perhaps as anarchistic a preservation of his political and intellectual independence as one might expect, and may be compared to his denial of literary influences. The 'anxiety of influence' in Silone's case extended to the intellectual as well as the literary sphere. He generally preferred in later life, as in 'Il pane di casa' (1971), to describe himself as a libertarian Socialist or as a Socialist without a party. Both descriptions could be regarded as synonyms of anarchist, and it is also noteworthy that by the late 1940s he had ceased to use the phrase 'democratic state', preferring instead to refer to 'democratic society'. Arnone suggests that Silone's experience of post-war politics caused him to become even more distrustful than before of authoritarian societies and helped clarify his libertarian convictions (Arnone 1980, 14). It may well be also that Silone wished to distinguish himself from contemporary anarchists on the grounds that his political philosophy, unlike theirs, had its roots in a particular reading of the Gospels influenced by the Joachimite tradition. In 'L'eredità cristiana', which precedes *L'avventura di un povero cristiano*, Silone wrote of 'una terza età del genere umano, senza Chiesa, senza Stato, senza esercitazioni, in una società egualitaria, sobria, umile, benigna, affidata alla spontanea carità degli uomini' [a third age of humankind, with no Church, no State, no compulsions, egalitarian, sober, humble, benevolent, relying on men's spontaneous charity] (Silone 1999, 555).

Ultimately, one has to attempt to define Silone's philosophical position on the basis of his novels, rather than on his empirical involvement with existing political parties. Anarchists were not agreed about the methods by which the transformation of present society, over-governed and over-regulated, into the free society of the future was to be brought about. The followers of Blanqui advocated the use of violence to seize power. Bakunin continued the Blanqui line, and his followers advocated a policy of individual acts of terrorism which came to be known as 'propaganda by the deed'. In both the popular imagination and the world of serious fiction it is this line of anarchism that has achieved greatest prominence. In the last decades of the nineteenth century and the early decades of this, a wave of anarchist violence swept Europe and America: it was a group of Italian anarchists living in New Jersey who planned and executed the assassination of King Umberto I in 1900. Anarchists of this stamp make an appearance in *The Princess Casamassima* by Henry James and *The Secret Agent* by Joseph Conrad. The Berardo of the early chapters of *Fontamara*, with his acts of ultimately unproductive violence, seems to be in the tradition of propaganda by the deed.

It could of course be argued that Berardo is simply engaging in what James C. Scott has called 'everyday forms of resistance'. Such forms of resistance include '"foot-dragging", dissimulation, false compliance, feigned ignorance, desertion, pilfering, smuggling, poaching, arson, slander, sabotage, surreptitious assault and murder, anonymous threats, and so on' (Scott 1989, 5). Berardo does indeed either advocate or engage in these techniques of 'first resort', but in the overall context of the novel and of Berardo's development, more seems to be at stake than the use of what Scott calls 'the weapons of the weak'.

In order to transform the justice-seeking but destructive Berardo into a self-sacrificing Christ-figure, Silone has to manipulate the events of his plot, as well as adding, in the course of revision, touches that stress the earlier Berardo's devotion to the ideals of friendship and justice, thus giving his terrorism a purpose it lacked in the earlier version. Silone also lays more stress in the 1940s on the child-like quality of his nature. Once Berardo openly declares his intention of marrying Elvira, he acquires a piece of land: his desire to marry and settle down then make him just as much of a self-seeking egoist as the other *fontamaresi* had been. He loses his interest in questions of justice and principle precisely at the moment when the other villagers are prepared to follow his earlier teachings. When they seek to enlist his support in their intended rebellion, he tells them he must now look after his own interests, thus adopting the selfish, familist philosophy he had previously scorned. He then fails in his attempt to find work in Rome, however, and he also learns of the death of Elvira. This is another shameless piece of manipulation on Silone's part, faced as he now is with a character who, as long as she is alive, is an impediment to Berardo's political and spiritual growth and must be removed.

Apart from Elvira's mysterious death, each of the events leading up to Berardo's failure to find work and settle down is plausible, if taken on its own. The wily Don Circostanza, who purchased Berardo's original plot of land in circumstances which strongly suggest fraud on the lawyer's part, sells him a piece of land in an exposed position on the mountain-side and therefore subject to flash-flooding, which washes away the scanty top-soil. Berardo will not find work in Rome because of regulations designed to restrict internal emigration. Nevertheless, there is about the sequence of events an invariable leaning towards disaster which reveals the hand of the author at work. Elvira's death is altogether too convenient, while the coincidence of Berardo's meeting with the Solito Sconosciuto in Rome – a city rather larger than Avezzano, after all – places a certain strain on our willingness to suspend our disbelief.

Berardo the conformist is no more of a Christ-figure than Berardo the terrorist, and so the circumstances of his life have to be manipulated in order to allow him to follow his vocation. In his despair, Berardo reverts to what Giuvà's son describes as his 'former way of thinking' (Silone 1998, 180). Once again without land, and therefore with nothing to lose, his ideas are channelled into a more positive direction by his encounter with the Solito Sconosciuto and his rediscovery of friendship. His mother had remarked earlier that if Berardo were to die in jail, it would be for the sake of friendship, not for money (Silone 1998, 72). The youthful narrator, observing with dismay the growth of Berardo's friendship with his fellow-prisoner, feels obscurely that his companion is 'lost', although he also registers Berardo's conviction that his life has now finally acquired a meaning (Silone 1998, 181). Silone probably has in mind at this point Jesus's saying that 'He who loses his life for my sake shall gain it' (Matthew 11:39). We already know that Berardo is capable of doing remarkable things for the sake of friendship, so that it is not out of character for him now to declare that he is the agitator the police are seeking in order to allow his new-found friend to escape.

That Berardo's self-sacrifice is Christ-like, in the sense of being completely altruistic, is stressed by a number of features of the text – more so in the 1940s versions than in the earlier one. He is thirty at the time of his death, which is an age sometimes attributed to Jesus at his crucifixion (thirty-three is the age more usually attributed to him). When he is dragged back to the cell, he is compared to Christ being taken down from the cross (Silone 1998, 185), and when he can hardly stand after being beaten he is a wretched 'ecce homo' (Silone 1998, 185). This last comparison is a 1949, not a 1947 addition, which suggests that Silone continued to look for language and imagery with which to emphasise Berardo's Christ-likeness.

D'Eramo finds that the revision process stresses that his death is not voluntary, maintaining that when declaring to the police that he was the Solito Sconosciuto, Berardo could not have envisaged his own death (D'Eramo 1971, 44). This is partly true, in the sense that, after his friend's release, Berardo seems about to tell the truth in order to secure his own freedom. It is the appearance of the clandestine newspaper bearing his own name and telling the story of his village, proof of his new friend's continuing loyalty, that dramatically hardens his resolve not to reveal his earlier stratagem. It is at this point that his death becomes both certain and freely accepted: 'Adesso piuttosto preferisco morire', he says, [Now I would rather die] (Silone 1998, 186), convinced that his death will introduce into his divided society a new unity. He will be the first *cafone* to die for others rather than for his own interests. The doubts which then assail him during the night are his equivalent of Jesus's agony in the garden of Gethsemane, when he prayed that this cup might be taken away from him, but nevertheless accepted what he regarded as God's will. Berardo's emphasis on the novelty of his sacrifice – 'Sarò il primo cafone che non muore per sé, ma per gli altri' [I shall be the first peasant to die for others, rather than for himself] (Silone 1998, 187) is also introduced in the 1947 Faro edition along with the references to 'novelty' or 'strangeness'.

Two further points need to be made at this stage about Berardo as Christ-figure. Firstly, it is natural enough that peasant characters, in a novel set in a region noted for its Franciscan associations, should express their reactions to events in religious terms and use Christian imagery. The exhausting journey of the women to see the new mayor, for example, is compared to a *via crucis*, but the image expresses suffering and humiliation, rather than suggesting that the women are a collective Christ-figure. That Berardo's mother, on the other hand, is compared to Mary at Calvary may express on one level the other women's perception of her as anxious and grieving, but on another level it reinforces, even at this early stage of the novel (Silone 1998, 72), our eventual perception of Berardo as Christ-like. Secondly, Silone is making use of an Abruzzo folk-belief, to which he refers explicitly in *Il seme sotto la neve*, that Jesus did not die on the cross but is eternally in agony. The crucifixion is thus seen – as it is by some theologians – as both an event in history and the expression of an eternal truth about the suffering inflicted on God by mankind's continuing sinfulness. Popular religion, moreover, linked both Jesus and St Francis with the early forms and the basic principles of Socialism (Nesti 1974, 35–6) – which is, no doubt, why it was possible for a young man from Ciociaria to say to Salvemini in a Roman prison in 1925: 'Let's hope that in Purgatory the holy soul of Lenin is praying for us' (Origo 1984, 152).

Salvemini saw this as Christianity living on in the Communist religion, just as Christianity had previously absorbed pagan elements, and something of this survival is reflected in Silone's novels. In *Una manciata di more*, a peasant woman has a vision of the Sacred Heart of Jesus on which are emblazoned the Hammer and Sickle.

But Silone's own perception is very different. In *Vino e pane* the lawyer Zabaglione remembers that in the office of the Peasant League at Fossa there had been, next to the portrait of Marx, a picture of Jesus in a red shirt – the Redeemer of the poor. Silone wrote in *Avanti!* in 1945 that democratic Socialism was the principal heir to Christian values (Mercuri 1979, xviii). By the time he came to write his *Memoriale dal carcere svizzero* in 1942 Silone was describing himself unambiguously as a Christian – although, it has to be remembered, his was a Christianity without superstructures, in which he conducted his spiritual life without the aid of priest or sacraments. His lay funeral fits easily into the tradition of lay, often anticlerical funerals described by Nesti (Nesti 1974, 16–17), but he chose to give it a specifically Christian dimension by asking for the Lord's prayer to be said over his body and for a simple cross to mark his grave.

Novels are not 'real life' and fictional characters are not 'real people': but how realistic is it to expect a peasant to become a Christ-figure? Is Silone holding up an ideal, urging us to reach out for a Utopia we have no hope of grasping: or has he, in this as in other ways, expressed in his fiction a phenomenon which is in fact to be encountered in peasant society? It comes as something of a surprise to find a social anthropologist reporting that in peasant society 'there may emerge certain figures who stand outside the competition and symbolize the common desire for communal harmony. These are Christ-like persons, whose reputation one would expect not to be assailed and who therefore should have no need to protect it' (Bailey 1971, 21). But, Bailey continues, very few such persons emerge and when they do, they are mocked: to be 'too good' is to be 'stupid'. A literary reflection of this robust attitude is to be found in the figure of Michele's father in Moravia's *La ciociara*, with his refrain of 'Qua, nessuno è fesso' [No one is stupid here]. Silone, however, has taken care to stress that Berardo, having neither wife nor land, is not only outside the normal competition but also, as Howe points out, 'free from the conservative inclinations of even those peasants who had nothing more than a strip of land' (Howe 1961, 125). He is also already greatly respected by the community, and the villagers, being more naturally pious than Moravia's peasant refugees, are not inclined to mock Berardo's Christ-likeness, although they are puzzled by it, seeing death in prison as a 'strange salvation' (Silone 1998, 190). Berardo is thus able to become the focus of aspirations which without him would never have been expressed

He is, of course, a demythologized Christ. There is no resurrection in the supernatural sense. Berardo can be said to live on, however, in two senses: as a figure who becomes a myth, who indeed was destined from the novel's early chapters to become a myth, presented as he is as being exceptional in every way. The *fontamaresi* can respect him even in his death and, because he died for them, can respect each other. They can now cooperate. They no longer wish to kill and destroy, which in Hobsbawm's analysis is the classical pattern of primitive rebellion: they have renounced anarchic violence in favour of cooperation and asking questions. Berardo can also be said to live on in the village's new sense of friendship.

Thus the village becomes the new collective, rather than individual hero. But, as we have seen, Silone's heroes are usually Christ-figures whose lives end in crucifixion – hence the second punitive expedition to Fontamara, which destroys the village and scatters the survivors. Hence, too, Silone's infidelity to history, for, as Hanne has pointed out, there were no such massacres in Fascist Italy (Hanne 1992, 136). Silone may also be looking back to the savage punitive expeditions already referred to in the introduction to this book and suggesting that they might recur; but at this point his myth seems to have taken over from history in shaping the novel.

If the early 'unconverted' Berardo was in the anarchist tradition, can the later Christ-like Berardo also have anarchist associations? At this point we must return to the peasant newspaper, *Che fare?*

We have already seen that its title seems to allude to one of Lenin's 'first and most influential' tracts (Rawson 1977, 5), although the peasants' practice is not that advocated by Lenin. But Judy Rawson also points out that in 1933 the paper's title was *Che dobbiamo fare?*, which possibly echoes both Tolstoy's *What*

then must we do? of 1886 and the gospel according to Luke 3:10–1: 'And the mul-
titudes asked him, "What then shall we do?" And he answered them, "He that
has two coats, let him share with him who has none; and he who has food, let
him do likewise"'. The way in which such passages can be used to give divine
authority to Socialist principles is obvious. The question is put by a shepherd to
Pietro Spina in this Tolstoyan form in *Il seme sotto la neve:* a shepherd, waiting for
the return of the Christ-like Infante, asks: 'E nel frattempo che dobbiamo fare?'
['And in the meantime what must we do?'] (Silone 1998, 986).

There were in fact two main trends in anarchist thought. While Blanqui and
his followers advocated violent revolution, the followers of Pierre-Joseph Proudhon (1809–65) – whom Silone had read – sought peaceful change. Tolstoy, who
greatly influenced the anarcho-pacifist tradition, gives one of the noblest expressions in Christian terms to this tradition. He sought to de-historicize Jesus, to discover the historically unconditioned core of his teaching, uncontaminated by
progress and the passage of time. That core, for Tolstoy, lay in Jesus's moral com-
mandments, especially in those which implied turning the other cheek, non-
resistance to evil, the forgiveness of one's enemies, and the relief of poverty and
suffering. The same period that saw the epidemic of anarchist violence referred
to earlier also saw the establishment of a number of communes or colonies in
which men and women tried to live simple, honest lives and to provide a practical demonstration of the efficacy of Tolstoy's ideas in resolving the dilemmas of
industrialized society. Both the Christian Socialist and the anarco-pacifist traditions, therefore, were strongly influenced by Tolstoy (Nesti 1974, 55).

It is clear from *Uscita di sicurezza* that Silone was familiar with Tolstoy's highly personal version of anarchism from an early age, probably initially at second
hand. He subsequently read a good deal of Tolstoy in Switzerland, and the title
of his pamphlet *What I Stand For* (1942) echoes Tolstoy's *What I Believe*. It seems
likely that the first title of Fontamara's newspaper is a tribute to the Russian
thinker who in *What then must we do?* advocates sharing wealth and land (Rawson 1981). The suggestion that the newspaper's changed title, *Che fare?*, is a reference to Lenin's tract is undermined, however, by the striking discrepancy
between what Lenin advocates and what the peasants actually do. Lenin pointed out the role of 'consciousness' in overcoming the 'spontaneity' of the masses
(Tarrow 1967, 5). He wanted to train propagandists, organizers and leaders who
would bring class consciousness to the workers from without, since it would
never arise solely from their own experience of struggle. Louis de Bernières
catches something of this in *Captain Corelli's Mandolin*, in which the 'sesquipeda-
lian' partisan leader, Hector, is seen by the illiterate Mandras as 'a man who
understood everything. He had a book called *What is to be done* and he knew
exactly where to look in it for guidance. […] it was by a man called Lenin, who
was even more important than Jesus' (de Bernières 1997, 209). Similarly, in

Gramsci's thought, the Party is the 'new Machiavelli' charged with organizing the popular will. At this point it becomes clear how far Silone's Solito Sconosciuto is from being a Leninist propagandist. Indeed, he at no point describes himself as a Communist. In the revision process Silone even excises his claim to incite insurrections. He is not a leader cast in the Leninist mould. He could, however, be an anarchist.

Judy Rawson (Rawson 1981) also draws our attention to a brief 1906 pamphlet by Tolstoy entitled in English *What's to be done?* – literally, *Che fare?* Several points in this text suggest that it was this essay that Silone had in mind, rather than Lenin's pamphlet, when he revised his novel. Tolstoy's pamphlet begins with a visit from two young men (and later a third, thus making up their number to that of Silone's narrators) who have been expelled from Moscow for their part in an armed rising. It expresses disapproval of the activities of revolutionary agitators who incite insurrection, and argues that the government must renounce its power. Evil cannot be conquered by evil. Tolstoy refuses to subscribe to a revolutionary newspaper. The law of loving one's neighbour is in his view the only possible moral response to oppression and injustice. In *The Kingdom of God Is within You*, Tolstoy writes that conscientious persons must resist – but non-violently – every act of government violence and should be prepared to suffer, as the early Christians did. Then, perhaps, their protests will inspire other similar protests and non-violent resistance will become widespread (Tolstoy 1935).

The argument that Silone is remaining within the Tolstoyan tradition is strengthened by those revisions in the novel which considerably tone down Berardo's early violence, and its pointlessness, while stressing his Christ-likeness. It is sometimes assumed that the *fontamaresi* intend to resist Fascist violence with violence (Virdia 1979, 49). This may be the case in chapter VII, but by chapter X they merely ask questions, which is the opposite of violent anarchist 'propaganda by the deed'. In opening a dialogue, the *fontamaresi* are asserting their humanity, as opposed to the sub-human status they had previously accepted. This may be construed as asserting that disturbing questions are ultimately more powerful than actions, while Berardo's conversion can be seen as being from active violence to an espousal of passive suffering.

It would of course have been natural in Italy in the 1940s to assume that the title *Che fare?* was a reference to Lenin's pamphlet, since it had been an important text in the training of young Communist leaders during the Fascist period (Asor Rosa 1975, 1537), and therefore of Silone too. Giovanni Amendola, writing in 1931, said that in Italy in 1926 Lenin's *Che fare?* exercised the same function as it had in Russia in 1898, pointing out to young intellectuals fighting Fascism that the only way to do so was to fight for the proletarian revolution (Ferri 1964, 435).

At this point it has to be said that a number of critics writing on Silone prefer to see him not as an anarchist but as a more or less unorthodox Communist, as though his *Che fare?* indicated that he still identified with the party (Virdia 1979, 50). Italian communism, however, was not always orthodox. Lenin had stressed the importance of the party's leadership of the masses, but Gramsci was concerned with the participation of the masses in the political decisions of the party. Silone seems to go even further than the 'heretical' Gramsci, in that he seems prepared to dispense with the party and its structures.

Virdia makes a more valid point when he goes on to argue that one of the functions of the newspaper's title is to involve Silone's readers, by addressing the question to them. Others recognise that Silone is indeed an anarchist of some sort, but assume that this must of necessity involve extreme individualism, and therefore constitutes a limitation to Silone's relevance, a limitation which is both intellectual and human (Salinari 1967, 322). Others merely assume that a withdrawal from the party political system must of necessity involve a more conservative stance (Annoni 1974, 35) or even a total withdrawal from history itself into the realm of the ontological (Padovani 1982, 103). Some light may be shed on these problems by an examination of the possible antecedents to Silone's ideas and of the anarcho-pacifist tradition.

That Silone saw an analogy between religious and political commitment from an early stage is clear from his use of Ignazio as a pseudonym and by the way in which he chose the Communist party for moral rather than exclusively political motives. He always spoke of his political creed in terms of faith and values, rather than of a system. For his veneration for Jesus, however, we do not need to go to Marxist sources: a similar veneration for a Jesus of social justice is expressed by Mazzini, a selection of whose writings Silone edited in *The Living Thoughts of Mazzini* in 1939. (A second edition was published in 1946.) Like Salvemini, Silone sees Mazzini as one of the forerunners of modern Socialism (Silone 1939, 26), but one who was merely used and exploited by Marx and Bakunin for their own ends. In this essay, which has been described as the first positive revaluation of Mazzini by an Italian Socialist (D'Eramo 1971, 514), Mazzini's religious thought is described sympathetically by Silone, who would later probably have been struck by Ernesto Buonaiuti's cry: 'Mazzini, Mazzini, ci sono italiani disposti a raccogliere il tuo mandato?' [Mazzini, Mazzini, are there any Italians ready to take up your command?] (Buonaiuti 1971, 400). In *Il Risveglio* of 14 March 1945, while he was still publishing Silone's *Fontamara*, Buonaiuti quoted Mazzini on the subject of Christianity:

> Noi veneriamo in Gesù il fondatore di un'epoca emancipatrice dell'individuo, l'Apostolo dell'unità, della legge, più vastamente intesa che non ne' tempi a lui anteriori, il profeta dell'uguaglianza delle anime e ci prostriamo davanti a Lui come davanti all'uomo che più amò, fra quanti sono nati e la cui vita, armonia senza esempio tra il pensiero e l'azione, promulgò [...] il santo dogma del sacrificio (Buonaiuti 1971, 56).

> We revere in Jesus the founder of an epoch emancipating the Individual, the Apostle of unity, of the law understood in a much wider sense than in times before him, the prophet of the equality of souls, and we prostrate ourselves before Him as before the man who most greatly loved, among all men born, and whose life, an unprecedented harmony between thought and action, promulgated [...] the holy dogma of sacrifice.

On 11 April 1945, Buonaiuti wrote that 'Il profetico sogno di Mazzini solo oggi forse sta per avere possibilità di attuazione' [Only today is Mazzini's prophetic dream perhaps about to have an opportunity to be realised] (Buonaiuti 1971, 86). The remarkable affinity of thought and culture between Silone and Buonaiuti, which has never been studied as it should, helps to explain Silone's choice of review in 1945.

It seems likely that Silone's break with the Communist party had led him to look at the origins of Marxism, and to look sympathetically at those who, like Mazzini, had not adhered wholeheartedly to orthodoxy but had gone on to develop the line of anarcho-pacifism. It would probably have struck him that this line of thought involved a rejection of party politics and of the power-struggle. Tolstoy, in his *What's to be Done?* of 1906 wrote:

> I know that to men suffering from that spiritual disease, political obsession, a plain and clear answer to the question What's to be done?, an answer telling them to obey the highest law common to all mankind – the law of love to one's neighbour – will appear abstract and mystical (Tolstoy 1937, 392–3).

Tolstoy's 'law of love to one's neighbour' looms large in anarchist thought, even when, as in Herbert Read's writings, it is rather incongruously linked with the idea of 'insurrectionary passion' (Read 1940, 2); but nowhere is the ethical principle of brotherly love and mutual aid given such a clear expression as it is in the writings of Peter Kropotkin. Studies of Silone do not normally cite Kropotkin, but such was the vogue for his writings that it is at least very likely that Silone read him. In his *Mutual Aid*, Kropotkin argued that the absorption of all social functions by the state necessarily favoured the development of an unbridled, narrow-minded individualism, since obligations towards the state have the effect of relieving citizens of their obligations towards one another, thus enabling people to seek their own happiness while disregarding the wants of others (Kropotkin 1972, 196).

Silone would have been able to see the application of this to Fascist Italy, with its all-inclusive state. Yet, Kropotkin maintained, the 'mutual-aid tendency in man' still survived, and ethical progress could be seen in terms of the extension of this principle from the tribe to always larger agglomerations, so as finally to embrace one day the whole of mankind. Silone's account of his ethical thought in the final paragraphs of *Uscita di sicurezza* is couched in very similar terms. Kropotkin's 'mutual aid' is akin to Silone's 'amicizia', which extends from Berardo and the Solito Sconosciuto to the village, which learns mutual aid in the production of its newspaper. Even the Solito Sconosciuto can be said to have an antecedent in Kropotkin's memoirs, where he asks: 'Where are those who will come to serve the masses – not to utilize them for their own ambitions?' (Kropotkin 1972, 1).

Not that Silone would have found in Kropotkin any comfortable optimism; writing of the 'communist fraternities of Moravia' – communist in the sense that they practised mutual aid – the Russian anarchist wrote bleakly that they were massacred 'by the thousands' (Kropotkin 1972, 195–6). Here, and in Tostoy's concern for the fate of the Russian Dukhovors one may perhaps see the literary and philosophical origins of the denouement of *Fontamara*, which, as we have seen, is very unhistorical. No such massacres took place in Fascist Italy, although violence was still the regime's main tool for controlling the peasantry. They did take place in German-occupied Europe in the course of the second world war. Silone's novel may have a prophetic quality. But in Italy, anarchists and anarchoid behaviour had always been identified in criminal terms; in Fascist Italy the anarchists were persecuted, driven into exile or killed.

Silone's concern with Christian anarcho-pacifism may have been deepened during during his Swiss exile by his reading of Tolstoy, and also by contact with the works of the Swiss pastor Leonhard Ragaz, whose *Von Christus zu Marx, von Marx zu Christus* was published in 1929, the year before Silone wrote *Fontamara*.

The metamorphoses of Berardo seem to me to mark his passage from one form of anarchism to another, from the violent to the Christ-like and loving, from the stream of Blanqui to that of Tolstoy and Kropotkin. At the same time I would see the revision of the text as reflecting not only Silone's greater commitment to what he sees as the central Christian values, but also his desire to adapt his novel to the changed circumstances in Abruzzo in the 1940s. In so doing he resolves what must be a basic problem for any writer who seeks to use the novel form to address specific social issues – the problem, that is, of avoiding writing simply a tract for the times that will cease to have anything other than a historical interest once those issues have been resolved. By making Berardo a Christ-figure and by making 'friendship' – in the sense of community or fellowship – a central issue in the novel, Silone has succeeded in relating his work to a central theme of western European culture. The Utopia towards which he urges us to reach is no nearer to realisation than it was in the 1930s. The political party is still the characteristic mode of government, and even devolution and decentralisation seem to involve the creation of ever larger central bureaucracies. Anarchism may strike the politically sophisticated reader as a naive faith, but it is a salutary naivety, like that of Silone's peasants, and even if the anarchists have failed to achieve their revolution, they – and none more than Silone – have provided a constant criticism of prevailing views and offered an ethical alternative to generally accepted social values by reminding us of the possibility of that 'third age of humankind, with no Church, no State'.

It is perhaps a limitation to Silone's thought that in his novels he tackles the problem of anarchist freedom only in relation to small, closed communities, but the Christ-like love or fraternity on which Silone's 'new way of living' is to be based is both contagious and subversive of the existing social order. It is not violent revolution; violence will come from those guardians of the status quo who respond to the open challenge of the question 'Che fare?' by seeking to defend with force what they interpret as their best interests.

Communism, as it was interpreted and understood within the peasant movement in the context of its post-war struggles, fused with the utopian, religious and mystical elements that were already present in peasant culture. Communism was, moreover, a dangerous kind of mysticism, since it was to be applied to property relationships (Ginsborg 1990, 126). Silone rejects Communism in favour of a movement even more utopian, but he is aware of the problems and dangers involved. He offers no facile solutions: nor would we believe him if he did. All his works end with a series of disasters, but always he insists on the need to reach out towards Utopia, for it is in the striving that our humanity and the imitation of Christ are most fully realized.

CHAPTER 9

Carlo Levi: a Turin intellectual and the problem of the South

INTRODUCTORY

Cristo si è fermato a Eboli is the remarkable account of one northerner's reaction to the experience of living in a small, remote village in southern Italy during the Fascist period. Carlo Levi, who came from Turin, was sentenced in 1935 to three years in *confino*, or internal exile, for his anti-Fascist activities. He was sent first to Grassano, an out-of-the-way hilltop village overlooking the Basento valley in Basilicata, one of Italy's poorest and most backward regions. Most of the area consists of mountain and hills. It had no industry, and its communications were poor. The Fascist government had rebaptized it with its ancient name of Lucania, as part of the process of 'Romanizing' Italy, but did little else for it. After a short time in Grassano, Levi was unexpectedly transferred to the much smaller and even more remote village of Aliano, to which in his book he gives the name of Gagliano, said to derive from the Latin 'Gallianus', possibly with the intention of suggesting that the conditions he was describing were not peculiar to one particular isolated village but were all too typical of the region as a whole. (There is, confusingly, a village named Gagliano del Capo in southern Puglia, in the very tip of the heel of Italy.) He consistently referred to the village as Gagliano in his other published works and interviews. Only in poems not published in his lifetime did he use the name Aliano (Levi 1998, 29, 33, 97), as well as Gagliano (ibid., 45). In a letter of 21 November 1935 to his family, Levi notes that in the local dialect, initial vowels are preceded by a kind of harsh expiration, rather like a 'g', so that 'Aliano' would be pronounced 'Galiano', 'Anna' would become 'Ganna' (ibid., 117).

In the opening paragraphs of *Cristo si è fermato a Eboli*, Levi writes of 'his' peasants, 'i miei contadini' (Levi 1965, 41) and of that land of 'his', devoid of comfort or gentleness, 'quella mia terra senza conforto o dolcezza' (Levi 1965, 42), and in so doing he makes it abundantly clear that he came eventually to identify with the peasants who inhabited the village. In this respect, as in others, he differs significantly from Stefano, the central character of Pavese's *Il carcere*, who rebels against the village to which he is confined and does all he can to distance himself from it psychologically. But it is also clear that Levi was far from feeling well-disposed towards the place when he first arrived there on, as he tells us, an August afternoon in 1935 in the only car in the village, which he describes as 'una piccola macchina sgangherata', [a tottering little car] (Levi 1965, 42). He was handcuffed and escorted by two robust representatives of the State – *cara-binieri*, in other words. 'Ci venivo malvolentieri, preparato a veder tutto brutto, perché avevo dovuto lasciare, per un ordine improvviso, Grassano, dove abitavo prima, e dove avevo imparato a conoscere la Lucania' [I went there reluctantly, ready to see everything in a bad light, because an unexpected order had com-pelled me to leave Grassano, where I had been living before, and where I had got to know Lucania] (Levi 1965, 42).

One can understand Levi's feelings. Gagliano (as I shall call it, following Levi) is singularly uninviting. Erosion of the topsoil has created a dramatic, almost lunar landscape, but as a place in which to live the village has few attractions. Most of the villages of Basilicata are cramped and crowded because of their hill-top situations. They are often many miles away from the nearest railway station – Gagliano's nearest station was eighty-five kilometres away at Grassano – and the poor state of the roads in the 1930s, together with the almost total lack of public transport, other than the trains, made them singularly difficult of access. This no doubt was their main attraction to an oppressive regime which wished to isolate and thus render harmless its critics and opponents. But Gagliano is even more remote than many villages of Basilicata, and the very nature of its site, which is accurately described by Levi as a straggling line of houses on an irreg-ular saddle between steep ravines, makes it even more constricted than other vil-lages I have seen in the area, with the possible exception of the even more squalid frazione of Gaglianello, which had been declared unfit for human habi-tation ten years earlier (but was still partly inhabited when I first saw it in 1988; the inhabitants had been moved to the new village of Alianello Nuovo or to tem-porary accommodation in prefabricated huts, from which some had returned). The sheer squalor of the peasants' one-room houses must also have been a depressing sight to one accustomed to the amenities of modern Turin. 'Le case dei contadini sono tutte eguali fatte di una sola stanza che serve da cucina, da camera da letto e quasi sempre anche da stalla per le bestie piccole...' [The peas-ants' houses are all alike, consisting of a single room which functions as kitchen, bedroom and, almost always, as stable for their small animals...] (Levi 1965, 140). Many of these houses have now disappeared, of course, replaced by blocks of flats which no doubt represent a considerable improvement in living stan-dards: some, however, remain, exactly as Levi describes them, although without the animals, which are now kept either in out-houses or in houses abandoned because of earth-quake damage. Levi describes the surrounding countryside as picturesque, dominated as it is by the 'calanchi', bare, steep slopes of furrowed clay from which the topsoil has been eroded and on which nothing can be grown.

Grassano, in contrast, was larger than Gagliano, and therefore offered, one supposes, a greater variety of people to meet, and so a greater possibility of finding, amongst its inhabitants, individuals whom Levi would find congenial: indeed, his account of his return visit to Grassano indicates that he had found there people with whom he was on good terms and with whom he could converse on subjects close to his heart. It also had the inestimable advantage of a much more open site which permitted greater freedom of movement to a 'confinato' who was required to remain at all times within sight of the built-up area of the village. All the same, Levi's opening statement about his exile is as interesting for what it omits as for what it includes.

Because he had qualified as a doctor, and was also a very talented painter with a national reputation, Levi was no doubt better equipped than many of his fellow-victims of Fascism not only to survive the experience of *confino* with his spirit unbroken – no mean feat in itself – but even to turn it into something positive. In this respect, his creative energy is amazing. In less than a year he painted over sixty pictures and wrote over fifty poems, as well as keeping up a steady stream of letters to family and friends. He was, moreover, rather better informed than most northerners in the Fascist period about conditions in the south and about the complexities – social and historical – of the southern problem. But on this aspect of his previous experience – about which most of his readers would be unaware – Levi maintains in his book a total silence: he merely tells us that he had got to know Lucania while at Grassano. In fact, since he already knew something about what he would find in the south, his stay at Gagliano had the effect of making him see the problem of the south in terms of human misery, poverty and deprivation, rather than as a set of abstract ideas, 'problems' or statistics. His concealment of his previous knowledge is a literary strategy, adopted in order to avoid alienating his readers, whom he reasonably assumes, after two decades of Fascist silence on the subject, to be uninformed about the southern problem. There is no one so annoying as the author who presents his readers with all the answers before they have begun even to understand the questions. Instead, we are as it were invited to share in Levi's discovery of the reality of the south. He can then go on to present his diagnosis and recommendations as arising naturally out of his – and our – discovery of that reality.

When and how, then, did Levi first get to know about the south?

A TURIN INTELLECTUAL AND THE PROBLEM OF THE SOUTH

Levi was born in Turin in November 1902, the son of a well-known and fairly well-to-do Jewish family, members of which were very active in Turinese literary and political circles. They were related to Treves, the publisher, and were to the left of the political spectrum. Levi once said that it was at home that he had got to know the 'general staff of Socialism'. His maternal uncle was Claudio Treves (1869–1933), a leading Socialist of the reformist school; and his cousin Carlo (1908–51) left Italy in 1938 as a result of the racial laws and broadcast for Radio London.

Levi took his degree in medicine and worked from 1924 to 1928 at the University Hospital in Turin. It was a promising start to a career, but he then gave up medicine in order to devote himself to painting. He began as a pupil of Felice Casorati, and exhibited works which showed the influence of his master at the Venice Biennale in 1924 – the same year in which he graduated – and at each Biennale until 1930. Regular visits to Paris brought him under the influence of the French post-impressionists, especially of Matisse. Together with Jessie Boswell, Gigi Chessa, Nicola Galante, Francesco Nunzio and Enrico Paolucci, Levi was a member of the group known as the 'Turin six' – 'i sei pittori di Torino' – who regularly exhibited together, in London and Paris, as well as in Italy, during the years 1929-30. They were eclectic in their styles, anti-academic, and chose deliberately to be European at a time when, under the influence of Fascism, official Italian culture was becoming ever more chauvinistic. The young English composer Edmund Rubbra did not greatly admire Levi's work: 'we didn't think greatly of them like a lot of modern art there was a straining after originality', he wrote, after seeing an exhibition which included some of Levi's work in 1930 (Bullock 2000, 678). Even so, another promising career was opening up for Levi in painting, and a whole room was devoted to his work at the Rome Quadriennale in 1934.

But Levi's life was not totally dedicated to painting and medicine, even during the period when he was successfully launching himself on a career in both fields simultaneously. He also took a keen and active interest in politics: and in Turin, which was the main centre of the intellectual opposition to Fascism, it was natural for him to gravitate towards the circles first of Piero Gobetti and then of Carlo Rosselli, rather than that of the Communist Antonio Gramsci.

Gobetti (1901–26) was only a year older than Levi, but his dynamic energy and his restlessly inquiring mind made him one of the leading figures in political journalism not only in Turin but in Italy. He founded his first journal, revealingly entitled *Energie nuove* (New Energies), in 1918. It was Levi's enthusiasm for the first number of *Energie nuove* which led him to get to know Gobetti. *Energie nuove* lasted for only two years, and in its rigorously moral approach to politics it was greatly influenced by the example of Salvemini's *Unità*, which was one of the first newspapers to tackle the problem of the south. It included among its contributors such eminent figures as Salvemini himself, Croce and Einaudi, as well as Antonio Gramsci, who in 1921 invited Gobetti to write theatre reviews for his *Ordine nuovo* (New Order).

In 1921 Gobetti founded the weekly review *La rivoluzione liberale* (The Liberal Revolution), which was to become one of the main organs of opposition to Fascism. In a long essay of the same title, which he published in 1924, he argued that the opposition between Liberalism and Fascism was the direct result of Italy's history, and that Fascism was, in a phrase which became famous, 'the autobiography of the nation'. As Gobetti saw Italian history, the process of *trasformismo*, of wheeling and dealing, of shifting alliances based on expediency rather than on principle or policy, had always stifled the growth of responsible political parties of both a conservative and a reforming nature. The Risorgimento, he argued, was a 'failed revolution', since it had in no sense been a popular movement, with the result that Government and the mass of the people were now separated from each other. In these circumstances, Fascism could not be the revolutionary movement it often presented itself as being; Mussolini, for Gobetti, was simply an opportunist, devoid of ideas. The middle classes were inadequate to discharge responsibly the role which history had forced upon them, while the working classes were divided into a by and large urban proletariat in the north and a rural proletariat in the south. They had somehow to be brought together to form the basis of a new, truly democratic state.

It required physical and moral courage of a high order to voice opposition of this kind to Fascism. On 1st June 1924, Mussolini sent a now notorious telegram to the prefect of Turin instructing him to make Gobetti's life 'difficult'. The instruction was obeyed. Gobetti was beaten up and arrested, while his periodicals were frequently either censored or confiscated after they had been printed, presumably with the intention of leaving him either with a bill for the work involved but no chance of recouping his expenses through sales, or else with a printer increasingly reluctant to take on work for a known 'subversive'. Persecution of this kind soon made it impossible for Gobetti to continue his work in Italy; in December 1925 he left for Paris, where he died in February 1926. It is generally believed that his health had been undermined by overwork and by the brutal treatment he had received from the Fascists. The early death of one so gifted was particularly tragic, but one cannot help being impressed by the youth, versatility and contagious sense of commitment of so many of the participants in his group.

Gobetti's departure and death were soon followed by the so-called 'special laws' of 1926, under the terms of which Gramsci and other leading Communists were arrested and imprisoned, while others took refuge abroad. All this naturally left a gap in both Turinese and Italian political life and in the intellectual opposition to Fascism. An attempt to continue Gobetti's work was made by Carlo Rosselli, who in 1929 founded the *Giustizia e Libertà* movement in Paris. Levi, who had contributed to Gobetti's reviews, established contact with Rosselli in the course of one of his frequent visits to Paris and was, with Leone Ginzburg, one of the founder members of the Piedmontese *Giustizia e Libertà* group. With

Nello Rosselli, Carlo Rosselli's brother, he also founded a review, *La lotta politica*, but it only lasted a few months.

The Rosselli brothers had been associated with Salvemini's anti-Fascist *Circolo di cultura* and its short-lived broad-sheet *Non mollare* [Don't give in]. Carlo Rosselli had also contributed to *La rivoluzione liberale*. After being arrested for organizing the escape from Italy of the Socialist leader Filippo Turati in 1926, he was sentenced to five years in *confino* on the island of Lipari. From there he made a sensational escape by speed-boat with the Republican Fausto Nitti and the former Sardinian Deputy Emilio Lussu, who later wrote a fiercely anti-militaristic (and therefore anti-Fascist) account of his first world war experiences, *Un anno sull'altipiano* (A Year on the Plateau, 1937), which had to be published in Paris.

Carlo Rosselli had at one time been a Socialist, but had come to reject Marxism on account of what he saw as its rigidly deterministic view of history, and moved instead towards a more liberal form of Socialism which he outlined in his book *Socialismo liberale* (Paris, 1930). His weekly journal, *Guistizia e Libertà*, and the twelve volumes of the *Quaderni di Guistizia e Libertà* (1932–5) had a necessarily limited clandestine circulation in Italy, but the group was not content to limit itself to discussion and theory. It also advocated violent action and armed resistance. Fascist repression was inevitably directed against members of the movement active in Italy: twenty-four were arrested in 1930, and the movement's Italian centre shifted from Turin to Milan. Further arrests followed in 1932 and 1934–5. Carlo Rosselli was by this time in France, but in 1936 he fought in the Spanish Civil war, which he saw as foreshadowing a forthcoming European conflict: his *Oggi in Spagna, domani in Italia* (Spain today, Italy tomorrow) was published posthumously in Paris in 1938. The Rosselli brothers were both murdered by Fascist-hired hit-men at Bagnole-de-l'Orne in 1937 when Carlo was recovering from war wounds.

Levi must have been marked down as a 'subversive' at an early stage. He had joined the 'Associazione nazionale per gli interessi del mezzogiorno' as early as 1921, and he published his first political article, 'Antonio Salandra', in Gobetti's *Rivoluzione liberale* on 27 August 1922, while still an undergraduate, but it was only in 1934 that he was arrested. He was taken into custody on 13 March and released on 9 May, with a two-year 'warning', which he proceeded to ignore. He was arrested for the second time on 15 May 1935, and on this occasion – inevitably – he was charged and sentenced to three years in *confino*. There is general agreement that the sentence was relatively light, but there was not much concrete evidence on which the State could build its case, and Levi had a remarkable capacity, in his dealings with the police, for telling bare-faced lies with an air of complete conviction. In the event, he served only ten months of his sentence before being released under the terms of an amnesty celebrating the fall of Addis Ababa in the Abyssinian campaign and the proclamation of the Empire.

Levi found Gobetti's approach to politics congenial. In June 1933 he published in the *Quaderni di Giustizia e Libertà* an essay entitled 'Gobetti e La rivoluzione liberale' (now in *Coraggio dei miti*) which reveals how impressive he found Gobetti's combination of courage, moral integrity and intellectual dynamism. He went so far as to say that, for him, to write about Gobetti was to write his own autobiography. Levi contributed a modest total of seven articles to *La rivoluzione liberale* and its literary and artistic supplement, *Il Baretti*, as well as writing regularly for the post-war newspaper *Giustizia e libertà*. It was Gobetti who suggested that he write on Salandra (1853–1931) at a time when he knew little about the south. His article anticipates attitudes which later find expression in *Cristo si è fermato a Eboli*.

Salandra, who had always asserted the authority of the State over and against reforming political parties, had soon begun openly to sympathize with Fascism: in 1923, in fact, Mussolini appointed him to represent Italy at the League of Nations in Geneva. Levi's essay relentlessly pursues the theme of Salandra's fundamental mediocrity, attacking what he sees as his basically anti-democratic attitudes. And since Salandra had also written on the southern question, Levi takes issue with him on that too. Salandra, according to Levi, had argued that the State should base itself on a class, not on a political party, and that class was to be the land-owning middle class, as the one most concerned to maintain the existing social and political order. (Prince Torlonia clearly had a similar perception of the role of the land-owning – or land-leasing – middle class in Abruzzo.) Levi points to the narrow-minded self-interest of this class, which made them totally unfit to serve that purpose:

> Il loro orizzonte politico non superava i confini del comune e del circondario; e mentre essi richiedevano uno stato forte per la difesa del privilegio, non si interessavano affatto alla sua vita, estraneo, romano; né amavano le seccature della libertà. Soprattutto nelle terre meridionali la mentalità dominante era ancora borbonica, arretrata, feudale (Levi 2001, 7).

> Their political horizon never extended beyond the boundaries of the commune and its administrative district; and while they demanded a strong state to defend privilege, they took no interest at all in its life, seeing it as foreign, Roman; nor did they like the bother of freedom. Particularly in the South, the dominant mentality was Bourbonic, backward, feudal.

The views which Levi expressed in this essay were, by and large, in harmony with those of Gobetti, but they could also have been voiced by a number of *meridionalisti* from Salvemini onwards. Gobetti had of course been profoundly influenced by Salvemini himself, and it is not surprising therefore to find that the problem of the south became a central feature of *La rivoluzione liberale*. In its first year the review had included a number of articles on the southern problem and related issues (such as protectionist policies favouring northern industry); but in 1923 Gobetti elicited contributions from a number of writers who were later to become noted *meridionalisti*, including Guido Dorso (1892–1947) and Tommaso Fiore (1884–1973). The latter were among the fourteen signatories of an article entitled 'Appello ai meridionali' which appeared in 1924. The language of the 'Appello' suggests that Dorso was the main if not the sole author, which would not be surprising since he is often seen as the leading *meridionalista* of his generation (Rossi-Doria 1956, 3). Gobetti then undertook in future to devote a page of each issue to the south, while Dorso stated his own views more fully in a book whose title – *La rivoluzione meridonale* – both echoes and contrasts with that of the Turinese review and Gobetti's own declaration of his political faith. Using some material from essays already published, including those in Gobetti's review, together with new material, Dorso described the Risorgimento not merely as a 'failed revolution', as Gobetti had done, but as a 'conquista regia' [royal conquest], that is, of the south by the Piedmontese dynasty, and saw the south as exploited by the north. The situation could be rectified, in his view, only by what he described as 'an autonomous southern movement' – akin, presumably, to Lussu's post world war 1 Sardinian Action Party, which the *Rivoluzione liberale* group greatly admired. Dorso's views conflicted both with those who, like the Fascists, believed in the efficacy of strong central government, and also those who, like Gobetti, believed that the way forward was to be found in an alliance of the southern peasantry with the northern proletariat. It comes as no surprise to find Levi, after the war, contributing to the Florence-based *Nazione del popolo* and then, as one of the leaders of the re-formed Partito d'Azione, editing and writing regularly for the populist *L'Italia libera*. Dorso republished his book in 1944, just as Levi was circulating *Cristo si è fermato a Eboli* in typescript and then publishing preliminary extracts from it in the Florentine review *Il Ponte* prior to its appearance in book form in 1945. Levi's work must therefore be considered in the context of both pre- and post-war debates about the south, the former necessarily restricted by censorship and real danger to a small number of participants, the latter conducted in a national forum. Levi's views were shaped by his experiences in the Fascist period, but, as with Silone's revision of *Fontamara*, they were published in the post-war period in order to bring home to Italians the reality of the south, and also to help democratic Italy avoid repeating the mistakes of previous governments. It is therefore worth dwelling on the close correspondence between the ideas of the *meridionalisti* writing for *La Rivoluzione liberale* and those expressed in *Cristo si è fermato a Eboli*.

The 'Appello ai meridionali' takes the problem of the south back historically to Roman times, and specifically to the devastation wrought by the lengthy second Punic war (218–201 BC) – a view with which a number of modern *meridion-*

alisti would concur. All subsequent Italian history is then seen in terms of an imposed and inappropriate centralization of power on the part of governments which have neither known nor understood the south. Fascism, which is seen as a northern phenomenon, has merely inherited its centralizing tendencies from previous regimes. Wealthy landowners, argues Dorso in 'Il Mezzogiorno dopo la guerra' (Basso 1961, 446), were happy to acquiesce in this situation, since the absence of effective government left them with almost feudal powers. The middle classes are seen as being totally to blame for conditions in the south; while on the one hand they have done nothing to help the peasantry improve their lot or develop any kind of political awareness, they have on the other hand relentlessly pursued their own material interests, conceived in the narrowest possible terms. Party politics in the south are reduced to the level of 'il partito del medico-condotto contro quello del farmicista, o del segretario comunale contro quello del maestro fiduciario: una lotta di feudalismo per impadronirsi del municipio e di là favorire i fedeli ed opprimere gli avversari' [the municipal doctor's party versus the chemist's, or the town clerk's party versus the elementary-school headmaster's: a feudalistic struggle to get control of the Town Hall and to use it to reward supporters and to crush opponents] (Basso 1961, 447). Levi had expressed a similar view in his essay on Salandra in the previous year.

The middle classes who control the Town Hall also control local finances and exploit the peasants mercilessly. Since the peasants are uneducated, and have neither class-consciousness nor political awareness – and consequently no opportunity of influencing the conditions in which they live and work – they have only a limited number of ways of responding to their situation. In the past, they have emigrated: but Giuseppe Gangale (1898–1978) – editor of the Baptist weekly *Conscientia* and author of *La rivoluzione protestante*, published by Gobetti in 1925 – argues in 'Il problema del Sud' that emigration has solved no problems. 'L'emigrazione non è servito a nulla; in una società giovane come l'America i nostri contadini vivono spiritualmente isolati; sfacchinano e mandano alle loro mogli i dollari in voto al santo protettore del paese' [Emigration has served no purpose; in a young civilization like America, our peasants live in spiritual isolation; they toil away and send dollars home to their wives as votive offerings to the village's patron saint] (Basso 1961, 493).

This reference to dollars and patron saints is part of Gangale's polemic against peasant superstition, which he believes gives to local priests a power of social control which they exercise through the womenfolk. He also mentions, as evidence of peasant backwardness, their belief in magic. Levi, as we shall see, takes up these themes, but makes very different use of them.

Gangale believes, however, that although emigration has not in itself solved any problems, its suppression – a process which had already begun at the time when he was writing – would exacerbate social tensions and problems: 'darà forse una certa pressione alla fredda caldaia meridionale' [It will perhaps increase pressure in the cold southern boiler] (ibid.). Tommaso Fiore, on the other hand, points briefly in the course of one of his 'Lettere meridionali' to the peasants' other, strangely contrasting responses to their plight – patience and resignation, punctuated by outbursts of impotent anger, the spontaneous uprisings referred to in chapter 2, of the kind that E.J. Hobsbawm would describe as 'primitive rebellion' (Hobsbawm 1963). The 'banditry' of the post-Risorgimento period carried out by the peasants was, in the view of the signatories of the 'Appello', no more than an expression of their resentment and of their 'thirst for social justice'. It seems impossible to deny this, but the label of 'banditismo', implying criminality, still sticks.

Tommaso Fiore, in his 'Lettere meridionali', came, like Dorso, to the most radical and far-reaching conclusion of all, namely that the southern peasants were completely divorced from the life of the state, and, under their successive conquerors, always have been:

> Ma, se le nostre idee sono giuste, la saggezza popolare, sia pure indistintamente, non può essere lontana. Non mi pare difficile penetrare nei bisogni di questi uomini, che non sono mutati da secoli. Come ai tempi degli Angioini e di tutti gli altri effemeri dominatori, che, col provvedere a Napoli, s'illusero, come ci si illude oggi, di aver fondati stati saldissimi, anzi modelli di Stato per l'Europa, le nostre plebi, in basso o in alto, restano completamente estranee alla vita dello Stato (Basso 1961, 512).

> But if our ideas are correct, popular wisdom cannot be far off, even if it is unclear. I don't think it is difficult to understand the needs of these people, who have not changed for centuries. As in the days of the Angevins and of all the other transient conquerors, who deluded themselves, as we delude ourselves today, that by taking care of Naples they had founded very sound states which would indeed be models for Europe, our common people, high and low, are completely outside the life of the State.

Little is said explicitly in the 'Appello' about ways of solving the problem of the south, since the main purpose of the article is to draw attention to a problem which the Fascists seemed determined to ignore, and would therefore exacerbate, but on one point the authors are clear. They uncompromisingly reject the idea of state intervention, of 'special laws' for the south, and of state subsidies, which they describe as 'the humiliating panacea of state charity'. But in other essays by Dorso and Fiore published in *La rivoluzione liberale* the view is stated with great clarity that decentralization is the only way forward. This, too, is in harmony with views put forward by Gobetti both in his review and also in his essay *La rivoluzione liberale*, in which he argues that it is the absence of real local authority that is responsible for the absence of an appropriately qualified and responsible governing élite in the south. The *Rivoluzione liberale* group takes the view that previous *meridionalisti*, even those they respect, such as Giustino Fortunato and Antonio De Viti De Marco – precisely because they were patriots, committed to Italian unity – were unable to see the benefits which would accrue from administrative decentralization, and so inevitably looked to the state for help. In *Cristo si è fermato a Eboli*, Levi unambiguously advocates decentralisation.

After reading Gobetti's review, one can be left in no doubt about the centrality of the southern problem in the thought of the *Rivoluzione liberale* group to which both Dorso and Levi belonged. Dorso himself repeatedly described it as 'the real Italian problem', while the 'Appello' called it 'the whole Italian problem'. *Cristo si è fermato a Eboli* is, in a sense, a counterpart to Dorso's *Rivoluzione meridionale*. When he republished his book in 1944 (with Einaudi of Turin, who also published *Cristo*), Dorso wrote in his new preface that he had had no time in which to revise his work in the light of the changed political situation, but that since it was in any case a book directed at specialists ('iniziati') and not the general public, his specialist readers would have no difficulty in separating out his central ideas from what was merely contingent. Levi, on the other hand, put flesh on the skeleton of Dorso's ideas, and gave the south a human face in a way which appealed instantly to general readers, many of whom could hardly have given the southern *cafoni* a thought before. But this is not to say that Levi followed Dorso's analysis in every respect: far from it, as we shall see.

CRISTO SI È FERMATO A EBOLI

Structure
Levi's book is couched not in the form of a systematic treatise, but of an autobiographical account that gives the impression – albeit without using precise dates – of covering a whole year in the life of Gagliano. The phrase 'in tutto l'anno che ci restai' [in the whole year that I was there] (Levi 1965, 206) clearly refers to time spent at Gagliano. Levi probably felt – as we have already seen that Silone did – that readers would allow him to tell them a story but not to preach at them. But although the structure seems to be that imposed by the calendar, it is not a day-by-day account of the life of either a *confinato* or the village: too many days would have been identical for such a method to be worthwhile. In any case, constant reference to the calendar would have undermined one of Levi's central theses, namely that peasant culture is, in a sense to be considered in chapter 11, outside time. Nevertheless, the references to the months and the seasons are maintained consistently enough to give us the impression that we are in fact following the sequence of events and experiences as they occurred. That we should

form this impression was, no doubt, Levi's intention. But a number of consider-ations suggest that the book is much more carefully constructed than might at first appear.

In the first place, the original surviving manuscript bears dates from 26 November 1940 to 18 July 1944, although the printed text is dated 'Firenze, dicembre 1943–luglio 1944' (De Donato 1998, 111), the period in which Levi was in hiding in Florence. Levi may have intended to indicate by this change of dates that even in the darkest period of the war, when Italy had become a battle-ground and the Germans were occupying the north, it was still possible to look to the future. No preparatory notes for the novel are known to have survived, but Grignani is certainly right to suggest that one of the functions of the poems Levi wrote in *confino* was to record events and experiences and so to act as notes for the later novel (Grignani 1998, xiv–xvii). It is also noteworthy that in the process of moving material from poems to novel, explicit literary references and allusions have been eliminated. Perhaps that is what Levi had in mind when he wrote in his preface to the 1963 edition that there was no place in it for 'ornamentation, experimentation, literature', but only 'real truth, in things and beyond things'. A recent edition of their *Paese del confino* edited by Valeria Barani and Maria Chiara Grignani puts poems and corresponding passages from *Cristo si è fermato a Eboli* on facing pages, together with drawings from the same period (Levi 1998, 1–101). Drawing and painting were for Levi ways of 'fixing' scenes and people in his memory. The manuscript of the novel in the Harry Ransom Humanities Research Centre is interspersed with drawings and sketches, while in a letter to a friend Levi wrote in February 1965 that his Lucanian pictures were the only original notes on which the book was based (Wells 1998, 167). In other words, the novel was written several years after the events and experiences it describes, and is clearly the result of much reflection on the underlying significance of those experiences. This might explain a minor but nevertheless puzzling inaccu-racy in Levi's account of his arrival at Gagliano in August. In fact, he arrived in Grassano on 3 August, and was not transferred to Gagliano until 3 October. Was this a simple and unimportant lapse of memory on the part of a Jewish author who, at the time of writing was in hiding in German-occupied Florence and may not have had access to notes or other materials? If so, it could have been cor-rected in a later edition. But the text of *Cristo si è fermato a Eboli*, unlike that of *Fontamara*, has undergone no major revision process in later editions. It follows that much of his account of August and September in the village, including his account of the 'patriotic assembly' organized by the mayor, (Levi 1965, 151–2) is fictional. Perhaps it was more important for Levi that readers should be given the impression that through his eyes they were witnessing an entire year in the life of Gagliano and therefore, given that the years are all identical in their rhythm, that they have seen all that there is to see. Levi's view of the static nature of peasant life is in this respect very like that which Silone puts forward in his preface to *Fontamara*. Sperduto has argued that it is this sense of timelessness, of a peasant culture that exists outside time that enables Levi to take liberties with chronology (Sperduto 1995). This may be a factor, but I suggest that his felt need to produce the account of a complete annual cycle was more important.

Thirdly, there are a number of omissions from Levi's account of his time in confino. The painter Guttuso has described meeting Levi at the Venice Biennale in 1936, walking with him through the *calli* and drinking coffee in the *campielli*, accompanied of course by the policeman whose function it was to keep an eye on him (Guttuso 1967). It is of course possible that Guttuso's memory was at fault, and that he met Levi either earlier, in 1934, when he was given special permission, as a *vigilato*, to go to Venice for the Biennale, or else later, after his release on 20 May 1936 (which means that he did not spend a whole year in *confino*). In either case, it is clear that Levi's status as a painter with an international reputation gave him a certain freedom of action and that he was able, while in Gagliano, to organize exhibitions of his work in the north: in May 1936, for example, he had an exhibition at the Galleria della Cometa in Milan about which he says nothing in *Cristo*. Levi's experiences have clearly been subjected to a process of selection and ordering in order to produce a book focusing primarily on the south and not on the person of Levi himself, or the details of his artistic career.

Further evidence that Levi has carefully selected and ordered his material is provided by the book's overall structure, which turns out on close examination to be thematic, rather than chronological. It is divided into unnumbered sections or chapters, which in recent editions are separated only by short gaps on the page. David Higgins has shown that Levi took considerable trouble to distribute his material into numerically symmetrical blocks of (unnumbered) chapters (Higgins 1970). The first chapter (Levi 1965, 41–2), ending with the words '*Cristo si è fermato a Eboli*', briefly evokes the world of Gagliano, while the second (Levi 1965, 42–7) describes Levi's arrival in the village and his first encounter with a group of peasants who want him to treat a dying man. These two chapters together constitute a kind of prologue, the first couched in general thematic terms, the second in more specific terms, but both anticipating in their different ways themes which will be developed at greater length in the course of the narrative. Then follows a group of seven chapters (Levi 1965, 47–90) dealing with the *galantuomini*, the impoverished and degenerate middle class of Gagliano. A second group of seven chapters (Levi 1965, 90–171) describes the peasants at greater length and with more sympathy than is shown to the gentry, while a third block of seven chapters (Levi 1965, 171–245) has as its unifying theme the conflict between galantuomini and peasants. Then follows a kind of epilogue or conclusion of two chapters corresponding to those with which the book began. The first of these describes Levi's brief return to Turin for a family funeral, and leads naturally to a discussion about the nature of the problem of the south, while the second relates, after his return to Gagliano, the news of the amnesty and his final departure. The opening and closing chapters are also linked by their references to the uncertain years of war during which the book was written. While reading, however, one does not perceive this symmetrical structure and this systematic distribution of material as something external, imposed on the raw material of experience by the writer's organizing mind: the structure seems, rather, to develop out of the experience itself. There are several reasons why this should be the case. The chapters are of varying length, and are not numbered, and the distribution of thematic material is not as strict or rigid as this account of the book's structure may seem to suggest. The way for later statements of themes is always carefully prepared.

Michael Aroumi has put forward an analysis of the structure of *Cristo si è fermato a Eboli* based on the premise that there are in fact twentyfour chapters, regarding the prologue as two chapters and subsuming the epilogue into the main body of the work (Aroumi 1994). I do not find this convincing.

LEVI AS PARTICIPANT OBSERVER

The first chapter of the prologue briefly evokes the circumstances in which *Cristo* was written. Levi was in hiding in German-occupied Florence, 'chiuso in una stanza, in un mondo chiuso'. Almost a prisoner, he recalls that other 'mondo chiuso', the closed world of the peasants of Gagliano. The process of association at work here is akin to that which he had carried out in an earlier period of imprisonment when he wrote the *Quaderno di prigione* dated 14 July 1934:

> Isolato dagli uomini, mi volgo alle immagini, richiamo il ricordo di un passato che pare pieno di luce come a trovarmi una prova di vita, una certezza oggettiva che nulla nel presente mi potrebbe fornire (Marcovecchio 1967, 103).

> Cut off from men, I turn to images, I recall the memory of a past which seems full of light, as if to discover a proof of life, an objective certainty that nothing in the present could provide. (Marcovecchio 1967, 103).

Since he also did a number of drawings in Turin prison, it is clear that it was through his twin arts, drawing and writing, that Levi came to terms with his experience. But in the case of the first chapter of *Cristo*, the perception which is initially presented is characterized by a series of negatives. 'Non', 'nulla', 'né' and 'senza' are the key words in this section. The peasants know no comfort, they are not 'Christians'. 'Cristiano', in their usage, common in the south, means simply 'human being'. Silone, writing in 1963, says that this usage was then still current in Abruzzo, quoting the example of a peasant who said incredulously: 'Hitler wanted to kill off the Jews? But aren't they *cristiani* too?' (Silone 1963, 81). Bronzini reports that Levi's title is simply a translation into Italian of a popular saying (Bronzini 1977, 155).

The peasants are regarded as sub-human, and have come to accept that estimate of their worth, just as Silone's 'cafoni' have become resigned to their lowly place in the social hierarchy. They are, Levi tells us, outside time, outside history, and outside the state. Yet these peasants, in their deprivation, have needs that are not being met. One of the functions of the second introductory chapter is to show us that the peasants do not receive even the most basic medical care, and also to show us the almost helpless compassion that makes Levi respond to their need, just as Yuri Zivagho responds to the needs of Russian peasants in Pasternak's novel. It is clear from the outset that Levi is an outsider: Muscetta points out that in southern literature this is not usually the case. In the case of Verga or Vittorini, say, or Silone and Jovine, to cite authors discussed in this book, it is always 'one of the tribe' who addresses us (Muscetta 1953, 100), although there are occasional exceptions to this general rule, such as Renato Fucini's *Napoli a occhio nudo* (1878). And as an outsider, from the north and endowed with professional skills, Levi enjoyed an immediate prestige. Natalia Ginzburg, writing in 'Inverno in Abruzzo' about her time in *confino* in Abruzzo with her husband Leone, describes him as enjoying a similar prestige. The peasants called him 'the professor', not being able to pronounce his outlandish Russian name correctly, and sought his advice on a wide variety of problems, from taxes to dental treatment (Ginzburg 1962, 14–15). John Berger, living in the Haute Savoie, wrote that because he was a foreigner and a writer he was treated with great tolerance (Berger 1979, 13). Berger was perceptive enough to see the fundamental contrast between himself and the peasants: he had chosen to live in the Haute Savoie, whereas they had not. Neither, of course had Levi had any choice in his place of residence, and he can to some extent therefore see a likeness between himself and the peasants and converts the notion of resemblance almost to one of kinship.

But if Levi is an outsider, he is also a participant in the life of the village, mixing with its inhabitants and, in certain cases, influencing the course of their lives by his skill. He is in the peasants' world, but not of it: he could have said of his medicine what Berger says of his writing: 'I am not a peasant. I am a writer: my writing is both a link and a barrier' (Berger 1979, 6). And whereas Silone makes a conscious and deliberate effort to distance himself from his material, using peasant narrators, who tell us themselves how they view their situation, Levi writes in the first person singular and tells us, not shows us what the villagers think and feel: because he does not distance himself from his *gaglianesi*, we rarely hear their voices. This degree of participation and identification enables Levi to speak with such rare and remarkable authority and insight that one is tempted to take for granted the truth and accuracy of Levi's account of 'his' village. Even the Marxist Asor Rosa, who takes a very different political point of view from Levi, in 1966 viewed *Cristo si è fermato a Eboli*, among all the books of the 40s which describe the people, as outstandingly the best informed and sociologically the most interesting (Asor Rosa 1972, 186).

Nevertheless, some questions do arise concerning the limitations of Levi's account of village life, and inaccuracies and misinterpretations that may arise from them.

In the first place, Levi's observations were limited by one material factor: as a *confinato* his movements were restricted to the built-up area of the village itself. He could not move about the countryside, except by special permission, and thus could not observe or talk to peasants at work. King points out that Levi's statements in *Cristo si è fermato a Eboli* that around Gagliano there were no shepherds or cultivated fields is at variance with the census data for the village in the 1930s (King 1988, 314). This discrepancy may be accounted for, at least in part, by Levi's limited knowledge of the more distant parts of the commune. It could be argued that these are relatively minor details, of course, and need not affect the general validity of his account of village life. In this more general area, however, a more serious problem has to be dealt with.

In the words of one social anthropologist writing on the south, 'Participant-observation is a powerful tool for uncovering the pattern of social relations, and its particular value lies in the access it can give to the meaning that people attach to those relations' (White 1980, 3). However, as White points out, there are two main problems inherent in the participant-observer role. One is that 'the very power of the lens has often immobilized researchers: their focus remains fixed on one small locality and their vision fails to adjust to the wider context in which it is set'. Since Levi sets his observation of Gagliano in the context both of an interpretation of Italian history since ancient times and of a discussion of relations between the local community and the state he would seem to be exempt from this criticism. It could also be argued that Levi wrote *Cristo si è fermato a Eboli* at least in part as a reply to Silone's *Fontamara*, which also suggests a wide perspective.

The second problem outlined by White is that in her experience 'many anthropologists seem[ed] to have become enmeshed in their informants' construction of reality'. The specific example she cites is that of anthropologists who accept at face value such assurances as 'We are all equal here', even though most Mediterranean villages are known to be highly stratified. In Levi's case, the question is perhaps more complex. One needs to ask whether he became enmeshed in his informants' construction of reality, or whether, in the light of his reading and thinking after *confino*, and of the circumstances in which he wrote his book, he enmeshed his informants in his own, highly polemical construction of reality. This problem will be dealt with in chapter 11. It is difficult, however, to accept the view (Russi 1967, 87) that Levi's presence changes nothing in Gagliano. But first, we need to consider Levi's account of the social groups which make up the village.

CHAPTER 10

Gentry and peasants in Levi's Gagliano

INTRODUCTORY

The second chapter of *Cristo si è fermato a Eboli* describes Levi's arrival in Gagliano and his initially unfavourable impressions of the village. He meets, briefly, the Mayor, the local *carabiniere* sergeant and the Town Clerk – the authorities, in other words, who will be responsible for him and who will be able to exercise real power over him during his enforced residence in the village. The Town Clerk finds him temporary lodgings with a widow who, since she has a little money and takes in occasional lodgers, occupies an intermediate position between the gentry and the peasants. Levi is then approached by a group of peasants who have heard that he is a doctor and who ask him to go and examine a sick man. Levi is reluctant to go, since his knowledge of medicine is now rusty, but they assure him that there are no doctors in Gagliano, and that their companion is dying. An old man, in a characteristic southern gesture to which Levi is unaccustomed and which he finds embarrassing, kisses his hand. How, he asks, could he resist their entreaties? Only when he reaches the patient's house does he learn that there are indeed doctors in the village, but that the peasants dislike and distrust them. They are not humane doctors, not 'medici cristiani'. But the man is dying of pernicious malaria: Levi's attempts to revive him are unsuccessful and he soon dies. The episode is emblematic. We are shown that the village consists of two main groups, the gentry, who exercise power through the offices they occupy or through their professions, and the peasants, who are oppressed and deprived.

Levi begins his novel by adjusting the facts of his biography to suit his purposes. His sister Luisa was visiting him from 17 September to 5 October and presumably accompanied him to Gagliano or would have arrived immediately after. His most recent biographers suggest her visit was the stimulus that made him return to medicine. (De Donato & D'Amaro 2001, 123–4). Levi chooses to record her visit and her account of the cave-dwellings at Matera as happening later. Why?

I do not know whether Levi had read Bronislaw Malinowski's *The Argonauts of the Southern Pacific*, but his arrangement of his material has the effect of putting him in the same relationship to his readers as does Malinowski's introduction:

Imagine yourself suddenly set down surrounded by all your gear, alone on a tropical beach close to a native village, while the launch or dinghy which has brought you sails away out of sight. Since you take up your abode in the compound of some neighbouring white man, trader or missionary, you have nothing to do but start at once your ethnographic work. Imagine further that you are a beginner, without previous experience, with nothing to guide you and no one to help you. For the white man is temporarily absent or else unable or unwilling to waste any of his time on you (Malinowski 1922, 4).

It is a masterly stroke. Levi positions himself as the personal narrator who will mediate between us and this mysterious other culture, with which we are totally unfamiliar; and, like Malinowski, he starts at once his ethnographic work, with medicine as the pass that allows him entry to all parts of the village.

THE GENTRY

It is the gentry who first come under Levi's close scrutiny and are presented to us in chapters 3 to 9 in a series of rapidly drawn, hostile caricatures. He meets them in the most natural way – in the village square in the evening, to which he returns immediately after leaving the home of the dead peasant and to which they betake themselves to enjoy the air and their evening conversation. Anyone who has stayed in an Italian village or town before the now almost universal television set came to dominate social life will recognise the scene Levi depicts, although he is careful to explain to his urban readers that the piazza in Gagliano is merely a widening of the road, lined on one side by houses and on the other by a low wall on which the gentry sit with their backs to a deep ravine, the Fossa del Bersagliere, so called because a Piedmontese soldier was thrown into it by local 'bandits' in the previous century. The mayor, Don Luigi Magalone, recognises Levi, calls him over, and either introduces him to other village notables or else identifies them as they pass. A line of *meridionalisti* from Fortunato to Salvemini and Dorso had prepared Levi to see the southern bourgeoisie as delinquent and morally corrupt. The reality of the south amply confirms his expectations.

Levi's portrait sketches tend to concentrate on a few features of face and dress, and then to reinforce the initial character impression by the dress, physical features and speech characteristics of the individual concerned, which are usually conveyed in indirect speech or indirect free style. In this way he avoids the problem of dialect. In Don Luigi's case, we are told that he is big and fat, his untidy hair is greasy, his face beardless and moon-shaped, and his eyes malevolent, insincere and self-satisfied. Stupidity, smugness and malice are his out-standing characteristics. He is also a snob, giving himself the title of *professore*, to which, as an elementary-school teacher, he is not entitled, and he is clearly delighted to have the opportunity of exercising his authority over a real doctor, a professional man and an artist, since he regards the other ten or so working-class *confinati* in the village as rabble, not worth mentioning, whereas Levi he considers to be a 'signore'. The irony of Levi's situation is therefore that the very class towards which he feels an immediate hostility regards him as one of their number. Later on, we learn that Don Luigi enjoys censoring the letters Levi writes, even delaying their dispatch, because he enjoys their style. The arrival of Levi's books gives him an opportunity to demonstrate both his power and his benevolence, since he graciously allows Levi to read Montaigne, whom he takes in his ignorance to be a dangerous French revolutionary.

It is not immediately clear how convinced a Fascist Don Luigi really is. He proudly tells Levi that the Prefect at Matera has described him as the most Fas-cist of the mayors in the province but, given the southern custom of taking the chances provided by national politics to further private, local interests, this is ambiguous praise. On the other hand, his habit of attempting to compel the peasants to listen to Mussolini's speeches on the wireless suggests a certain naive commitment on his part. Levi's description of him certainly implies that he is a Fascist of sorts. His riding-trousers and boots have all the air of a rustic parody of the fasces. The riding-whip with which he toys also suggests a streak of sadism in his make-up. But Levi is not taken in by Don Luigi's superficial brand of Fas-cism: as in Silone's *Fontamara*, the gentry are merely using the opportunities presented by political changes at national level to promote their local ambitions. Don Luigi is a party member, and he goes through some of the motions required of a Fascist mayor, but one of his main reasons for doing so is fear of what his enemies might report to the authorities in Matera, rather than ideo-logical commitment. Indeed, he sounds less than convinced, and is totally unconvincing, when he attempts half-heartedly to persuade Levi that the father-land is on the threshold of new glory in the Abyssinian campaign.

Pomposity and self-importance are also the characteristics of Dr Gibilisco, who is one of Don Luigi's principal enemies. He is described in terms of his worn and shiny black suit, his black hat, and the black umbrella which he always carries, perfectly vertical, like a canopy over the sacred tabernacle of his own authority. The village's second doctor, Milillo, who is Don Luigi's uncle, is almost senile, and is described as having the sagging cheeks and lachrymose eyes of an old hunting-dog. Both doctors are ignorant and despise their patients, regarding them as ignorant and superstitious. The peasants exist, in their view, merely as a source of income that is theirs by right, which is why Don Carlo de Risio becomes a doctor in Jovine's *Signora Ava*, and they strongly advise Levi to insist that the peasants pay him at the official national rate, despite their poverty. Their attitudes in this respect are reminiscent of those of Don Circostanza, who insists on paying peasants at the national rate only because agricultural wages have been reduced, and of the de Risio family in *Signora Ava*. Gagliano's doctors provide a useful yardstick by which to measure Levi's attitudes when he finds himself compelled reluctantly to resume the practice of medicine.

As people come and go in the square, one portrait leads into another in a sequence that is almost cinematographic. Levi's sense of colour, line and movement reveal the painter in the writer; but these chapters also introduce us to the tangled web of personal and political rivalries and alliances in the village in terms which Dorso or Gramsci would have recognized instantly, and which indeed bring to mind Levi's own early essay on Salandra, with its scathing – and almost prophetic – reference to southern politics as being conducted in terms of the elementary-schoolmaster's party and the local doctor's party (see chapter 9). There is, however, no Impresario-type figure in Gagliano, partly because the area is even poorer than Fontamara and, lacking any resource comparable to the Fucino plain, offers no scope for capitalistic exploitation. Perhaps for this reason, and perhaps, too, because the peasants here for the most part own their own land, it seems at first that clientelistic relationships play little or no part in the life of the village. Indeed, Levi does not even mention clientelism. But traces of clientelism can nevertheless be found in Gagliano. The peasants follow the ancient custom of offering Christmas presents to the relatively wealthy, including Levi himself (Levi 1965, 207). This kind of gift-giving is very different from that practiced in other parts of the south, including Calabria, for example, in which the gifts given and received balance each other out, so that no one is better off as a result of the process. Don Luigino owns some land, which he must employ peasants to cultivate (Levi 1965, 161), as Silone's Don Circostanza does, and the mayor's assurance to Levi that his sister will find him a suitable housekeeper is an obvious attempt to buy his services as a doctor. Gibilisco is able to obtain, through the influence of a friend at Matera, a wholly irregular permission for the local pharmacy to remain open, under the management of his totally unqualified nieces, until stocks run out – which will naturally not happen since all medicines are now adulterated (Levi 1965, 52). Patients' gifts to their doctor are also perhaps a relic of clientelism, and while Don Trajella is by no means a typical southern priest, he bitterly resents not receiving from the flock he despises the customary gifts in kind and in cash (Levi 1965, 73, 210). The *carabiniere* sergeant is as well placed as any to exploit his position, and local rumour has it that in three years his prudent use of his authority over the peasants has enabled him to put aside forty thousand *lire* (Levi 1965, 52).

I take all this to be evidence that clientelism flourished to such an extent that it forced itself on Levi's attention even though he appears not to have been familiar with the term and was not looking for signs of it. It could be argued that Levi is describing in Dorsian terms as bastardised versions of feudal rights phenomena which sociologists would now unhesitatingly describe as clientelism. This might also explain why certain posts, such as that of the schoolmaster, are thought of by their occupants as being hereditary. This might also lead one to ask whether Levi's accounts of peasant generosity and hospitality are not really descriptions of traditional attitudes towards a patron. Is not Levi himself perhaps a patron, with the favour he distributes taking the form of medical attention, and the peasants' payment taking the traditional form of food and hospitality? This might explain why the barber who assisted Levi in his work subsequently complained that he had done nothing for the village (*Il Paese* 1985,122).

It follows that a reading of the text which suggests that there is no class conflict in Gagliano, and that oppression is exercised only by central government and by government and party officials (Crovi 1960, 274) is wide of the mark.

Be that as it may, Levi finds himself drawn into the system, since Don Luigi and his sister, Donna Caterina, who is perhaps the most forceful personality in the village, are at odds with Gibilisco. Because their uncle, Milillo, is virtually senile, they are eager to enlist Levi's support in an attempt to drive Gibilisco out of business. Levi is understandably reluctant to become involved in local disputes, and in any case wishes to concentrate on his painting: but he is subjected to a two-fold pressure. He would perhaps have been able to resist that exerted by Don Luigi and Donna Caterina alone, but he is helpless in the face of the plight of the peasantry, and eventually resigns himself to his new role in the village. The second chapter of the book therefore has the function of emphasising that, since he responded promptly to a perceived need, it was compassion for his patients rather than a willingness to take part in petty local intrigues that prompted his return to medicine, a point he reinforces later when, in describing the peasants, he observes that he had resigned himself to resuming his profession because so many of them had come to him for treatment. (Letters to his mother and family, however, suggest that income from his medical practice was useful, especially as he was judged not to qualify for the subsidy granted to the poorer *confinati*.)

But Levi can hardly have been an ordinary doctor. Not that he tells us about 'miracle' cures or lives dramatically saved: if anything he dwells rather more on his failures. Nor is it simply that he tried very quickly to bring his medical knowledge up to date. What is impressive, rather, is his combination of compassion, energy and resourcefulness. The qualities that one may be inclined to take for granted in the medical profession were singularly lacking in Milillo and Gibilisco. Levi's energy was no doubt a function of his youth, while his resourcefulness was necessary in a situation in which he had neither colleagues nor hospital services to call upon. But in more general terms, Levi's qualities also throw into relief what Fortunato often referred to as the 'idleness of spirit and heart' of the southern middle class, or, rather, their assumption that they had the right, even the duty, to be idle. It is perhaps in relation to the gentry of the village that one has to see Levi's sister. As a doctor, she gives a 'healthy' northern reaction to the squalor of the south, which exceeds all that she had anticipated: she is horrified that no one is doing anything to combat the state of affairs which she sees.

Levi was clearly a strong individual. His powerfully optimistic personality and his artistic skills would no doubt have enabled him not merely to survive the experience of *confino* but to turn it into something positive; his paintings and poems from this period are proof enough of that, since they have greater vitality that any of his previous work. But it should not be forgotten that the effects of *confino* on sensitive individuals could be devastating, once they found themselves cut off from the family and friends who normally supported them and from the amenities of civilization and culture. Don Trajella, Gagliano's priest, previously taught at a seminary and has been 'exiled' to Gaglianello by the ecclesiastical authorities (though he resides in Gagliano) because he took what are referred to as 'liberties' with his pupils. The humiliated homosexual now lives with his senile mother in a squalor which he passively accepts in a spirit of self-castigation. Don Trajella is an educated and cultured man. He once wrote lives of saints and painted devotional pictures in which Levi can see some talent, but he has now totally abandoned these pursuits. He stands as a reminder of what a weaker man than Levi could have become in this kind of exile.

According to the 1936 census, the *comune* of Gagliano had only 1574 inhabitants. It would therefore have been relatively easy for Levi, as a doctor, to get to know many of them and to learn their secrets. His account of the gentry not surprisingly aroused great resentment. When *Cristo* appeared, the mayor wrote indignant letters to several local newspapers, including *Il Gazzettino* of Matera (14 October 1946), in which he not only revealed his true identity as Luigi Garambone – an exposure which Levi had spared him – but also accused the author of spreading lies and despising 'the simple and honest purity of life' as lived in the rural south. When Levi campaigned as a candidate for the Partito d'Azione in 1948, he was not allowed to hold a meeting in the village. According to one report (*Epoca*, 15 March, 1978), they made their peace with him only in 1974.

THE PEASANTS

A number of recent writers on the south have tended to suggest that it is excessively limited and limiting to see social relations in the south purely in terms of poverty-stricken peasants struggling against a middle class which is taking advantage of the remains of a bastardized feudalism. Alongside such factors as the formation of what is sometimes described as a 'pseudo-bourgeoisie' that lacks the civic sense of the former aristocracy, and the absence of developed urban centres which could act as regional capitals, it is argued that one should take into account such 'objective' factors as the degradation of the soil, the prevalence of malaria, and the loss of civic rights and common lands. Since all these factors are man-made, and responsibility for them can be attributed, it is not clear in what sense they are 'objective'. They are all treated by Levi, however, in his discussion of the peasants.

The main body of Levi's account of the peasantry, important aspects of which are anticipated in the second chapter of the prologue, begins, as does his account of the gentry, with a portrait. He uses the same basic technique to describe the peasants as he does to portray the gentry, but it is immediately obvious not only that the former are presented more sympathetically than their exploiters, but also that they are seen by Levi as belonging to a totally different culture. Both points can be exemplified in the initial portrait of the village gravedigger cum town crier and in the later portrait of Giulia la Santarcangelese, the witch who became his housekeeper.

To describe the peasants Levi frequently has recourse to nature imagery. The gravedigger's skin is wrinkled like that of an apple, his sternum protrudes like that of a fowl. Giulia has the strength of an animal and her eyes are flecked like those of a dog, while her teeth are as strong as those of a wolf. This kind of language is not confined to 'set-piece' portraits, of which there are in fact very few, but is also to be found in other, more generalized accounts of the peasants as well. The women are like 'animali del bosco' (Levi 1965, 63), and as they wait motionless at the single fountain from which Gagliano di Sotto still drew its water in 1988, they are compared to a flock of sheep (Levi 1965, 79). Giulia's daughter is like a kind of little wild goat (Levi 1965, 126). The image of those peasants who have made the mistake of coming back from America as having the disappointed air of whipped dogs is particularly vivid. One is aware here of Levi's visual awareness and of his ability to find words to put before our eyes what he has seen, but enabling the reader to visualise a person or a scene is not the only purpose or effect of such imagery. Levi wishes to suggest that the peasants are close to nature, and for this reason also indicates the passage of time in terms of the seasons.

Other images, on the other hand, suggest that the peasants are part of an ancient culture. The gravedigger's face is 'outside time', and he is not so much aged as strangely ageless, his powers magical and mysterious. Giulia is compared to a classical amphora, while her face, now wrinkled and yellow from malaria, has the severe structural beauty of a classical temple, the form and proportions of which can still be appreciated although it has lost the marble which once adorned it. Such individual portraits of peasants, however, while reminding the reader of the themes of natural magic and a culture that is alien to the modern state, are exceptional in Levi's account of the peasants, whom he tends to describe more frequently in groups or in general terms. Individualism, with its concomitant vices of egoism and self-seeking, is the prerogative of the gentry: the peasants think and act as a group, and it is as such that they are seen standing in the village square on Levi's first evening in Gagliano, symbolically standing apart from their social superiors. In keeping with this group presentation, he mostly gives the peasants no individual names; and his naming of 'Giulia Venere' is mythic – a Roman first name and Greek surname.

Peasants and artisans

Since he tends to describe the villagers other than the gentry as a group, Levi may at first give the impression of being unaware that rural society is stratified and that there will in any village be a group, however small, of artisans and craftsmen. Indeed, he states quite specifically that at Grassano there was an intermediary class of craftsmen, especially of carpenters, whose presence and whose splendid American tools gave a particular character to the life of the village, whereas at Gagliano there were only peasants and gentry (Levi 1965, 178–9). According to the 1936 census, 922, or 86.4 per cent, of the economically active population of 1067 were engaged in agriculture (King 1988, 310). 6 per cent, including a pharmacist, three barbers and a tailor, worked in 'industry and commerce', but since the barbers and the tailor are as poor as the peasants, Levi finds that the social distinction between peasants and tradespeople is hardly worth drawing. The gentry – the mayor, local government officials, police and doctors – no doubt account for most of the remaining 7.6 per cent. The point is emphasized by the fact that one of the barbers owns and works a piece of land, with the result that his shop is hardly ever open. If there is a gap between the peasants and the artisans and shopkeepers, it is negligible compared to that which separates peasants and artisans alike from the gentry, who alone can prefix the particle 'Don' to their names. But while poverty is a great leveller, it does not immediately, any more than in Fontamara, change traditional social attitudes: the implication of Levi's comments is that the craftsmen still think of themselves as socially superior to the peasants. The tailor, for example, tries to dress his children better than those of the peasants, and bitterly regrets that he will not be able to make *galantuomini* of them. They will be condemned to live, as most of the *Gaglianesi* are, in one-room windowless hovels identical to those described by Silone. Readers of Italian literature – of Pirandello's tale 'L'altro figlio', for example – would have been familiar with accounts of such hovels, but may well have supposed them to be a thing of the past.

Peasants and the land

Levi is aware that there is a fundamental difference between the peasants of Gagliano and those of Grassano. The latter are landless labourers, *braccianti*, and they work on the estates of the local gentry. Levi thus sees in two separate villages the two peasant social groups that Silone sees in Fontamara; and, like the Abruzzese novelist, he sees them living in the same poverty. He is, however, anxious to make the point that the *latifondi* are not the sole source of the south's social problems, and in this respect he may be writing against Silone (Moloney 2002).

The peasants of Gagliano own small plots of land; 270 out of 387 holdings in 1930 were less than five hectares in size. Only nine were larger than fifty hectares, but since most of these probably consisted of clayey slopes and precipices, they could not have offered much of a living (King 1988). These holdings often lie at some distance from the village, sometimes up to four hours' walk away (Levi 1965, 68). We have already seen that one possible limitation of Levi's account of peasant life is that he cannot visit these distant fields. He does, however, see or hear their cheerless departure for work in the dark, early hours of the morning, when he notices that, like the *fontamaresi*, they do not sing on their way to work; and he sees them return in the evening, toiling up the steep paths to the village like souls in a Dantesque hell (Levi 1965, 195), and he knows that after a strenuous day's work their backs will ache and they will be dirty with dust and sweat (Levi 1965, 95).

He knows, too, that the peasants work in unhealthy conditions, since the nearby valleys of the Agri and the Sauro are breeding-grounds for the malaria-bearing mosquitoes that were eliminated only after the second world war. As a doctor, he attempts to treat malarial cases, while his sister is accosted in Matera by children begging for quinine. He is aware that deforestation is one of the prime causes of the degradation of the soil, and comments on the constant threat of landslides after heavy rain. He is convinced that the land could be improved and the danger of malaria reduced by prophylactic measures, even with limited expenditure of resources and energy. The problem is that the authorities cannot solve problems whose very existence is officially denied. Indeed, Levi sees the authorities, at national and at local level, as exacerbating the peasants' problems. On the national level, the 'battle for grain' compels the cultivation of cereal crops on land that is unsuitable for them (Levi 1965, 195). The tax on goats, imposed to encourage the planting of wheat, and which the peasants cannot afford to pay, forces them to slaughter the animals which represent their principal capital investment and are an important source of cheese and milk in an area in which malnutrition is a serious problem. The skinning of a dead goat by means of inflation of the skin prompts one of Levi's most vivid descriptions (Levi 1965, 76–8). At the local level, the mayor attempts to force the peasants to assemble to listen to patriotic broadcasts on the radio, thus compelling them to lose a day's work.

Peasants and politics

The order to grow grain and the tax on goats are cited by Levi as examples of the fundamentally harmful ways in which the central authority of the state impinges on the lives of the peasants. The state brings them no benefits; the provisions made for their education and welfare are grossly inadequate, while their inability to pay taxes meets only the punitive response of the confiscation of their already meagre property. Levi might seem here to be echoing Fortunato's view of the relations between peasants and the state. Fortunato in 1898 described the peasants as 'powerless against a political order whose principal function was that of the tax collector, and whose customs and excise verge on a regime of confiscation' (Fortunato 1982, 23). Levi, however, is not content to follow Fortunato only and, like most of the *Rivoluzione Liberale* group, he specifically repudiates what he sees as Fortunato's essentially negative outlook.

The voice of Fortunato is represented in the novel by signor Orlando of Grassano. He was the brother of Mario Soldati, who was to become famous as a writer of narrative fiction and film director. Levi had been working on his portrait for the cover of Soldati's *America primo amore* when he was arrested. Levi records conversations with Orlando about the southern problem and reports that Orlando had concluded that nothing could be done to solve the insoluble problem. Orlando's 'Niente' [Nothing] is seen by Levi as echoing the view of Fortunato, whom he describes as 'the best and most humane thinker' on the subject, but who was fond of calling himself 'the politician of nothing' (Levi 1965, 195–6). 'Nothing' also characterizes, in Levi's view, the fundamentally negative outlook of southerners in general, which he sees as deriving from a deep-rooted inferiority complex.

In what sense, then, can the peasants of Gagliano be said to be 'outside history' and 'outside the state', as Levi repeatedly asserts them to be? According to Falaschi, Levi fails to realise that the state and the peasants constitute a single organism in which the dominated guarantee the existence of the dominators (Falaschi 1978, 43). This seems to be a misreading of the text. Levi does indeed see that, in terms of exploitation, the peasants are inevitably within the state. Its fiscal and agricultural policies impinge forcefully on their daily lives. What Elsa Morante would call la Storia (with a capital S, just as Levi ironically writes 'Stato' with a capital S) is making them poorer all the time. Levi's point is that they are within the state but not of it; its values are not theirs, and it has contributed little of value to their lives. In terms of their essential values – as we shall see in the next chapter – they are outside history.

CHAPTER 11

Cristo si è fermato a Eboli and the problem of the North

It is now taken for granted that *Cristo si è fermato a Eboli* needs to be interpreted in the light of *Paura della libertà*, the essay which Levi wrote in France in 1939 but did not publish until 1964. Remo Catani, for example, wrote in 1979:

> The resurgence over the last decade in critical studies on Levi has large-ly been based on a recognition that convictions first expressed theoreti-cally in *Paura della libertà* (1939) offer a key to a deeper understanding of his work (Catani 1979, 213).

Cristo si è fermato a Eboli has so far been discussed mainly in terms of the problem of the south, and it is natural that this should have been the case. From time to time, however, it has been suggested that *Paura della libertà* is 'a book packed with ideas on the rebirth and rediscovery of civilization' (Falaschi 1978, 13–14), but the implications of this for the interpretation of Levi's account of Gagliano have not yet been fully worked out.

Paura della libertà was originally intended to be merely the introductory section of a much longer and very ambitious work, which was never completed, in which Levi planned to analyse the problem of what so ailed European society that it had spawned the monstrosities of Fascism in Italy and Spain and Nazism in Germany, with strong Fascist movements in other countries, with the result that the world was about to be plunged into war. Levi wrote in his preface to *Paura della libertà*, written shortly after the publication of *Cristo si è fermato a Eboli*, that:

> Se il passato era morto, il presente incerto e terribile, il futuro misterioso, si sentiva il bisogno di fare il punto; di fermarsi a considerare le ragioni di quella cruenta rivoluzione che incominciava (Levi 1964, 10).

> If the past was dead, the present uncertain and terrible, the future myste-rious, one felt the need to take stock: to pause and explore the reasons for the bloody revolution that was beginning.

The relevance of *Paura della libertà* for the interpretation of *Cristo si è ferma-to a Eboli* is that the earlier work strongly suggests that the later book has a dual purpose. It does indeed denounce as unworthy of a civilised society the poverty and deprivation in which the peasants of the south live, and it criticises the state for its failure to tackle the problem of the south. But it also suggests that the subordinate culture has positive values that the dominant culture signally lacks, and implies that the lack of these values, and their replacement by other, more sinister, values, is the root cause of modern mass society's malaise. That Levi identifies positive values in peasant culture, and argues that they should be preserved, has long been recognised (Asor Rosa 1972, 189). But it has not been recognised that these values are intended, cumulatively, to offer both a critique of modern mass society and an alternative to it. Nor is there general agreement on what, precisely, these positive values are.

The central thesis of *Paura della libertà* is that Western European culture is characterized above all by a fear of freedom, since freedom involves the need to commit oneself to social relations and accept one's responsibilities. The idea is not new, either in the absolute sense, or in Levi's writings. In the 'Seconda lettera dall'Italia' of March 1932, published in the second *Quaderno di Giustizia e Libertà*, he had criticised what he described as 'an historic Italian tradition', which found in Fascism its appropriate organisation:

> È la ereditata incapacità ad essere liberi, l'abitudine della indulgenza liberatrice, della dimenticanza del peccato nella facile obbedienza, degli intermediari còn Dio. È la paura della passione e della responsabilità, che porta a ricercare adorando chi ce ne privi e ce ne liberi (Levi 1975 (2), 33–4).

> It is our inherited inability to be free, the habit of liberating indulgence, of forgetfulness of sin in easy obedience, of intermediaries with God. It is fear of passion and responsibility, which leads us to seek adoringly someone who will deprive us of them, and free us from them.

This theme is developed in the eighth essay in *Paura della libertà*, entitled 'Storia sacra', in which Levi treats the account of the Fall in *Genesis* as a mythical account of the development in human beings of a sense of separation or alienation, which in turn led to the loss of the original sense of perfect freedom which had characterised mankind before the Fall (Levi 1964, 119–26).

Levi wrote in the preface to the first edition of *Paura della libertà* (Levi 1964, 11) that he had had no books with him when writing it, and no means of acquiring information or documentation on the particular problems he was dealing with; but a number of critics have asserted that he had available a copy of the Bible and the works of Vico, although it is not clear whether he had all or only some of the latter (Camerino 1982, 96). There is certainly abundant evidence in Levi's work of his familiarity with the Bible (both Old and New Testaments), while his sense of the importance of myth, his interest in the primitive and his cyclical view of history seem to echo Vico. What is also probable is that Levi was familiar with other attempts to diagnose the malaise of twentieth-century society; at any rate, his work displays striking affinities with the thought of a number of other writers, ranging from Carl Gustav Jung to Wilhelm Reich and Erich Fromm. Wilhelm Reich (1897–1957) published *The Mass Psychology of Fascism* in 1934; Erich Fromm (1900–80) published his *Escape from Freedom*, known in the United Kingdom as *The Fear of Freedom*, in 1941.

In his notable attempt to survey Jung's influence in Italy from 1903 to 1976, Carotenuto does not even mention Levi (Carotenuto 1977), but Camerino is nevertheless right to see the Swiss psychoanalyst as providing the basis of *Paura della libertà* (Camerino 1982, 97) – and therefore, one might add, of *Cristo si è fermato a Eboli* too. De Donato sees Levi as grafting on to Gobetti's thought a Jungian analysis of the crisis afflicting European civilization, while rejecting Jung's basic pessimism (De Donato 1974, 52). One could, however, go further, and argue that Jungian psychology provides Levi with the conceptual framework that supports his total view of human nature and of society.

Much of Jung's later work is concerned with the process of individuation, the process, that is, by which individuals emerge from the undifferentiated collective and establish their personal identities. Levi, however, is also concerned with the undifferentiated collective as well as with the process of differentiation; he is therefore interested in some of Jung's relatively early works, including especially his more anthropological writings on primitive psychology. There is a striking affinity, for example, between Jung's essay 'Archaic Man', published in *Seelenprobleme der Gegenwart* in 1931, and Levi's account of certain aspects of magic and the supernatural in Gagliano.

Modern man, says Jung, has learned to distinguish between what is subjective and psychic from what is objective and 'natural'. Primitive man had not:

> His country is neither a geographical nor a political entity. It is that territory which contains his thinking and feeling in so far as he is unconscious of these functions. His fear is localized in certain places that are 'not good'. The spirits of the departed inhabit such and such a wood. That cave harbours devils who strangle any man who enters. In yonder mountain lives the great serpent; that hill is the grave of the legendary king; near this spring or rock or tree every woman becomes pregnant; that ford is guarded by snake-demons; this towering tree has a voice that can call certain people (Jung 1964, 63).

Jung would certainly have recognised as archaic the world of the *gaglianesi*, with its elves and sprites, its witches and sorcerers, its demons who waylay travellers by night, and the spirits of infants who died unbaptised, and who may, if captured, be compelled to reveal the location of fabulous treasures buried by the *briganti*. Jung relates that in Africa an old woman may also be a crocodile, or a leopard; similarly, Levi relates that a Gaglianese woman may also be a cow, or a man also a wolf. Even his dog, Barone, shares this double nature, and is by virtue of his name part animal and part aristocrat. And in case we are not ready to take the point, Levi directs our interpretation of his world by explicitly describing it as archaic; the large loaf on the table at his first lodging is shaped like a Mexican time-stone, while the wine-jug is shaped like an archaic female image (Levi 1965, 63).

The psychology of the *gaglianesi* resembles that of Jung's archaic man in other important respects as well. Neither, unlike modern people, believes in rigorous connections of cause and effect linking events (Levi 1965, 103; Jung 1964, 56). Both believe in omens which rational modern people reject (Levi 1965, 103; Jung 1964, 58). Yet in spite of these differences, Jung insists, the psychology of archaic man 'is the psychology also of modern, civilized man, and not merely of individual "throw-backs" in modern society. On the contrary, every civilized human being, however high his conscious development, is still an archaic man at the deeper levels of his psyche' (Jung 1964, 51). This is undoubtedly what Levi has in mind when he refers, repeatedly, to 'the Lucania which is in each of us', and to 'all the Lucanias in every corner of the world'.

Levi is clearly asserting that there is in humankind a core of historically unconditioned values or characteristics. It is to these values that he gives the name of 'civiltà contadina' or 'peasant culture'; but he makes it clear that what he calls peasant culture 'non è certamente limitato nello spazio né riservato agli uomini che zappano la terra o portano i greggi sui pascoli' [is certainly not restricted in space or limited to men who dig the soil or take their flocks to pasture] (Levi 1975 (2), 58). These values are, he said when commemorating Gramsci, 'quei valori fondamentali che qui ho imparato a conoscere' [those fundamental human values that I learned here] (Levi 1975 (1), 72), that is, in Lucania. And in the documentary film, *Lucania dentro di noi*, which was directed by Libero Bizzarri with a commentary by Levi, he referred to a culture which is the very root of our being. What, then, are these values, and in what way does their survival in peasant society represent a critique of modern mass society?

The very survival of these positive values is for Levi in itself an indication that peasant culture, although still subject to the pressures of history, exists outside time. Levi insists that here, 'il tempo non scorre' [time does not flow] (Levi 1965, 96). The gravedigger may be about ninety years old, but his face is 'fuori del tempo, rugoso e sformato come una mela vizza' [outside time, wrinkled and shapeless like a withered apple] (Levi 1965, 94). Giulia la Santarcangelese has a similar agelessness (Levi 1965, 127). But this quality of timelessness or atemporality is attributed only to the peasants; the world of the gentry is, on the other hand, characterised by a sense of tedium, of a time which passes very slowly because it is empty (Levi 1965, 90–1). They are also historically contextualised in a way the peasants are not.

As a northerner, Levi brings with him into this timeless world a sense of time passing more or less quickly, depending on one's sense of commitment or fulfillment. For the exile, time often drags (Levi 1965, 170), to such an extent, indeed, that he describes time itself as a 'dreary prison' (Levi 1965, 218). The thought of having to spend two more years in Gagliano dismays him: 'Ancora due anni quaggiú! Il senso della noia degli identici giorni futuri mi scese improvviso nel cuore'. [Two more years here! the sense of the tedium of those identical days suddenly sank into my heart] (Levi 1965, 254). There are then for Levi two different kinds of time – the linear time of the calendar and of history, and the natural rhythm of the peasants' world, marked by the recurrence of the seasons. His sister's brief visit has the effect of making him realise that these 'two times' are irreconcilable (Levi 1965, 106).

All the more remarkable, then, are the episodes in which Levi describes himself as being granted – as though in some moment of grace – a sense of being himself outside time. The episode in which he sits up to see the New Year in, only to find that his watch has stopped, is surely symbolic of his escape – even if only temporary – from the artificial restrictions of linear time. It constitutes, indeed, an escape from history – or rather, from History – which elsewhere is wreaking such havoc. Historical time is inhuman: only the peasants' timelessness has a human dimension:

> Il mio orologio si era fermato, e nessun rintocco di fuori poteva giunger-mi e indicarmi il passare del tempo, dove il tempo non scorre. Così finì, in un momento indeterminato, l'anno 1935, quest'anno fastidioso, pieno di noia legittima, e cominciò il 1936, identico al precedente, e a tutti quelli che verranno poi, nel loro indifferente corso disumano (Levi 1965, 213).

> My watch had stopped, and no chime could reach me from outside, to indicate the passage of time, where time does not flow. Thus, in an inde-terminate moment, the year 1935 finished, that irksome year, filled with justified boredom, and 1936 began, identical to its predecessor, and to all those which had come before, and which will come later, in their indif-ferent, inhuman course.

Shortly after this episode, there occurs the sequence of events that lead to Levi's visit to Il Pantano, to tend a man dying of peritonitis. As a doctor, Levi is helpless and humiliated. Having given his patient a pain-killing injection, he can only rest, while listening to the cries of the dying man and the muttered prayers of the women of the household. Yet at precisely this moment, there descends on him a great sense of peace and happiness, which derives from his sense of identification with the world and from his sense of timelessness. The Jungian language of the passage suggests that the experience of timelessness is the result of a return to an undifferentiated sense of collectivity:

> Mi pareva di essere staccato da ogni cosa, da ogni luogo, remotissimo da ogni determinazione, perduto fuori del tempo, in un infinito altrove [...] mi pareva di essere entrato, d'un tratto, nel cuore stesso del mondo (Levi 1965, 229).

> I seemed to be detached from everything and everywhere, quite remote from all determination, lost outside time, in an infinite elsewhere [...] I seemed all at once to have entered the very heart of the world.

Miccinesi has written of 'a break in mathematical time, as measured, in other words, by our watches' (Miccinesi 1979, 55), but, although he writes of Levi discovering 'a new temporal dimension', he seems to miss the experience of the totally atemporal. Guy Raffa perceptively observes that it is precisely through what he calls Levi's 'sacred art of healing' that the painter/doctor is so completely able to identify with peasant culture as to achieve this state of timelessness, albeit only temporarily (Raffa 1997).

It is not surprising that some of Levi's Marxist readers have described him as a mystic. He seems to be describing what T.S. Eliot would describe, in Christian terms, as 'the point of intersection of the timeless / with time', and – in a brilliant oxymoron, 'the intersection of the timeless moment' (Eliot 1974, 212, 215). Indeed, one of the most immediately striking features of *Paura della libertà* is its religious vocabulary and imagery. The title of the opening chapter, 'Ab Jove principium', is an oblique reference to Gaetano Salvemini's use of the phrase in 'La questione meridionale' of 1898–9 (Salvemini 1955, 32–54), which reinforces the suggestion that the malaise of modern Europe and the healthy values of the south are closely associated in Levi's mind. After a somewhat opaque opening paragraph on a Jove who resembles a worm rather than an eagle, and who is to be found on earth rather than in the heavens, Levi states clearly and unambiguously that we shall not be able to understand anything human unless we start from the sense of the sacred; conversely, we shall not be able to understand the social unless we begin with the concept of the religious. The sacred and the religious are being contrasted. In 'Il contadino e l'orologio' – a revealing title to which we shall have cause to return – Levi argues, in Jungian terms, that:

> Poiché la civiltà contadina è posta al limite dell'indistinzione, vive e perdura in quell'ambigua regione nella quale per la prima volta l'individuo si

distacca, si forma e prende coscienza di sé, ed attorno a lui è sempre pre-
sente e incombente il senso del sacro, della originaria indistinzione. (Levi
1975 (2), 58).

Since peasant culture is set at the limits of indistinctiveness, it lives and
persists in that ambiguous region in which the individual is separated for
the first time, is shaped and becomes aware of himself, and around him
there is always present and incumbent the sense of the sacred, of original
indistinctiveness.

Moreover, Levi continues, 'this same moment, this same initial poetic condition, is in each of us'. This is, as he frequently puts it, 'the Lucania in each one
of us'.

At this point it becomes clear why we first see the peasantry in the village
square at Gagliano as a group, whereas we see the gentry as a series of individuals; the former still belong to a collectivity whose individual components are
only just beginning to achieve self-awareness. The suggestion that Levi depicts
the bourgeoisie with greater facility because that is his class, misses the point that
Levi is making, namely that the village notables represent extreme individuation, whereas the peasants are only at the beginning of differentiation
(Aurigemma 1982, 6465–7). Commenting on the peasants' lack of political
awareness, which he perhaps exaggerates, Levi writes:

Non possono avere neppure una vera coscienza individuale, dove tutto è
legato da influenze reciproche, dove ogni cosa è un potere che agisce
insensibilmente, dove non esistono limiti che non siano rotti da un influs-
so magico (Levi 1965, 103).

They cannot have even an individual awareness, when everything is connected by reciprocal influences, when everything is a power that acts
imperceptibly, when there are no limits which are not broken by a magic
influence.

For that reason, in Levi's view, there is in Gagliano an all-pervasive sense of the
sacred. The peasants' belief in magic is far from being merely a manifestation of
their ignorance and superstition, or of Levi's taste for the exotic. It is, rather, an
indication of their sense of the numinous in all that surrounds them. Here, says
Levi, 'tutto partecipa alla divinità' [everything here partakes of divinity] (Levi
1965, 137); there is a 'numinous atmosphere' (Levi 1965, 167). Levi follows
Jung, one of whose recurrent themes was that what he calls 'modern man' has
lost all his old metaphysical certainties, while every step in material 'progress'
threatens him with a catastrophe even more destructive than the first world war

(Jung 1964, 81–2). What Jung calls 'archaic man', on the other hand, has always been in touch with the life of the spirit. There is something of 'archaic man' in 'modern man', but there are still examples of 'archaic men' to be found in the modern world:

> Great innovations never come from above; they come invariably from below, just as trees never grow from the sky downward, but upward from the earth. The upheaval of our world and the upheaval of our consciousness are one and the same. Everything has become relative and doubtful. And while man, hesitant and questioning, contemplates a world that is distracted with treaties of peace and pacts of friendship, with democracy and dictatorship, capitalism and Bolshevism, his spirit yearns for an answer that will allay the turmoil of doubt and uncertainty. And it is just the people from the obscurer levels who follow the unconscious drive of the psyche; it is the much-derided silent folk of the land, who are less infected with academic prejudices than the shining celebrities are wont to be. Looked at from above, they often present a dreary or laughable spectacle; yet they are as impressively simple as those Galileans who were once called blessed (Jung 1964, 87).

De Donato has already drawn attention to the Jungian origin of Levi's 1935 prison writings (De Donato 1974, 51, 247). With this in mind, it becomes clear that Levi's reading of Jung had prepared him to discover positive values in the peasants of Gagliano, just as his study of the *meridionalisti* had prepared him to relate the peasants' poverty to the structures of their society. Bronzini also points out that Levi's observations on the sacred in the family – 'the sacred, mysterious, magic sense of a community' (Levi 1965, 112) – are important, and were made before Lévi-Strauss and others (Bronzini 1977, 211). De Martino also stresses that the element of magic in peasant life is not to be regarded merely as the expression of a 'primitive mentality'; it is often an important aspect of the religious life of a society (De Martino 1987, 193n).

Opposed to this natural sense of the sacred is the religion of the State, which in Levi's view characterizes mass society, according to which the State is an expression or embodiment of the Spirit and transcends the individuals who make it up. When Levi writes of 'the Ethical State of the Hegelians of Naples' (Levi 1965, 158), he is attacking the philosophical tradition nurtured by the Neapolitan school, and especially by Giovanni Gentile (1875–1944), who was the leading ideologist of Fascism. But, as he makes clear, Fascism is merely the most recent manifestation of what he calls 'statalismo' (Levi 1965, 250). 'Statalismo', or faith in the State, is not peculiar to Fascism, but is a manifestation of Italy's petty bourgeois society. In this same section of his book, he refers to Italy's 'eternal Fascism' (Levi 1965, 251), implying that the centralised structures of Italian society since the Risorgimento are the root cause of the problem.

But why, one asks, does Levi use a religious vocabulary to contrast what he calls 'the sacred' with the religion of the State? Levi was aware that the modern sacralization of politics had been carried much further by Fascism, which had usurped narratives of perdition and redemption for its own content, re-casting them in the form of a religion of the State. This religion, focusing on the charisma of Mussolini, expressed millenarian longings and conjured up the mystical notion of an imminent age which would see the culmination of Italy's 'civilising mission'. Mussolini's commitment to this as his 'core myth' (Griffin 1998, 9) seems to have been intuited by Levi, who seeks to present peasant culture as an authentic alternative to Fascism's spurious restoration of the numinous in its festivities, rituals and rallies. Nazism in this respect 'improved' on Fascism and Victor Klemperer has recorded the way in which Nazism systematically appropriated the language of the gospel (Klemperer 2000, 103–18).

And why does mass society come into being? In Levi's thought, each act that produces differentiation, represents an act of freedom. In great cities, on the other hand, membership of mass society produces a new form of indifferentiation, in which individual identity is lost. Only in isolated families, in villages and in towns of a modest size, can life be lived on a human scale, with individuals known and recognised, duly differentiated, while still retaining a sense of community. In mass society, the mass State becomes a religion, which demands sacrifices (Levi 1964, 105–10). These sacrifices take the form of the surrender of the individual will, and therefore of responsibility, and, in time of war, even of life. Mass society seems destined, in Levi's view, to become a totalitarian society. One is reminded of the way in which, for Lewis Mumford, New York in 1938 inspired a vision of the insensate commercial megalopolis, marked by 'sprawl and shapelessness' and portending the triumph of totalitarian militarism (Mumford 1938, 289–92).

Possibly the most important of the values which Levi finds in peasant culture is its sense of fraternity and solidarity:

> Non possono avere neppure una vera coscienza individuale [...] Ma in essi è vivo il senso umano di un comune destino, e di una comune accettazione. È un senso, non un atto di coscienza; non si esprime in discorsi o in parole, ma si porta con sé in tutti i momenti, in tutti i gesti della vita, in tutti i giorni uguali che si stendono su questi deserti (Levi 1965, 103).

> They cannot have an individual awareness either [...] But the human feeling of a common destiny, of a common lot, is felt by them. This is a feeling, not an act of awareness; it is not expressed in speech or words, but

they carry it with them at all times, in all the acts of their life, in all the identical days which stretch out over these desert places (Levi 1965, 103).

This is why the peasants of Gagliano freely offer hospitality to strangers – 'quella non servile ospitalità antica, che mette gli uomini alla pari' [that ancient, unservile hospitality, which puts men on terms of equality (Levi 1965, 228 and cf. 172). They feel and actively show concern for a sick member of their community, even the man who lives in the remote and isolated il Pantano. 'Tutti, in paese, conoscevano il morto, e l'amavano' [Everyone in the village knew and loved the dead man] (Levi 1965, 231).

This ancient, unspoken sense of fraternity is also the basis of the peasants' natural, instinctive sense of justice. They know that if the Abyssinian war involves taking land from those who already own it, it cannot be just (Levi 1965, 150). They consider the *confinati* as their brothers in misfortune. Since this 'true brotherhood' and 'sober hospitality' are also the themes of some of the first poems Levi wrote while in *confino*, they must have made an immediate impression on him (Levi 1990).

Bronzini confirms the general accuracy of Levi's account of Lucania; 'Levi's book was not a work of the imagination, he had written the truth, things he had seen with his own eyes'. He sees this 'reciprocal solidarity between members of the same community' as a fundamental feature of peasant culture in Lucania (Bronzini 1977, 38 and 46); elsewhere, he writes of 'the duty of mutual aid, the sense of human solidarity' (Bronzini 1969, 770). Indeed it was this aspect of Levi's account of Gagliano that prompted Ernesto De Martino to begin his investigations into Lucanian peasant culture. But more is at stake here than the question of the accuracy of Levi's account of peasant culture in Lucania. Falaschi seems to interpret Levi's attitude towards the humanity of the peasants purely in literary terms, comparing it to Vittorini's view that the poor and oppressed are more human simply because they are poor and oppressed (Falaschi 1971, 37). What is at stake, rather, is a conviction on Levi's part that peasant society serves as a model for the future, in that it makes the individual the basis of all relationships (Levi 1965, 252). The State, in its present form, is for Levi the source of problems; the idea of the State, and the relationship of the individual to the State, need to be completely rethought, in order to produce a new form of state. In his account of the reaction of the peasants to the death of the man at il Pantano, Levi gives us a glimpse of the peasants' sense of community in action:

> La loro avversità per lo Stato, estraneo e nemico, si accompagna (e la cosa potrà parere strana, e non lo è) a un senso naturale del diritto, a una spontanea intuizione di quello che, per loro, dovrebbe essere veramente lo Stato: una volontà comune, che diventa legge (Levi 1965, 232).

Their hostility towards the State, as an external enemy, is accompanied (and this may seem strange, but it is not) by a natural sense of right, by a spontaneous intuition of what, for them, the State ought really to be, a common will, which becomes law.

The episode of the compilation of the petition, requesting that Levi be allowed to continue to practice medicine, demonstrates that in a free society the peasants would be capable of self-government. In his final summing-up of his conclusions, Levi argues that the only way forward for Italy lies in the creation of autonomous rural communes. This, in turn, would require the restructuring of all forms of Italian social life into a series of autonomous organisations – factories, schools and cities alike. The autonomous rural commune is the only form of state which would allow the two cultures to co-exist (Levi 1965, 252–3).

Here, and in parenthesis, one might note that Levi (and Silone) offer an interesting anticipation of the thought of Franz Fanon, who argued that:

In an underdeveloped country the party ought to be organised in such a fashion that it is not simply content with having contacts with the masses. The party is not an administration responsible for transmitting orders; it is the energetic spokesman and the incorruptible defender of the masses. In order to arrive at this conception of the party, we must above all rid ourselves of the very Western, very bourgeois and therefore contemptuous attitude that the masses are incapable of governing themselves. In fact, experience proves that the masses understand perfectly the most complicated problems (Fanon 1971, 151–2).

At this point Levi both continues and develops a line of thought which derives from Gobetti and Dorso, and at the same time parts company with them. Moderates among the architects of the Risorgimento had admired the English system of local government, and accepted French liberal criticisms of the highly centralized Napoleonic state. Faced with the realities of the problem of the south, however, Italian politicians had centralized power, thus exacerbating the problem (Lyttleton, 1973, 6–7). *Meridionalisti* such as Fortunato described a situation similar to that observed by Levi, with a government that was not representative but 'a dictatorship, in prey to obsession and paroxysm', bent on colonial expansion (Fortunato 1982, 23–4), but with the difference that, for Fortunato, the unity of the state was sacred and not to be undermined in any way. Salvemini, however, developed the idea of the autonomy of the region and the commune (Pogliano 1976, 141). Dorso had then seen local autonomy as one of the ideals of the Risorgimento which had been abandoned as a result of the 'conquista regia'. Levi takes up the idea and makes it the basis of Italy's future.

For Dorso, however, the coming 'Southern revolution' would need to be based on a rural block of 'small capitalists' and – after that group – a peasant working-class block which would find in autonomy the political solution to the southern problem (Dorso 1972, 264–5). But the peasants, in this block, would inevitably be in a subordinate, supporting position. Levi, in his 1957 essay on Dorso, endorses the latter's view that there could be no Italian revolution without the south (Levi 1975 (2), 132), but he also distances himself from Dorso – and also from Gobetti – in one important respect. Dorso believed firmly that the key to the solution of the southern problem lay in the creation of a new class of intellectuals who could offer a leadership of which the present corrupt southern bourgeoisie was incapable. Leadership, in other words, is to exercised by an elite (Dorso 1972, 279). Levi, on the other hand, places his faith in the natural and instinctive virtues of the peasantry, who are thus not to be reduced to a subordinate or supporting role, while leadership is to be exercised by the collectivity, rather than by an elite. Levi is able to do this on the basis of his analysis of positive values in peasant culture, whereas Dorso had denied that the south had any such original culture (Dorso 1972, 105). One has the impression that 'culture' for Dorso meant a modern, urban 'high' culture, as it does for many of Levi's readers. One also has the impression that, in spite of Dorso's advocacy of local autonomy, he is still thinking in terms of the State (with a capital S) as the source of reform, which will therefore come from above. It is possible that Levi was strongly influenced by Gramsci's advocacy of factory councils, which were intended to be the pattern for a future society. Dorso's review of *Cristo si è fermato a Eboli*, first published in April 1946, makes it clear that he agrees with much of Levi's analysis but regards reform as a national problem, not to be solved at the local level (Dorso 1986, 169–79) A new democracy based on local autonomy was Action Party policy by the time Levi wrote his novel.

But Levi also distances himself from Gramsci – by implication – since Gramsci had seen the peasantry as subordinate to the urban working-class movement and – in his pre-prison writings – had been unable to suggest any institution analogous to the Turinese factory councils around which the peasant movement could organise itself (Gramsci 1974, 14). Spriano points out that Gramsci was thinking merely in terms of transferring the paradigm of the factory council to the village (Spriano 1963, 62). Levi, on the other hand, was thinking in terms of the village generating its own paradigm.

At this point, the difficult question arises – as it did in chapter 9 – of whether, and to what extent, Levi has become enmeshed in his informants' construction of reality, or whether he has enmeshed them in his. Several considerations suggest that the peasants' sense of brotherhood, to which he attributes such importance, is in reality less pervasive than he suggests.

When Levi is looking for a housekeeper, he is assured that dozens of the women of Gagliano would compete for the work and the income it represents

(Levi 1965, 121). Competition for scarce jobs is not conducive to social cohesion. It is, moreover, Donna Caterina, the mayor's sister, who finds him a suitable housekeeper, in an exercise of what looks very much like clientelism. Clientelism is, traditionally, conducive to the development of vertical relationships between patrons and their individual clients, but not to class solidarity, as we have already seen in the case of *Fontamara* (see chapter 6).

Levi has difficulty in recruiting a housekeeper because he is a bachelor, living alone. Local custom does not permit an unaccompanied woman to enter the house of a lone man. The assumption is that they would immediately make love (Levi 1965, 121). Levi has much less to say about sexual mores than Silone, whose narrators are inclined ironically to attribute the repeated pregnancies of certain women to the intervention of the Holy Spirit, since their husbands have either died or emigrated to the United States. But we do learn that the husband of one Gaglianese witch, Maria C., has already served a prison sentence for a murder committed out of jealousy, while the same emotion makes the current lover of Giulia la Santarcangelese terminate her services in Levi's house (Levi 1965, 241–2, 254–5). Bronzini makes the point that one of the functions of the neighbourhood – 'il vicinato' – was to give mutual aid, which in part confirms Levi's view, but he also says that another function was to ensure the observation of social norms (Bronzini 1977, 218). Levi emphasises the positive, supportive, function of the neighbourhood, but also documents the element of control by his references to breaches of the social norms.

Certain aspects of witchcraft and magic also suggest that social harmony in Gagliano is far from complete. Illness, whether of animals or human beings, is attributed to spells cast out of malevolence. There are spells to transfer one's pains to someone else. There are even spells to make one's enemies die (Levi 1965, 241). All are expressions of tensions and enmities.

To what extent, then, do these indications of social tensions undermine Levi's message that peasant society is characterised by its strong sense of brotherhood and social support? In themselves, they may not at first seem significant, but one has also to consider the possibility, raised in chapter 10, that Levi's presence, and particularly his activity as a doctor, are themselves conducive to displays of social harmony. The participant observer does, by virtue of his or her very presence, change the environment which he or she is observing; all the more so, if he or she is active in that environment. The Glaswegian Ralph Glasser, commenting on the time which he spent in San Giorgio Albanese in Calabria, writes: 'By this time the group discussions were springing up spontaneously wherever I happened to be' (Glasser, 1977, 82), and one of the local nuns later confirms that the villagers have talked about their community's problems only during, and as a result of, his stay with them. The same Sister Valeria expresses a wish that Glasser would remain in the village (ibid., 138), just as the *gaglianesi* wish that Levi would remain with them.

Perhaps inevitably, Levi's views were dismissed by some as mere mysticism, even as mystification, representing a failure on his part to provide a concrete political solution to the problem. His account of the mass state as religious experience inevitably attracted the hostility of Marxist critics such as Mario Alicata (Alicata 1968). One of Levi's more temperate critics, Asor Rosa, finds in Levi a cultural seriousness in which other, more 'progressive', writers are deficient, but he nevertheless sees in *Cristo si è fermato a Eboli* a tendency towards aestheticism and mysticism, as well as a defective ideology. Levi's political and ideological error, in Asor Rosa's view, lies precisely in his 'anti-historical' identification of positive values in peasant culture, and his decision to make these, rather than the class struggle, the basis of his political programme (Asor Rosa 1972, 153–60, 190–1).

Levi himself was well aware that he had not offered in *Cristo si è fermato a Eboli* a specific programme of reform. Certainly, he was convinced that the second world war had brought civilization to a crisis point, and that the resistance had been fought to construct a new society, not to restore the old:

> Siamo davanti alle rovine, che dobbiamo finire di abbattere per riedificare. E la nuova città non può rifarsi sulla pianta dell'antica (Levi 1975 (2), 54).

> We are faced with ruins, which we must finish knocking down in order to rebuild. And the new city cannot be rebuilt on the plan of the old one.

At the time of writing *Cristo si è fermato a Eboli*, Levi had no clear idea of what form of government or what institutions would emerge in the post-war period. There were, however, a number of developments which Levi did not foresee.

The first of these was that there was in post-war Italy no significant and far-reaching agrarian reform. Ginsborg's verdict on the reform is basically negative (Ginsborg 1990, 137–40). Italy's postwar 'economic miracle' then prompted an exodus from the countryside to the cities, as the peasants sought work and prosperity in the north. It was argued that the continuing power of the land-owning feudal aristocracy in southern Italy had restricted the growth of cities in the eleventh century, the period when, in the north, feudalism was declining and cities were growing (Campagna 1967, 58). Only in the second half of the twentieth century, Campagna argues, did the landowning classes cease to dominate absolutely the social pyramid, allowing room for other, urban, forces to develop. The south is being transformed, he agrees:

> Hence that celebrated book by Carlo Levi – which in the immediate post-war years had seemed to be an interpretation of the values of 'peasant culture', of a culture which could have a future of its own [...] today

we can read or reread it as a beautiful funeral ode to that so-called 'peasant culture' (Campagna 1967, 58).

Emigration, he goes on, marks the aspiration of the southern peasantry towards an urban culture which is seen by them as superior. They acquire also the values of that urban culture, and so feel no regrets when they leave for distant cities, not being able to leave for nearer cities. In a similar vein, writing of a Scottish crafting community, Alasdair Maclean observes that 'There's nothing like a dose of realism to rid the system of cant. The people who actually lived in the black houses of Ardnamurchan were the first to want out of them' (Maclean 1986, 201). It follows, in Campagna's view, that industrialisation is the only way in which modern Italy can give new life to the south.

In the event, the south has not been industrialised. Living standards have indeed risen, partly as a result of the exodus towards the north of which Campagna wrote, and material prosperity has done much to undermine the quality of life which Levi admired. Ralph Glasser, writing in 1977, maintained that:

> the advanced countries need thoroughgoing decentralization and social and economic restructuring to produce a basic pattern of small townships of network size, with a necessary return to the belief that localised relationships are the stuff of life (Glasser 1977, 206).

There is a striking affinity between the views put forward by Glasser and those of Levi. Like Levi, Glasser distrusts the desire to lapse into total dependence, and to flee from freedom and responsibility (Glasser 1977, 155–6). True humanity, for Glasser, can flourish in what is regarded as a 'backward culture' (Glasser 1977, 11). It therefore comes as a surprise to find Glasser attributing to Levi a view of southern peasants as subhuman which, in *Cristo si è fermato a Eboli*, the peasants attribute in fact to the 'Christians beyond the horizon' (Levi, 1965, 41). This is a fundamental misunderstanding of the text, which prevents Glasser from ever seeing how close is his own position to Levi's.

But Glasser, in 1977, was able to record phenomena which Levi could not have anticipated. He describes San Giorgio Albanese, not far from Gagliano, as indicating compellingly that:

> a certain type and size of small self-regenerating township – or growth unit – is the right social model to strive for, one that can be fully known to itself and therefore helps the individual to maintain the reciprocal relationships of obligation and response needed to support the community's emotional network (Glasser 1977, 26).

But returning to the village after a long absence, Levi discovers that the ubiquitous television set has fractionalised social relations, that the washing-machine has transformed washing the laundry from a public, communal activity, into a private one, and that the motor car has enabled people to travel separately to their fields, rather than together. The old sense of community has disappeared. History has continued to impinge on the life-style of the peasants to such an extent that there is now no space left that is 'outside time'. Levi wrote in 1955:

> Questo mondo della Lucania era profondamente cambiato. Non era più, e non era più effettivamente, non era più il mondo immobile precedente alla fine della guerra; non era più il mondo immobile che è scritto nel mio libro *Cristo si è fermato a Eboli* (Bronzini 1977, 145).

> That world of Lucania had changed profoundly. It no longer existed, in reality it no longer existed. It was no longer the immobile world of before the end of the war; it was no longer the immobile world described in my book *Cristo si è fermato a Eboli*.

Here we may hear what Campagna described as the 'beautiful funeral ode' to peasant culture – although Levi would never have been so patronising as to describe peasant culture as 'so-called', or to write 'peasant culture' in inverted commas, as Campagna did.

CHAPTER 12

Signora Ava and the Risorgimento as peasant crisis

THE AUTHOR

We have already seen that Jovine's first novel, *Un uomo provvisorio* (1934), had undertones of Fascist ruralism, and was also streaked with the influence of D'Annunzio. Since it was a psychological study of a provincial misfit in Rome, it is not surprising to find in it also echoes of Svevo, Borgese and Moravia. Yet shortly after Jovine died in 1950, at the age of only forty-seven, his final novel, *Le terre del Sacramento*, was hailed as one of the finest achievements of neo-realism. In the 1920s, he had supported Fascism, although probably only in limited fashion; but by 1945, he was a member of the Action Party and taking part in the resistance. In 1948, he joined the Communist Party. On both the artistic and on the ideological level, a remarkable transformation had taken place. His second full-length novel, *Signora Ava* (1942), can be seen as occupying a crucial place in that process of transformation.

Jovine was born in 1902 in the village of Guardialfiera, in Molise. Since some 75 per cent of the region's work force was employed in agriculture, it was known in Fascist ruralist propaganda as 'la provincia "ruralissima"', which meant, in effect, that it was the poorest region of Italy. It remained poor throughout his lifetime. In 1961, eleven years after his death, 58.2 per cent of the work force in Molise – as compared to 37.4 per cent in the south generally and 25.4 per cent nationally – still worked on the land (Izzo 1967, 355). Jovine spent much of his life in Molise, which is the setting of most of his narrative fiction. When his heroes (or anti-heroes) – Giulio Sabò in *Un uomo provvisorio* and Siro Baghini in *Uno che si salva* – move to Rome, they find themselves out of their element and have to return to their native village to recover their health and their moral equilibrium. Similarly, Maria, in *Ragazza sola* (1936–7) moves from Rome to the country to regain her moral equilibrium.

The experiences lived out by his characters, of course, do not represent a simple transcription into literature of Jovine's own experience of life. He was educated at Larino and Velletri, in Molise, qualifying as an elementary school teacher at the age of sixteen. He taught locally for a time, probably to help support his family, but moved to Rome in 1925. He continued to teach, contributing to various educational journals, but also enrolled at the University of Rome, where he took a degree in philosophy. His professor, the Gentilean Giuseppe Lombardo Radice, was a *meridionalista* who knew Giustino Fortunato and Gaetano Salvemini.

At this point the problematical issue of Jovine's involvement with Fascism arises. Some sort of commitment to Fascism, even if only a nominal one, would have been necessary to pursue a career in teaching. It would also have been natural for an idealistic young teacher to be attracted by Giovanni Gentile's educational reforms of 1923, and possibly even to equate Fascism with those reforms. The absence of any reference to Fascism in his early fiction has been seen as 'a silently polemical way of reacting to the hated reality of the time: by ignoring it altogether' (Finocchiaro Chimirri 1968, 363), which takes for granted a certain hostility towards the regime on Jovine's part – a hostility which one could also deduce from his explicitly Crocean standpoint in certain essays (Carducci 1977, 13). Carducci, in fact, sees Jovine as involved in a compromise with Fascism, with his adherence as nominal or skin-deep (ibid., 16). He would have had to hold a Fascist party membership card in order to hold a state teaching post, after all. The British Library, however, attributes to Jovine part-authorship, with Lino Domenighini, of a book entitled *La patria fascista. Storia di ieri e di oggi*, which is basically a Fascist children's history of Italy, reaching its climax in the March on Rome. It also includes the rules of the Opera Nazionale Balilla and the Milizia Avanguardia. The cover and the title-page do not give the authors' initials or first names, merely their surnames, but the Keeper of Italian Books at the British Library tells me in private correspondence that he is 80 per cent sure of the attribution. The British Library catalogue dates the book 'c. 1930'. If this is the case, Jovine's Fascism was rather more than skin-deep. Todini also argues that an article of 1929 in *I diritti della scuola* shows a certain support for Fascism (Todini 1979, 7003).

It was paradoxical then, that Fascism should have reacted so negatively to *Un uomo provvisorio*. Sergio Lupi, writing in *Roma fascista* on 18 July 1935, rejected it on the grounds that 'We have found a moral reason for living, and do not think one can live indifferently or provisionally'. The second adverb is a cut at Jovine, while the first is a stab at Moravia, and to link the two together was perceptive. It was in the mid-1930s that the term 'neorealism' was first applied to literature and to novelists such as Moravia, Silone and Jovine in particular. Like *Gli indifferenti*, *Un uomo provvisorio* is set in Rome; the insistence of both authors on grey skies and rain provides an appropriate setting for the uniform dreariness of their central characters' lives, and both authors frequently use the word *noia* to describe their protagonists' condition. A proposed second edition of Jovine's novel was banned.

It would not be altogether unfair to describe *Un uomo provvisorio* as a confused mish-mash of undigested influences. Perhaps the same could be said of the young Jovine's politics. Here, then, is a crucial difference between Jovine on the one hand and Silone and Levi on the other. Silone and Levi were politically committed and had a clear awareness of the problem of the south before they began to write their fiction; Jovine, although born in the south, came to understand the problem of the south more slowly. By about 1937, however, he was clearly finding Fascism uncongenial. Declaring himself an anti-militarist, he applied for a transfer to North Africa, teaching first in Tunisia (1937–9) and then in Cairo (1939–40). It is of course unlikely that a post of this kind would have been allocated to anyone regarded as a dangerous opponent of the regime.

Jovine returned to Italy in May of 1940, shortly before Italy entered the war. In the same year, he published a volume of short stories entitled *Ladro di galline*, all of which deal with southern village life. Although only two of them can be said to be memorable – 'Malfuta, o della fondazione di un villaggio' and 'Ladro di galline', which gives the collection its title – it is clear that Jovine has by now discovered his subject-matter, namely the province of Molise. He has also discovered that his narrative work needs to be based on careful historical research.

SIGNORA AVA

The composition of *Signora Ava*, the novel which marks the beginning of Jovine's maturity as a writer, must have overlapped with that of *Ladro di galline*, since the novel is dated 1938–41. These dates are perhaps misleading, however; in an interview in 1949, Jovine said that he had had the idea for *Signora Ava* in 1928–9 and wrote 'the first four chapters' of the novel before writing *Un uomo provvisorio* (Carducci 1977, 33). He resumed work on it in 1935, only to abandon it again. The final version was written in Tunisia and Cairo between 1937 and 1940. Since the novel in its final form is divided into unnumbered sections, rather than chapters, it is difficult to be sure how much of the novel dates back to he author's youth. In any case, the early sections of the novel so strongly express the narrator's sense of the injustice of the social order in nineteenth-century Molise – a sense of injustice which is conspicuously absent from *Un uomo provvisorio* – that one suspects that a good deal of revision and rewriting has taken place in the intervening years.

At the same time as he was beginning *Signora Ava*, Jovine was beginning to advocate a return to complex, well-constructed works of narrative (Finocchiaro Chimirri 1968, 357). Manzoni's *I promessi sposi* was clearly one of his models, Nievo's *Confessioni di un italiano*, although hardly well-constructed, another. His reading of Nievo may have suggested setting the novel during the Risorgimento, and he may indeed have had in mind the possibility of creating a Molisan version of the Castle of Fratta; but it was surely Manzoni who provided the example of an historical novel that was well researched.

Critics tend now to point to the many liberties Manzoni took with history, rather than to his accuracy. While there can be no doubt that *Signora Ava* is well researched, there has been considerable disagreement about Jovine's fidelity to history. Even though Martelli accepts that 'history is the great protagonist of the novel', he doubts whether it is really an historical novel, on the grounds that events seem to be determined by a vague destiny (Martelli, 1970, 55–6). Grillandi simply doubts the historical accuracy of the novel (Grillandi 1971, 58). Salinari, on the other hand, admires the 'precision and care' of Jovine's historical reconstruction (Salinari 1967, 81), while Mauro lauds his 'historical rigour' (Mauro, 1965, 57) and Martelli documents his use of historical sources (Martelli 1978). Evidence of Jovine's historical reading and personal observation is to be found in his *Viaggio nel Molise*, a series of articles written for *Il Giornale d'Italia* between June and August 1941, and from which it is clear that his accounts of Molise are based on both close personal observation and wide historical reading and research. D'Episcopo has also been able to show that a number of characters, including Don Matteo, derive from archival sources, and the historical and sociological material which is presented in the newspaper articles is transformed imaginatively in the novel.

If read without reference to its date of publication, the *Viaggio nel Molise* may seem bland and inoffensive. It can, however, be read, with reference to its publication in the Fascist period, as having a certain concealed cutting edge. Its emphasis on the poverty of the soil and the harshness of peasant life can be seen as undermining the ruralist propaganda of the period, while Jovine's statement that peasants hoped that their labour, which had made the land fertile, would give them the right to ownership, runs counter to Fascist policy and anticipates one of the themes of the dénouement of *Le terre del Sacramento*. One's perception of the historicity or otherwise of *Signora Ava* similarly depends on reading it in the context of its publication. In that context, Jovine's agreement with one point of Levi's analysis of the southern problem is noteworthy:

> Il cafone sapeva che tra i due padroni, il duca o il marchese che abitavano a Napoli o Parigi e che conoscevano appena l'ubicazione delle loro terre, e l'avvocato, l'usuraio locale che avevano tutto l'impeto e l'avidità di una classe nuova in progresso, che lesinava invece di sperperare, che conosceva il valore del danaro che era la sua unica arma di dominio, preferiva il duca e il marchese (Jovine 1976, 118–19).

> The peasant knew that of his two masters, the Duke or Marquis who lived in Naples or Rome and hardly knew where their lands were locat-

ed, and the lawyer, the local usurer, who had all the grasping energy of a new class on its way up, who skimped instead of spending, who knew the value of the money which was his only means of domination, he preferred the Duke and the Marquis.

Signora Ava is a popular folk-figure, personifying an age fabulously distant from our own. (One of the peasants in 'Malfuta' says 'Caduta una casa? Non ne cadeva una dal tempo della *Signora Ava*' [A house has fallen down? One's not fallen down since the days of Mrs Ava.].) The novel is prefaced by a quotation from a southern folk song:

> O tiempo da Gnora Ava
> nu viecchio imperatore
> a morte condannava
> chi faceva a' 'mmore.
>
> In Missus Ava's time
> an old emperor
> sentenced to death
> those who went a-courting.

The name 'Ava' may mean either 'grandmother' or 'ancestress'.

It was clearly this quotation and the dedication – 'Alla memoria di mio padre, ingenuo rapsodo di questo mondo defunto' – which enabled Russo and other critics to insist on the element of the *favoloso*, and it may well have been this aspect of the novel which brought Jovine fame when it first appeared, but in seizing on this aspect of the novel, sometimes to the exclusion of all else, critics have followed the unsound procedure of applying to the author words which he uses to describe certain of his characters;

> [...] i più vecchi [...] si compiacevano di questa funzione di cronisti e, senza volerlo, con quella operazione della mente che è volta a rendere armoniche le disarmonie del passato davano ai semplici fatti narrati un ritmo di favolosa invenzione [...] Il passato cosí inconsapevolmente composto e armonizzato si coloriva di bellezza (Jovine 1990, 90–1).

> The older people took pleasure in their function as chroniclers and, unintentionally, in the way the mind works when it is intent on harmonising the discords of the past, gave to the simple facts they related the cadence of a fabulous invention [...] The past, unconsciously composed and harmonised in this way, took on a beautiful colouring.

One of the themes of the first part of the novel is undoubtedly that of the essentially static, indeed unchangeable nature of the structures of southern society, as it is perceived by almost all the characters – which is not to say that the narrator perceives it in the same way. The novel might be said to have two main characters. One is Don Matteo Tridone, a poverty-stricken priest and part-time poacher, a man of peasant origin, who ekes out a living as best he can, having no parish of his own, by saying mass and taking peasant funerals here and there and, in winter, by working as an assistant in Colonel Giovannino De Risio's private school, in which he functions as a kind of domestic bursar. The other is Pietro Veleno, a young peasant who is employed as an odd-job man by the De Risio family. It is Don Matteo who is presented to the reader first, and with touches of humour:

> i contadini morivano in genere di colpo cadendo di picchio sui solchi e i figli gli mettevano un po' di terra in bocca: e poi si facevano il segno della croce. E a Don Matteo niente: se capitava, qualche giorno dopo, lo portavano sul luogo e lo invitavano a dire un Requiem: due uova (Jovine 1990, 24).

> the peasants generally died suddenly, collapsing over their furrows, and their children put some earth in their mouths and then crossed themselves. And nothing for Don Matteo; sometimes, if he turned up, a few days later, they would take him to the spot and invite him to say a Requiem: two eggs.

Don Matteo's normal fee for performing the last rites is a chicken.

The narrator's gentle humour, together with the practical jokes played on Don Matteo, might give the impression that this is a stable, cosy society, isolated from whatever changes might take place elsewhere. Fugnitta, in the De Risio kitchen, chats inconsequentially to Don Matteo:

> Ricostruiva a brani la sua mattinata, analizzandola in ogni piccolo momento. Sapeva di dire cose che il suo muto interlocutore conosceva, ma le diceva ugualmente come se avesse voluto dare una consistenza al tempo che ormai da anni le si svolgeva con un ritmo uguale senza apportare nella sua vita e nella vita delle cose che la circondavano alcun cambiamento (Jovine 1990, 15).

> She was reconstructing her morning piece by piece, analysing its every little moment. She knew she was saying things her silent interlocutor already knew, but she said them all the same, as if wanting to give some consistency to time, which for years had been unwinding round her with

unvarying rhythm without bringing any change to her life or the life of the things about her.

Fugnitta and Don Matteo may not realize it, but change is in the air; the action of the novel begins in 1859. King Ferdinando II had crushed the uprising of 1848 and re-established his absolute authority; but in 1860 Giuseppe Garibaldi was to invade Sicily with his famous 'Thousand', swollen by Piedmontese reinforcements to 20,000, and later that same year the Kingdom of Naples would be annexed to Italy. The first event in the action of the novel is the return from Naples of Don Carlo de Risio, newly graduated in medicine. In the capital he has mixed with young men

> che erano mischiati alla vita della capitale, conoscevano personaggi di gran conto, aspiravano a diventare cavalieri dell'ordine di Francesco I, volevano la costituzione, temevano l'evoluzione dei cafoni, giocavano volterrianamente sull'autorità della Santa Madre Chiesa, e avevano tutti un canonico o un monsignore in famiglia (Jovine 1990, 17).

> who had joined in the life of the capital, knew important people, aspired to become knights of the order of Francesco I, wanted a constitution, feared the development of the peasants, played in Voltairean fashion on the authority of Holy Mother Church, and all had a Canon or a Monsignore in their family.

All this suggests that any liberalism they may profess is self-interested and only skin-deep, and that what really matters to them is the protection, preferably the extension, of their own rights and privileges within the existing social framework.

It is the duty of the novel's second central character, Pietro Veleno, to take a horse to meet Don Carlo at nearby Petrella and escort him on the final stage of his return to Guardialfiera. All the details of the journey are calculated to emphasise the places of Don Carlo and Pietro in the social hierarchy, including the fact that the former is carried across the river, while Pietro has to lead the horse and get wet. When Pietro admits that he would willingly become a monk, Don Carlo chooses to give him a mocking lecture on the social order:

> Monaco; ma tu non sai che andiamo verso tempi di progresso, non sai che i conventi verranno aboliti, l'ozio dei frati condannato; tu vorresti abbandonare i campi, tu contadino a cui la società degli uomini liberi assegna l'alta e sacra funzione di trarre dalla madre terra quei frutti che alimentano la scienza e il progresso delle umane lettere (Jovine 1990, 21–2).

A monk. But you don't realize that we are moving into progressive times, convents will be abolished and the idleness of monks condemned; you would like to forsake the fields, you, a peasant to whom the society of free men has assigned the lofty, sacred function of extracting from mother earth those fruits which nourish science and the progress of the humanities.

Although the semi-literate Pietro cannot catch the distant echoes of Enlightenment thought carried by his superior's inflated language, he understands only too well that Don Carlo is joking; but in case he has not taken the point, Don Carlo speaks more plainly:

> Se con la zappa in mano tu sei nato
> devi zappar come sempre hai zappato.
> Capito adesso? (Jovine 1990, 22).

> If you were born with a spade in your hand
> You must dig as you have always dug.
> Understand now?

Indeed:

> Pietro aveva capito: ma il proverbio non l'offese come l'altro immaginava: l'aveva sempre sentito ripetere fin da bambino ed era convinto che non potesse essere che giusto (ibid.).

> Pietro had understood, but the proverb did not offend him as the other imagined; he had heard it repeated continually ever since he was a baby and was convinced of its rightness.

If change is to come to this immobile society, then, it will not come about as the result of liberal initiatives taken by the local land-owners, or as a consequence of revolt on the part of the peasants, who seem as resigned to their lot as the *fontamaresi* at the beginning of Silone's novel. It will come about as the result of external pressures; unless, of course, the shock of those pressures is simply absorbed or diverted.

Structurally, the novel is divided into two parts, the first of which focuses on Don Matteo, the second on Pietro Veleno. The novel is consequently unevenly balanced. Humour dominates in the first part, pathos in the second; there is too much caricature in the first part, too much melodrama in the second. However, the first part succeeds in evoking a society and a way of life, and around Pietro and Don Matteo is grouped a rich gallery of vivid characters: Don Eutichio, the head of the De Risio household, who unscrupulously exploits the peasants by lending them seed corn at exorbitant rates of interest, scheming to get possession of the common land; his son, Don Carlo, slothful, ignorant and fat, who practices medicine, like Levi's Gibilisco, as though it were a hereditary feudal right; Don Giovannino, a former *carbonaro*, who runs a private school to prepare young men for university; his students, youthfully idealistic, vaguely dreaming of a new Italy and a better life; and a number of lesser figures, servants and peasants. Private schools of this kind flourished in the Kingdom of the Two Sicilies; many of the best were in Naples, but others flourished in the provinces. Their pupils had manned the barricades in 1848 and Jovine suggests that the same was to happen in 1860–1.

It does not seem to me, however, that Jovine presents this world as fabulous or remote. His sense of history is too sharp for that, his observation of detail too accurate and sympathetic. Don Matteo is idealistic, talking of justice and bread for all, which ensures his reputation as a Liberal and a revolutionary, even though he cannot envisage a different way of ordering society. The landowners are on whichever side suits their interest, which might be defined as the preservation of the existing social hierarchy and the acquisition of the peasants' land. The intellectuals, cherishing vague ideals of liberty, side with Garibaldi, and, while there is in their behaviour a good deal of attitudinizing and a considerable absence of practical common sense, there is also much nobility of mind. For the peasants, on the other hand, liberty is essentially freedom from exploitation and oppression and the right to the ownership of land. All these attitudes are authentic and convincing; all could equally well be set in the period of the so-called revolution of the Fascists, which provides the setting for *Le terre del Sacramento*. Certain themes are, in fact, common to both novels.

In his essay 'Come ho visto la società meridionale', Jovine wrote that the key dates in the history of the south were, in his view, 1799 and 1860.

> Nel 1799, quando a Napoli gli illuminati e nobili giacobini elaboravano le loro teorie politiche sul *Monitore* e scioglievano inni alla libertà, nelle campagne la lotta prendeva la sua vera fisionomia.[...] Sessanta anni dopo, in un altro periodo, ancora il contadino meridionale combatterà per il re, accanto ai preti ed ai superstiti dell'aristocrazia. Combatterà per il Borbone che egli riterrà suo padre e protettore di fronte ai galantuomini che si appoggiano ancora una volta agli stranieri. Nel '99 gli stranieri erano i francesi, ora sono i piemontesi (Jovine 1979, 119–20).

> In 1799, when enlightened and noble Jacobins in Naples were working out their political theories in the *Monitor* and intoning hymns to liberty, the struggle in the countryside was showing its real face. [...] Sixty years

later, in another era, the southern peasant fought once more for his king, alongside the priests and the survivors of the aristocracy. He fought for the Bourbon whom he considered to be his father and protector against the gentry who once again were supporting the foreigners. In '99 the foreigners had been the French, now they were the Piedmontese.

I hypothesize that Jovine started out to write an historical novel about Molise in 1860, and that a novel which was originally intended to evoke a vanished world became, as his political awareness developed, an account of an historical period in which a hitherto rigid and unchanging society is threatened by new ideas, but which are then absorbed and used to reinforce the existing structures. All these attitudes are convincing; but it is as though *Signora Ava*'s comments on the Risorgimento as a failed revolution are intended to be read as equally valid comments on Fascism as a failed revolution. These comments could hardly have been voiced openly in the early 1940s, but, like many historical novels, this one could also be read as a commentary on the author's own times.

The first part of the novel, then, is not totally dominated by the timeless and the fabulous; it carefully paves the way for the prevalence of social issues in the second part. In the slightly shorter second part of the novel, political disturbances increase. Pietro Veleno and another peasant are compromised when, on the instructions of the De Risio family, they replace in the village church a portrait of the King of Naples, previously removed by the revolutionaries, who now seem to be losing the campaign. The substitution of the portrait of one monarch for that of another in an out-of-the-way country church may seem a trivial incident for the course of the novel to turn on; but images in fact play a crucial part in the establishment of a new régime (or in the disestablishment of an old one, as the toppling of statues of Lenin clearly showed when Communism collapsed). The image of Vittorio Emanuele had to be treated in southern Italy with particular respect. The accidental breaking of a plaster bust of the new king in the Guardia Nazionale barracks at Casalnuovo (now Villapiana) led to that body being dissolved and the arrest of the troops concerned, two of whom were shot while being transferred to Naples (Martucci 1999, 327). The death penalty by firing squad was imposed for insulting the King's portrait (Dickie 1999, 44). Pietro's misfortune is that the Redshirts return. Northerners, they know nothing about local injustices and the peasants' hunger for land, although they do realize that they need the cooperation and support of local power-brokers, who are quick to seize their opportunity. The De Risio family makes Pietro their scapegoat, responsible for moving the portrait; he flees and eventually joins a group of bandits loyal to the Bourbon monarchy. The novel thus incorporates Jovine's analysis of banditry as peasant protest, rather than basic criminality. Characters and incidents in the novel correspond, almost point by point, to his

later essay 'Del brigantaggio meridionale', which is clearly based on his historical reading, and by emphasizing Pietro's naivety and his tender love for Annetta, Jovine seeks to subvert the stereotypes of 'bandits' as sub-human beasts.

When Jovine wrote *Signora Ava*, the peasant banditry of the 1960s, in which
some 100,000 peasants took part, was still regarded as anti-patriotic disorder,
which it had been right to suppress. Jovine argues, in 'Del brigantaggio meridionale', that it had not been criminally motivated and that the wide support it
had received showed that it had had underlying motives which had yet to be
examined, springing from the need to be free:

> per loro essere liberi è riscattarsi dal bisogno, dalle angherie dei signori,
> dalle usure, godere beni materiali adeguati alla loro antica fame e che la
> sorte e l'ingiustizia degli uomini congiunte hanno sottratto (Jovine 1970,
> 640).

> Freedom for them meant redemption from their needs, from oppression
> by the gentry, from usury, freedom to enjoy material goods sufficient for
> their ancient hunger, of which fate and men's injustice have combined to
> deprive them.

Since the landowners side with the *garibaldini* and the Piedmontese, the peasants instinctively fight against them, and consequently against the tide of history. Their defeat is inevitable. Don Eutichio's treachery, however, has the effect
of destroying Pietro's previously unthinking loyalty to the old system, much as
Don Circostanza's betrayal makes the *fontamaresi* conceive of the possibility of
change.

THE DENOUEMENT

The band of which Pietro is a member attacks a convent, which, by one of those
coincidences that reveal the flimsiness of the novel's construction, is the very one
at which Antonietta De Risio is convalescing after an illness. To save her from his
companions – for Jovine does not at all idealize banditry – Pietro seizes her as his
share of the booty and discovers that his love for her is returned. There follows
a brief, tender idyll, which culminates in Antonietta's pregnancy. They then
attempt to escape to the Papal States, which Pietro naively imagines must be an
earthly paradise where all repentant sinners are pardoned, instead of an area in
which 'brigands' who took King Francesco's money enjoyed political sanctuary
(Mack Smith 1959, 71). Jovine's readers would also have known that King
Francesco II had taken refuge there, welcomed by the Pope, who had agreed to

allow Papal territory to be used for political sanctuary. Instead of reaching this promised land, Pietro and Don Matteo are arrested as they are about to cross the border. General Enrico della Rocca, commander of the army in southern Italy, decided in 1861 to carry out summary executions in the countryside, on the grounds that terror was the only form of government that could succeed. Nino Bixio wrote to Cavour that the Neapolitans understood nothing but force (Moe 2002, 160). Jovine wants to show them instead as good but ignorant Christians who seek justice. Pietro Veleno and his peasant companions are what Eric Hobsbawm would call 'pre-political people who have not yet found, or only begun to find, a specific language in which to express their aspirations about the world' (Hobsbawm 1963, 2). Their 'social banditry' is perhaps inevitably concerned with the righting of individual wrongs and the restoration of an imagined traditional world where justice prevailed.

Pietro's mother had warned her son at their last meeting: 'Hanno fucilato tutti quelli che hanno preso' [They've shot all those they've caught] (Jovine 1990, 225); since other peasants captured in similar circumstances have been summarily shot, we assume that the same fate awaits Pietro Veleno, in spite of his conviction of invulnerability. Not only was it forbidden at the time to spend the night in the open country, as Pietro and Annetta had done, but the penalty for bearing arms was immediate execution, which Piedmontese patrols were ordered to carry out on the spot (Martucci 1999, 324–7). Mack Smith also observes that 'there were renegade priests who celebrated clandestine masses in the woods' (Mack Smith 1959, 72). General Pinelli, in charge of the campaign against the 'brigands', blamed uprisings on priestly plotting (Dickie 199, 162 n.51), and Jovine knew that, on occasion, priests had been executed for openly siding with the peasants, thus carrying to an unacceptable extreme the Church's known opposition to the unification of Italy.

In *Signora Ava*, the Risorgimento is seen as a peasant crisis which remains unresolved. Political change, imposed by external pressures, changes nothing. Jovine indeed seems to anticipate Tomasi di Lampedusa's cynical Tancredi, who tells his uncle, Prince Fabrizio, that if everything is to stay the same, everything must change. In Jovine's novel, the Risorgimento is a political revolution in which the peasants do not participate and which brings about no social revolution. At the same time, it is a valuable prologue to *Le terre del Sacramento*, the symbolism of which seems to imply at least a certain cautious optimism, while *Signora Ava* reflects Jovine's feeling that in the Fascist period no change was possible.

CHAPTER 13

Le terre del Sacramento and the occupation of the land

COMMUNITY AND THE ORGANIC INTELLECTUAL

The question of community has recurred in key chapters of this book since it is a central concern of the authors discussed, probably because Gramsci and other Communist writers consistently refer to peasants as an amorphous 'mass' rather than a class, assuming them to be incapable of autonomous action and needing leadership provided from outside. In *Fontamara*, Silone presents the peasants of his fictional village as divided by the system of clientelism and at odds with each other over such issues as the scarcity of work and the shortage of water. They become united and therefore capable of cooperation only as the result of the Christ-like self-sacrifice of Berardo and with the help of the Solito Sconosciuto. Levi, on the other hand, on the basis of his experience and observation at Gagliano, takes the view that there already exists among the peasants a strong sense of brotherhood and a common sense of social justice. Jovine hardly touched on the issue in *Signora Ava*, in which we see a small group of individuals becoming political refugees and attempting to find political asylum in the Papal States. But in the years between writing that novel and *Le terre del Sacramento*, Jovine both continued his research into the history of Molise, bringing it up to the Fascist period, and developed politically, becoming a member of the Italian Communist Party. In his last and finest novel, which was published posthumously, he takes up the issue of the kind of leadership required to convince peasants of the need – and of their ability – to act together. In Luca Marano, the central character of the novel, he depicts what Gramsci would have described as an 'organic intellectual'.

Gramsci is clearly using the term 'intellectual' in a very wide sense indeed. For Gramsci, almost everyone is an intellectual, even members of political parties, and he rejects the conventional distinction between intellectuals and non-intellectuals, although he agrees that not everyone in reality exercises in society the function of an intellectual. Gramsci would regard as an intellectual an entrepreneur who has to organize his business, manage his workforce and persuade customers to buy his products. The organic intellectual is one who works alongside other members of his class to persuade and to organize them, primarily of course for the political struggle. He is thus much more than a mere speechmak-

196

er. This is a topic on which Gramsci wrote in his *Quaderni del carcere* [Prison Note-books], according to which each new class, historically, creates its own organic intellectuals (Gramsci 1974, 3–19). The striking exception to this otherwise general rule is the amorphous peasant mass, which neither produces its own organic intellectuals nor assimilates intellectuals from other social groups, even though the latter take many of their intellectuals from among the peasantry. In rural society, intellectuals become priests, lawyers or doctors, all of whom enjoy a standard of living superior to that of the peasants. Consequently they represent a social model for peasant aspirations and the peasant thinks that at least one of his sons could or should become an intellectual, usually a priest, and so raise the family's social standing. Once a peasant's son becomes a priest or lawyer, however, he has 'arrived'; he ceases to be a member of the peasant class and does not speak or work for that class; he becomes instead what Gramsci would call a 'traditional intellectual', a member, that is, of the power structures that oppress and exploit the peasantry. He becomes conservative, disinclined to risk changing the social order (Izzo 1967, 367). Luca Marano, however, has long been recognized as a Gramscian organic intellectual, but the question of how Jovine could convincingly represent a phenomenon that Gramsci said could not exist remains to be considered.

THE HISTORY OF THE NOVEL

As seems also to have been the case with *Signora Ava*, Jovine seems with *Le terre del Sacramento* to have set out to write a very different novel from that which was finally published. He wrote in *La fiera letteraria* of 10 October 1946 that he had been thinking for ten years about a novel 'di vastissime proporzioni' [on a very large scale]. The models he had in mind probably included Manzoni's *I promessi sposi* and Nievo's *Le confessioni di un italiano*, both of which had influenced *Signora Ava*. He added that he had begun to write a novel entitled *La capra del diavolo* [The Devil's Goat]. Since Enrico Cannavale, the lawyer and landowner who is the first character we meet in *Le terre del Sacramento*, is known locally as 'capra del diavolo', partly on account of his 'barba caprina' [goatee], and partly on account of his lechery, we may assume that Jovine's original intention was to chronicle the decline of a once wealthy family, with Enrico Cannavale as his protagonist. It could be that he intended to write a sort of reply to De Roberto's *I vicerè*, which shows a southern family adapting to the unification of Italy in order to consolidate its power. In 1947, in the essay 'Come ho visto la società meridionale', he makes it clear that he considers his work from *Signora Ava* onwards to be an imaginative history of Molise (Jovine 1947). He also makes it clear that he regards the history of the province as having a continuity based on the fundamental problem of land ownership. In fact the novel at one stage was to have been entitled *Terre di redenzione* (Cattanei 1986, 135). Jovine thus seems in 1946 to have had in mind two separate novels which at some stage must have become fused.

The novel finally produced does indeed feature 'la capra del diavolo', but its title draws initial attention not to a character but to the basic problem of the struggle for land ownership and the peasants' developing class consciousness and aspirations. It derives its title from the name of an estate that was confiscated from the church in 1867 by the government of the newly united Italy and sold to Enrico's grandfather, much as the forebears of Silone's Don Carlo Magna had purchased church land. The action is set in the 1920s and the estate has passed into Enrico Cannavale's ineffectual hands. The priests of the area insist that the land rightfully belongs to the Church and that any attempt to cultivate it will be cursed by God. In the eyes of the superstitious peasantry, the estate's history seems to confirm this view, since the chapel has twice been struck by lightning and now lies in ruins and at least one former owner died a violent death, while Enrico Cannavale, dissolute and in debt, seems to heading for much the same kind of fate. Not that this superstitious fear prevents the peasants from cutting down trees on the estate for fuel in winter. They also illicitly pasture their animals there and encroach on the estate when they plough. Early references to these activities are an indication that the uncultivated land will be the subject of the novel. Felice Protto, Enrico's administrator, also introduces at an early stage the idea of the need to reclaim the land if it is to be sold (Jovine 1972, 3–5).

By setting the action in the early years of the Fascist period while referring back to the Risorgimento, Jovine establishes an historical perspective; one failed revolution echoes another. Manacorda in fact sees Jovine as the only neo-realist writer of the period 1940–65 to present southern history in perspective, focussing on the peasantry (Manacorda 1967, 109). On the other hand, Manacorda also expressed the view, in an essay first published in 1950, that history in Jovine's works is static, unchanging and pre-determined (Manacorda 1972, 31). I do not believe this to be the case in *Signora Ava*, in which the pressure of events compels Pietro Veleno to change his views and to attempt to change the circumstances of his own life, albeit not those of his fellow-peasants. I also hope to show that in *Le terre del Sacramento* there is a wider sense of the movement of history.

CHARACTERS IN THE NOVEL

Enrico Cannavale

There are three main characters in the novel. They are Enrico Cannavale, his wife Laura, and Luca Marano. The emphasis falls first of all on Enrico, then on the relationship between his wife and Luca, and finally on Luca and the peasants. The early appearances of Enrico characterize him well. In the very first chapter, in an almost cinematographic sequence, he stampedes a flock of animals illegally grazing on his land, instead of taking effective measures to discover whose they are and gain compensation, generally treating the matter as a joke; then he seduces his orphaned cousin Clelia, who has come to keep house for him. Idle and in debt, he is incapable of taking his affairs in hand. Then Laura appears on the scene. Young and beautiful, she has been studying music at Naples. As time passes, her Neapolitan life comes to appear more glamorous in retrospect than it was in reality, but she soon loses touch with her former student friends. When she and Clelia meet, the latter quickly resigns herself to defeat. Laura, more sophisticated and provocatively beautiful than the unsophisticated and conventionally pious Clelia, makes herself indispensable to Enrico while prudently keeping him at a distance. Unable to win her as easily as his previous conquests, Enrico proposes marriage. Laura accepts, her mind full of vague idealistic plans for reforming Enrico's way of life, setting his patrimony in order, giving work to the peasants and leading a calm and virtuous life. Around this relationship Jovine groups the little society of provincial Calena, Enrico's household, his servants and estate manager, Laura's family, and behind them the empty, trivial round of under-employed professional men, lawyers and teachers, all neatly introduced through Laura's father, the retired President of the Appeal Court De Martiis. The fictional Calena is based on the real town of Isernia, which Jovine regarded, with its surrounding villages, as a centre of reactionary thought and attitudes (Carducci 1977, 87–8).

Enrico, who has already made an appearance in the short story 'Terra vecchia', is a lawyer. Fundamentally an orator, he deals in words, not deeds; he professes to be a Socialist but despises those workers who want to organise themselves (Jovine 1972, 125). He is a conventional bourgeois intellectual, belonging to the class of southern gentry who wish to live on the income from their land without working it and who speak the language of democracy and justice solely in order to promote their own interests (Lalli 1981, 71). They also profess, like Silone's Don Circostanza, to be the friends of the people. It was by no means unusual for landlords to embrace Socialism or Republicanism, promising reform if elected but in fact doing nothing to bring it about (Snowden 1985, 75–9). In Gramscian terms, Enrico is a traditional intellectual who has discovered the poor but has not been absorbed into the political vanguard party. He limits the application of his Socialism to not collecting rents, thus making his personal situation worse, although an unfounded rumour circulates to the effect that he intends donating the uncultivated *terre del Sacramento* to the peasants.

Enrico becomes more ineffectual than ever and he hands over the administration of his business matters to Laura. Inevitably, given the rising tensions of post-war Italy, his professions of Socialism inevitably attract the hostility of the younger Fascists. He is given a beating from which he never recovers; a semi-invalid, he is nursed by the ever faithful and undemanding Clelia.

Luca Marano

With Enrico increasingly ineffectual and his wife in charge of his affairs, the stage is set for the introduction of Luca Marano, who is to be brought into contact with Laura. Their meeting is effected with admirable skill and economy, as well as humour.

Luca is the oldest son of a peasant family from the nearby village of Morutri. The village priest, impressed by his intelligence, sent him at the age of ten to a seminary as a candidate for the priesthood, hoping the boy would become his successor. But Luca discovers that he has no vocation for the religious life and realizes that his career has been imposed on him from without. Religious practices gradually lose all meaning and he accepts as natural a world without God. His innate honesty compels him to reveal his state of mind to his superiors and, at the age of fifteen, he leaves the seminary. He eventually continues his education as a law student at the University of Naples as one of those numerous students who live at home and visit the University only to take examinations. He lives with his parents for half the year, doing little manual work but helping with the harvest, and during the winter months he lives with his uncle, Filoteo Natalizio, the *ufficiale giudiziario* [court bailiff] of Calena, as well as working in the office of the lawyer Jannacone, copying documents by hand and bored by his repetitive, intellectually undemanding work. On occasions when his Calena friends want to insult him, they call him angrily 'un cafone schifoso' [a disgusting cafone] (Jovine 1972, 60).

Luca is known as 'il toro di Morutri' [the bull of Morutri] on account of his exceptional strength, which he no doubt owes to Silone's Berardo. He is also depicted as having a fundamentally gentle nature. These qualities, together with his keen intelligence, set him apart from the other young people we meet in Calena. He is also poverty-stricken – the poorest of the poor students of the area. At the same time, he feels a great sense of frustration and injustice, which could easily find expression in violence. Luca has only one pair of shoes, so that he has to stay at home whenever they are being repaired. His shirt is multi-coloured, being composed of parts from two worn-out shirts joined together, 'in sé e per sé fatiscenti e inutili, ma decenti e valide nella loro ingegnosa unione' [in and by themselves dilapidated and useless, but presentable in their ingenious union], as Filoteo puts it in his deliberately cultivated pompous manner. Luca cuts a grotesque figure when he tries to solve the problem of how to wear trousers that are now too short for him, since he has been growing rapidly – whether to wear his belt at its normal level and so expose his shins, or slacken

his belt and make it look as though his trousers are about to fall down. He opts
for the latter solution, only to be told by his friends, later that same day, firstly
that his trousers are falling down – he naturally knows why – and then that he
has holes in the heels of his socks – which strikes him as eminently possible –
and finally that his shirt-tail is hanging out – which in his confusion seems quite
likely. By this time, as far as Luca is concerned, things have gone beyond a joke.

> La camicia era tutto entro i suoi leggitimi confini. Si calmò un poco. Era
> stato, ancora una volta, vittima di uno scherzo, ma non era disposto a rid-
> ere. Aveva i muscoli duramente tesi e sapeva che se Gesualdo o Elpidio gli
> fossero capitati tra le mani, li avrebbe picchiati a sangue (Jovine 1972, 46).

> His shirt was within its legitimate boundaries. He calmed down somewhat.
> Once again he had been the victim of a joke, but he did not feel like laugh-
> ing. His muscles were tensed and hard and he knew that if he had got his
> hands on Gesualdo or Elpidio he would have beat them till they bled.

The use of irony here is interesting. The boundary image refers back to the
peasants' habit of encroaching on to the Cannavale estate, while the legal language in which it is couched is appropriate both to the image and to Luca's
employment in a lawyer's office. Irony is also used, more bitingly but also with
appropriate imagery, after the episode in which Enrico is beaten up by a group
of Fascists, mainly students. 'Giancarlo Pistalli sosteneva la tesi della provo-
cazione' [Giancarlo Pistalli argued the provocation thesis] (Jovine 1972, 177),
with the image of a student defending his degree thesis deriving from the fact
that Pistalli, like Luca, is a student, albeit behaving in a non-academic fashion.
Luca's sense of impotent rage at the practical joke is the first indication of something in his character other than gentleness, patience and humour. It is more
than personal pique; it is, one comes to realize, the as yet unexpressed rage of a
disappointed and frustrated generation. Luca and his friends nurture no hope
and underneath their facetious air, their cigarette-scrounging, their occasional
gambling and their furtive fornications, they are uneasy about the future. In the
young people of Calena Jovine portrays the period of post world war I unemployment and unrest, when those too young to have served were bitterly envi-
ous of those who had and who, because of their absence on military service, were
awarded passes in examinations they had not taken. This resentment is extended to include the whole social structure. Gesualdo says:

> Con tutti me la piglio. Bisogna spaccare tutto. Anche qui, questo lurido
> buco di Calena. Non ci pensi che succede? Tutto in mano ai vecchi. Aria
> ci vuole (Jovine 1972, 81).

> I'm picking a fight with the lot of them. We've got to smash everything.
> Including this place, this filthy hole, Calena. Can't you see what's going
> on? Everything controlled by the old-timers. We need a breath of air.

What Luca might have become is shown in a number of minor characters.
Pietro De Santis is an orphan who was confined in a reformatory for killing
another boy; he returns to Calena ten years later 'vestito con vistosa eleganza, con
una testa di morto in argento appuntata sul soprabito' [dressed with striking ele-
gance, with a silver death's-head pinned on his overcoat] (Jovine 1972, 117).
Shortly after his arrival, Fascist demonstrations begin take place on Sundays in
the main square of Calena, breaking up Socialist meetings. Giancarlo Jannacone,
the lawyer's son, is soon under his influence, as are other young men whose families are wealthy enough to permit them to reside in Naples in term-time, and not
merely for the duration of the examinations. The young Fascists are exempted
from their end of year examinations. Luca, politically uninformed and naïve, does
not understand the conflicting ideologies behind the Fascist-Socialist brawls, but
he concludes that Fascism is a revolution by the rich and, by implication, for the
rich. As is the case with the peasants of Silone's Fontamara, his naiveté is a device
for exposing the self-seeking sophistry of the middle classes.

One of Luca's fellow-students in Naples, Giulio D'Angelo, is in a position
similar to his. He comes from a poor family and is in his sixth year of medical
studies. He fails an examination and has to repeat the year. Since his father is
heavily in debt on his account, he marries a forty year-old spinster for the sake
of her dowry. When Luca asks what he will do when he has taken his degree, he
replies that there are already four other doctors in his village, Caccavone:

> Ci sono altri quattro medici a Caccavone. Io sarei il quinto. Quelli sono
> figli di signori, e anche se guadagnono poco per loro va bene lo stesso. Io,
> se rimango, andrò con le pezze al culo per tutta la vita (Jovine 1972, 103).

> There are four other doctors in Caccavone. I would be the fifth. They are
> all sons of gentry, and even if they don't earn very much, they'll still be all
> right. If I stay there, I'll wear rags on my arse for the rest of my life.

Luca already knows that there is a surfeit of lawyers in southern towns and villages and that his professional prospects are bleak indeed, since there are already
'cinquanta avvocati a Calena' [fifty lawyers in Calena] (Jovine 1972, 49). He
gradually comes to see how most of these law students will inevitably become
intellectuals of the traditional type:

> Giovani come lui, che si lasciavano intossicare l'anima senza speranza.
> Domani avrebbero vissuto sfruttando, derubando subdolamente i conta-

dini dei loro villaggi che erano legati alla loro stessa sorte dalla stessa ingiustizia (Jovine 1972, 228).

Young men like himself, who had allowed their minds to be hopelessly poisoned. Tomorrow they would make a living by exploiting, craftily robbing the peasants of their villages, who were linked to their fates by the same injustice.

In these circumstances, Fascism's call for revolution and its promise of change and fresh ideas inevitably appeal to the discontented young, like Luca's friends Gesualdo and Elpidio, even though they sense that ex-service-men will have first priority when it comes to jobs. In the meantime they are happy to be given pass marks without having to take their examinations, while their frustrations find expression in fights with Socialists in both Naples and Calena. But it is also clear that Fascism also appeals to the wealthier people of Calena. Whereas Gesualdo, an idealist, can believe that he is helping to further common interests, Giancarlo Jannacone and Pistalli, on the other hand, ignorant of the way Fascism is developing in the north, are merely furthering the interests of their class, supporting the landowners, even lowering agricultural wages. Labourers who protest, or who want wage increases, are suitably dealt with by a combination of Fascists and *carabinieri*, which brings to mind episodes on the Fucino plain and elsewhere in the south in the 1940s. Such episodes from the Molise countryside are reported by Luca's father, Seppe Marano, to his friend Arduino. Seppe assumes that the civilians wear black shirts in order to be able to recognize one another, while the *carabinieri* must be enforcing the law: 'C'è legge, Arduino' [There's the law, Arduino] (Jovine, 1972, 100). Luca, a law student, distinguishes between law and justice and he cannot understand why the peasants do not combine to work together and obtain justice. It is his sense of their need for both solidarity and work that makes him decide to cooperate with Laura's plan to employ peasants from Morutri to cultivate the *terre del Sacramento*.

Laura Cannevale

Laura, like Luca, is highly intelligent. She soon realizes that her marriage, not based on love or even mutual respect, is a disaster and that life in provincial Calena is tedious after Naples. Its stagnation and lethargy threaten to entrap her. Her early desire to return to Naples or Rome (Jovine 1972, 24–5) is perhaps an anticipation of her eventual flight, suggesting that her motives are at all times very mixed. She acquires financial and business experience and shows practical sense when she puts her dead brother's affairs in order. She is a relatively emancipated or free young woman, able to visit Enrico unchaperoned, unlike 'le figlie degli avvocati' who cannot leave home unescorted. She even has her own chequebook. Her plan to bring order to Enrico's affairs is not entirely unrealistic.

When an IOU signed by Enrico is passed by a client to the lawyer Jannacone for action, he sends Filoteo Natalizio to the Cannavale house to make a legal attachment of goods to the value of the relatively small debt. Filoteo takes with him both witnesses and, since his eyes are not what they were, a clerk, who is naturally his nephew Luca. They arrive during one of Enrico's frequent absences and it is Laura, not yet married to Enrico, who takes charge of the situation, producing her chequebook to pay the debt.

The contrast between Laura's beauty, sophistication and decisiveness on the one hand and Luca's timidity, embarrassment and poverty on the other could hardly be greater. He is understandably embarrassed when Laura asks him if she is to give the cheque to him. His reaction is ambiguous: it could be a sign of his sense of social inferiority or of incipient sexual attraction, perhaps the uneasy mixture of both which is to characterize their relationship. When they meet again in the street on the evening after their first encounter, Laura, 'come aveva fatto nel pomeriggio, lo squadrò dapprima con uno sguardo investigativo lungo tutta la persona, poi gli piantò nelle pupille i suoi occhi azzurri' [looked him up and down, from top to toe, with an inquiring gaze, then fixed his pupils with her blue eyes] (Jovine 1972, 46). Jovine thus makes Luca's awkwardness visible. Yet, uncomfortable though all his meetings with Laura are, she invariably treats him with courtesy. Their first, casual, encounters in Calena are followed by another, this time in Morutri, where she creates a minor sensation by wearing trousers; since she is riding a horse, causing the shocked parish priest to take refuge in his presbytery and his housekeeper to describe her, under her breath, as a whore. Enrico and Laura, on a visit to 'le terre', come across Luca, unshaven, barefoot and idle. Enrico treats him in seigneurial manner, using the familiar *tu*; Laura uses the more courteous – and in the rural south, unusual – *Lei*, as she had done on their first meeting. When speaking earlier to Enrico's lawyer, avvocato Colonna, she had used the formal and more usual *voi*, which makes the *Lei* stand out even more. When they leave, Luca is conscious only of resentment:

> Per un quarto d'ora egli aveva rappresentato il pretesto della sosta in un luogo dove si è giunti per noia e nel quale si cerca qualcosa che la sotto-linei perché diventi memorabile (Jovine 1972, 66).

> For a quarter of an hour he had been the excuse for lingering in a village which they had visited out of boredom and where they had looked for something lend it some emphasis and make it memorable.

Laura, who is taking over the management of Enrico's affairs, invites Luca to the Cannavale palace to enlist his help in her schemes. Once again, he is made aware of his poverty and lack of social skills. His humiliation is conveyed in a series of touches which are now allowed to speak for themselves – Laura's taste for expensive cigarettes, for instance, which immediately makes one think by contrast of the students cadging a cheaper variety, and the infinite caution with which Luca puts down his wine-glass, which shows how afraid he is of his own clumsiness. In spite of his embarrassment, however, Laura fascinates him and he becomes her willing ally. At this stage there is no discernable duplicity on her part: she seems merely to wish to reclaim uncultivated land to the benefit of all concerned.

Luca's attempts to put a stop to the illegal felling of trees are unsuccessful, but when Laura produces her plan to induce the peasants of Morutri to cultivate the neglected land, he is completely successful. Laura is the brains behind the scheme: it is she who persuades her Neapolitan backers to employ peasants on a day-labour basis, it is she who has the idea of rebuilding the ruined chapel – this time, prudently, with a lightning-conductor – and of having it re-consecrated, in order to overcome the peasants' superstitious hesitations. Luca acts as her inter-mediary. Taking advantage of his prestige and of the peasants' trust in him, he convinces them because he is himself convinced and also because he is one of them. When, at a village meeting, a girl calls out: 'Ma ci vuole uno che non ci tradisca. Tu non ci devi tradire, Luca' [But we need someone who won't betray us. You mustn't betray us, Luca.], she is voicing the sentiments of the whole com-munity (Jovine 1972, 175). This trust in Luca remains unshaken. A crisis arises while he is in Naples, but they are confident he will return to help them. 'Ma noi dicevamo che saresti tornato' [But we said you'd come back.]. And when things finally go wrong, it is again to Luca that they naturally turn (Jovine, 1972, 227).

In order to raise the capital necessary to clear the land, Laura and her back-ers, among whom is Baron Santasilia, who has banking connections, float a com-pany. Luca is warned in Naples, too late, that Santasilia is a hard man. When the land has been reclaimed by means of cheap labour, they issue eviction notices to the peasants, offering some of them the less fertile land in order that they them-selves may farm the best land, employing other peasants on the traditional day-labour basis. It is to this crisis that Luca returns. Laura, meanwhile, has fled to San Remo with her share of the profits and, possibly, with Santasilia. Since we see her mainly through Luca's eyes, it is not entirely clear whether this had always been her intention, or whether she had originally embarked on the scheme in an idealistic spirit but had been driven to escape by the unattractive prospect of life in Calena with a prematurely senile husband.

THE DÉNOUEMENT

Luca's reaction to the situation is to feel that he has been betrayed: 'Mi hanno tradito' [They've betrayed me] (Jovine 1972, 232), since, on the basis of Laura's assurances, he has given his word to the peasants that they would become tenants with perpetual leases on the land they were clearing. But his experience of Fascism in Naples has enabled him to see himself no longer as an isolated but a typical or even representative figure:

> Luca Marano, figlio di Giuseppe, non era più una vittima solitaria. Il suo destino, la sua tristezza di ventenne miserabile era simile a quella di Gesualdo, del canonico, di Ferdinando, delle migliaia di studenti che piovevano a Napoli tra ottobre e novembre, per esporre ai professori le nozioni lette nei manuali di Diritto Civile durante le desolate stagioni trascorse in villaggi come Morutri (Jovine 1972, 228).

> Luca Marano, son of Giuseppe, was no longer a solitary victim. His destiny, his sadness, that of a poverty-stricken twenty year-old, was like that of Gesualdo, the Canon, Ferdinando, of the thousands of students who rained down on Naples between October and November to expound to their professors the notions they had read in their civil law textbooks during the dreary summers they had spent in villages like Morutri.

Thus he is able now to identify completely with the peasants: 'E il lavoro dei contadini [...] Hanno grattato la terra per sei mesi!' [And the peasants' labour [...] They've been scratching the ground for six months!] (Jovine 1972, 233). It is no longer a matter simply of betrayal of himself, or of the peasants alone, but of a collective us. 'Io sono tornato per dirvi che ci hanno traditi' [I've come back to tell you they have betrayed us], he tells them (Jovine 1972, 239). They also exploited the peasants' religious scruples: 'Hanno ingannato noi e Cristo' [They deceived us and Christ] (Jovine 1972, 239) and all Luca's innate idealism is offended. Still ingenuous in spite of the deceit practised on him, he leads the peasants out to occupy the land as they had done in 1898, but this time in a non-violent protest, with the intention of sowing corn – which had also been the intention of the occupying peasants on the Fucino plain in 1943. This time, they will wait for justice to be done – real justice, as opposed to mere legality. Justice is not done. They are attacked by a force consisting of *Carabinieri* and Fascist irregulars, and in the struggle Luca and two others are killed.

Luca's part in this peasant revolt is the expression of a maturity and a feeling of solidarity with the oppressed which he had reached in Naples. There, he found many of his fellow-students prepared to compromise with society, ready to exploit and be exploited: others turned to Fascism, including, he noticed, those who already belonged to the privileged class, who were using Fascism for their own ends. He is appalled by this intricate web of self-seeking and his first open gesture of revolt takes place in a cheap restaurant frequented by poor students like himself, where a group of Fascists attempt to 'purge' another student who earlier had led an act of resistance to their bullying tactics. This time it is

Luca who leads the resistance in defence of his friend. This incident follows immediately after the realization that he and the peasants of Morutri have been betrayed and is a natural consequence of it, marking the step from disillusionment to rebellion and preparing the reader for what is to come.

In the narrative, this act is separated from the realization that he has been betrayed by an episode in which Luca is persuaded by two urchins to buy an umbrella that opens and closes automatically, although, as it turns out, somewhat unpredictably. As he goes into the restaurant in which the skirmish with the Fascists is to take place, the waiter tells him that in view of recent brawls umbrellas, being potential weapons, are not allowed, and takes it from him. It promptly opens, much to the delight of the students. Neither the waiter nor the proprietor can close it, and the latter, enraged, throws it at the noisiest of them. It lands perfectly furled. The episode is delightful in itself, but it raises two questions. The first relates to the relevance of this and one or two other minor episodes, and the second relates to Jovine's use of humour. On the issue of relevance, it is possible to argue that Jovine is using farce here to separate and set off two serious and significant events and is at the same time commenting obliquely on Luca's gullibility. In the structure of the novel, he is also providing a counterpoint to an earlier episode in which the same pretentious waiter had joked at Luca's expense. Luca's defence of his friend D'Angelo against the Fascists can also be read as anticipating the novel's dénouement.

Other episodes cannot be justified in the same way, however. At a luncheon party given by Laura on the Frassino farm for her Neapolitan friends, who have come to see work in progress on the estate, Luca's gaucheness and embarrassment are again revealed, but the episode after lunch, in which Luca and the Baronessa di Santasilia make love in a hay-loft, seems gratuitous, and it must be admitted that at times the narrative is not conducted with the strictest economy. The humour of the umbrella episode is interesting, since it shows that Jovine, for all his fundamental seriousness, is capable of writing humorously. He uses humour to bring his characters down to earth – in one case at least, literally. Filoteo Natalizio and Luca at one stage discuss, somewhat flippantly, the sacrifice of Christ and elaborate the metaphor of a cheque that can be cashed only at the bank of heaven. On the way to the peasant revolt, Filoteo takes up the metaphor again:

> Quando tu volevi presentare la cambiale in protesto dei nostri contadini alla Banca del cielo, io non ero d'accordo con te. Ma ora la presentiamo alla Banca della storia – concluse con voce trionfale, alzando il capo in alto. Inciampò e cadde (Jovine 1972, 244).

> When you wanted to present the draft in favour of our peasants at the Bank of Heaven, I didn't agree with you. But now we're presenting it to

the Bank of History – he concluded in a triumphant tone, raising his
head high.
He stumbled and fell.

Then Luca has to pick him up from the mud and brush his clothes. Jovine refuses to be carried away by rhetoric; he prefers to let events speak directly to the reader.

With the end of the revolt, a striking change comes over the tone of the novel. The three corpses are laid out on the ground where they fell. The women, including Luca's mother, sit for a time in silence. As night falls, the old men – the young have fled or been arrested – light fires. The silence is broken by a cry of grief from Immacolata, after which the women begin their traditional wailing and lamentations. This 'duolo' was a custom which had clearly made a great impression on Jovine, since he had earlier described it in *Un uomo provvisorio*.

> Poi tra le teste delle donne se ne levò una che incominciò a fare il 'duolo' a voce alta, cantando le lodi del defunto, commisurando con estro inconsapevole il concetto alla monodia; le lasse del canto terminavano con un ah! svolto in un tema di tre note strazianti che le donne in circolo riprendevano in tono più rapido (Jovine 1934, 179–80).

> Then one of the women raised her head and began to keen aloud, singing the praises of the dead man, adapting her thought to the monody with unconscious inspiration; the verses of her song ended with an Ah! sung to a tune of three heart-rending notes which the women in the circle took up in a more rapid tone.

In the earlier novel, the description had remained at the level of unassimilated folk-custom, reported rather than made alive. In *Le terre del Sacramento*, on the other hand, Jovine lets us hear the women's lament, with its litany-like repetitions, its rhymes and assonances; the narrator refrains from comment and adjectives such as 'strazianti' are suppressed. Ernesto De Martino, a friend of Jovine in his last years, describes the traditional lamentation as consisting of short verses, without metre or rhyme, usually ending with an emotional refrain and often referring to the dead person's work or accomplishments. Villages had their own traditional melodic lines. He also reported that the custom of the *pianto* was still widespread in southern country districts.

> Quando la notte divenne buia, i vecchi accesero i fuochi alle spalle dei morti. A un tratto Immacolata Marano urlò:
> – Luca, oh Luca! – e si mise le mani intrecciate sul capo dondolando sul busto.

- Luca, spada brillante, – gridò una voce giovanile.
- Spada brillante, – ripeterono in coro le altre.
- Stai sulla terra sanguinante.

Via via le donne si misero le mani intrecciate sulle teste, altre presero le cocche dei fazzoletti nei pugni chiusi e li percuotevano facendo:
- Oh! oh! Spada brillante, stai sulla terra sanguinante!
- T'hanno ammazzato, Luca Marano.
- A tradimento, Luca Marano.
- Non vuole la terra il tuo sangue cristiano.
- Difendevi le terre del Sacramento.
- Erano nostre, nostre le terre.
- Avevamo le ossa per testamento.
- Le avevamo scavate con le nostre mani.
- T'hanno ucciso, Luca Marano.
- A tradimento, Luca Marano (Jovine 1972, 250).

When night set in, the old men lit fires by the dead men's shoulders. Suddenly, Immacolata Marano howled:
- Luca, oh Luca! And put her entwined hands over her head, rocking backwards and forwards.
- Luca, shining sword, – cried a youthful voice.
- Shining sword, – chorused the others.
- You lie on the blood-stained ground.

One by one the women put their entwined hands over their heads, others grasped the knots of their kerchiefs in their fists, striking them and saying:
Oh! Oh! Shining sword, you lie on the blood-stained ground!
- They've killed you, Luca Marano.
- By treachery, Luca Marano.
- The earth doesn't want your Christian blood.
- You were defending the Sacramento lands.
- They were ours, ours those lands.
- We had the bones as our testament.
- We had dug them out with our own hands.
- They've killed you, Luca Marano.
- By treachery, Luca Marano.

After this, the last sentence of the novel, rather than a mere factual observation, may be read as a symbol of hope: 'La notte era buia e le voci si perdevano sulla terra desolata oltre il circolo della luce che faceva il fuoco, ancora vivo' [The night was dark and their voices were lost over the desolate land beyond the circle of light cast by the fire, that was still alive] (Jovine 1972, 251). The revolution has failed, the darkness of oppression has again descended, but the protest the peasants have made is like a fire piercing the darkness, which does not overcome it. This optimism is perhaps anticipated by Marco Cece's observation, as he and the other peasants move to occupy the land: 'Vento del Timbrone [...] Rompe le nuvole. Avremo un po' di sole, domani' [Wind from the Timbrone [...] It's breaking the clouds. We'll have a bit of sun, tomorrow] (Jovine 1972, 243).

HISTORY AND SYMBOL

Marco Cece, who is killed along with Luca and his friend Gesualdo, is an elderly peasant who had taken part in the 1898 occupation, for which he had served a jail sentence. Since there had been a '98 occupation in many of the villages of Molise, Marco Cece is both a representative figure and a reminder of the continuities of southern history. The San Carlo warehouse, where the peasants meet to decide firstly to cultivate and then to occupy the land, is another reminder of the continuities of southern history, since it had once housed the corn bank from which peasants had once borrowed seed corn at a 25 per cent interest rate, borrowing damp corn in level containers in November and repaying dry corn in August, in heaped containers. Readers are also reminded of Don Eutichio's system of lending seed corn to his peasants in *Signora Ava*. The peasants of Morutri had pillaged and burnt the corn bank in 1898, since when it had remained unoccupied.

Two things have changed the situation in the period in which Jovine now sets his novel. In the first place, peasants like Seppe Marano, Luca's father, who had always been inclined, like the peasants of Silone's Fontamara, to accept the immutability of the existing state of affairs, have had their perceptions changed by war-time propaganda promising land to the peasants. Occupations had become frequent in the post-war period, with peasants regarding the land as rightfully theirs. The peasants' discussions about the land in *Le terre del Sacramento* take place in this atmosphere of unrest and occupations. Now, however, the peasants of Morutri succeed in finding a sense of solidarity and common purpose. The process begins when Luca warns them not to take out loans if they do not want to lose their land. All know that this was how much land had in the past become the property of Don Benedetto Ciampitti. Their agreement and the steps they take to avoid debt contrast with their earlier quarrels (Jovine 1972, 191–5). At the end of the novel, the mourning women are able to say 'Nostre erano le terre'. Peasant logic, as in *Fontamara*, argues that land worked by no one belongs to no one (Jovine 1972, 99); now that they have worked it, the same logic convinces them it belongs to them. Cooperating to work together on the land and agreeing to occupy it has created a sense of community which previously was non-existent. This process is slow but irreversible.

But Jovine is careful to set the action of the novel on either side of the Fascist march on Rome. As the peasants asserted their rights, so the middle-class defenders of law and order – the social status quo – began to take the law into their own hands, with a resultant growth of violence on the right. Landowners came to use *squadristi* as their own private police force, with which to break strikes and enforce new labour contracts, lowering wages and cancelling perpetual leases. Historians point out that the *squadre* were sometimes accompanied by *carabinieri* in uniform on their punitive expeditions. Luca's belief that 'legalmente non possono agire' [legally they can't act] (Jovine 1972, 247) is naïve. He returns to Morutri just as the Fascists are beginning their march on Rome, between 26 and 30 October 1922. With their success, the Fascists become even bolder and more ruthless and have no hesitation in using armed force to crush the occupation. From 1922 onwards, occupations virtually ceased and peasants sometimes lost land previously gained (Caracciolo 1950, 40). This suggests that one of Jovine's aims was to remind his readers of the way in which the campaign for land in the post 1915–18 war had been defeated and to draw a parallel with what was happening in the 1940s.

In the light of that defeat, Gramsci took the view that spontaneous peasant occupations served no useful purpose. Dorso went further, arguing in *La rivoluzione meridionale*, republished in 1944, that they made the situation even worse, using, interestingly, the image of light and darkness. Occupations, he states, seemed to be the beginnings of revolt against the system but in reality were merely deceptive flashes of light that made the darkness worse (Dorso 1944, 166). This is in clear contrast to Jovine's description of fires lighted almost as a protest and defiance against the gathering gloom. Dorso had also assumed that the new revolutionary elite needed to reform the south would come from the ranks of the southern petty bourgeoisie, not from the peasantry. Gobetti, in *La rivoluzione liberale*, had taken the view that peasants were not capable of anything more than 'una rivoluzione fanatica' – 'primitive rebellion' in Hobsbawm's terms. Why should Jovine take a more optimistic view?

Partly, no doubt, the tone and imagery of Jovine's dénouement are an expression of the changed expectations of the situation of the 1940s. between the summer of 1944 and that of 1946, the minister of agriculture was the Communist Fausto Gullo, who issued a complex series of decrees intended to transform peasant-landlord relations in the south. In part he was responding to the 1943–4 wave of peasant agitation; in part he was attempting to ensure the nation's food supply. In October 1944, he decreed that uncultivated or partly cultivated land could be occupied and farmed by peasants for four years in the first instance, provided that the peasants organised production cooperatives. The legislation appeared to recognize the validity of the peasants' fight for justice and gave them a powerful incentive for corporate action. Hundreds of cooperatives were formed, often aiming at the occupation of ex-demesne land or common land that had been usurped. The Gullo reforms were fiercely opposed by landowners. The Christian Democrats succeeded in having Gullo replaced with one of their own, Antonio Segni, while the Communist Party failed to mount its own campaign to back Gullo's reforms. In the 1944 elections the Christian democrats won a clear victory, putting an end to hopes of land reform. But southern peasants had been linked with regional and national politics for the first time (Ginsborg 1984).

Jovine seems to have hoped that justice was finally about to be done, that the injustices of the past could not be repeated. His optimism finds expression in his depiction of Luca, son of Giuseppe and mourned by his mother Immacolata, as a laicized Christ-figure.

Luca was originally destined for the priesthood, but leaves the seminary when he looses his faith. The church is depicted as, at best, concerned only with personal salvation, as when the village Lent mission takes place, failing to preach a social gospel or, at worst, worldly and corrupt, its priests part of local power-structures. The exception to this is don Giacomo Fontana, who D'Episcopo rightly sees as a key character in the novel (D'Episcopo 1984, 91). As a missionary in Egypt for forty years, Don Giacomo had not made converts, judging that the Egyptians were not ready for such enlightenment. He had, instead, sought to replace their resignation with hope. There is a hint that perhaps, like Luca, he did not have a real vocation for the priesthood. Now, he develops Luca's ethical sense and encourages him to rebel, urging him to see Christ's sense of justice not in his resurrection but in his self-sacrifice, thus preparing Luca to sacrifice himself for a just cause, helping the peasants to achieve a sense of community and human dignity, replacing their resignation with hope.

CHAPTER 14

Pavese as historian: *La luna e i falò*

In his diary, *Il mestiere di vivere*, under the date of 17 November 1949, Pavese wrote:

> Hai concluso il ciclo storico del tuo tempo: *Carcere* (antifascismo confinario, *Compagno* (antifascismo clandestino), *Casa in collina* (resistenza), *Luna e i falò* (postresistenza). [...] La saga è completa. (Pavese 1990, 375).

> You have concluded the historical cycle of your time: *Carcere* (anti-Fascism, internal exile), *Compagno* (clandestine anti-Fascism), *Casa in collina* (resistance), *Luna e i falò* (post-resistance). The saga is complete.

Pavese, in other words, soon after the completion of most mature and complex work, looked back over all that he had written and singled out these four short novels as constituting an historical cycle that has a thematic unity deriving from his treatment of Italian history. His last novel was also intended to be 'a modest *Divina commedia*' (Pavese 1966, 659) – a summary, that is, of Pavese's artistry and view of the world. Just under nine months later, Pavese committed suicide in a Turinese hotel room, where his body was discovered on Sunday 27 August. By the side of his bed, in a copy of his *Dialoghi con Leucò*, he left a suicide note that concluded with the words 'Non fate troppi petegolezzi' [Don't gossip too much].

The majority of critics, however, ignored Pavese's advice – or was it a plea? – and have chosen not to regard Pavese as an historian of his own time. Gioanola, indeed, has pointed out that critics have chosen to focus more on the Pavese 'case' than on his works, as the titles of their books indicate: *Il vizio assurdo, La maturità impossibile, Il mito Pavese, L'échec de Pavese* (Gioanola 1971, 7). Inevitably, the authors of titles such as these have tended to focus on Pavese's works as the expression of his unresolved personal problems and failures, of which there were many. Remote, introspective, incapable of commitment or identification with either 'the people' or a political party, how could such a novelist have anything relevant to say about the state of Italian society or the interpretation of Italian history? Even Gioanola, whose study of Pavese is probably the most positive assessment of the novelist by an Italian critic, seeks to 'rescue' him from these negative views by presenting him in Heideggerian terms as a writer who dramatically participates in western culture's discovery that we are 'beings-towards-death'; in other words that death is not the end or goal of life, but that we are dying all the time. Pavese's is an intensely personal experience but one which also has exemplary or universal value. Gioanola thus interprets Pavese as a writer whose concern is with the individual and the ontological, not with the societal or historical. It follows from this approach that allusions to history and politics in *La luna e i falò* are 'inserts' and constitute the novel's 'weakest moments' (Beccaria 2000, v).

Yet since Pavese is, in Gioanola's words, one of the few 'thinking writers' in the history of Italian literature (Gioanola 1972, 67–8), whose creative writings are invariably accompanied by probing reflections on the purpose and techniques of those writings, it would be prudent to take seriously his bold claim to be writing the history of his time. His works have both an existential and a societal dimension, as has been recognised in the generally more positive approaches of critics writing in the United States and the UK (Biasin 1968, Thompson 1982, Davis 1984, Moloney 1990), although I would argue that it is only in the novels and tales of his maturity that Pavese succeeded in balancing successfully the demands of expressing both existential perceptions and incisive comment on the course of Italian history. In his last works Pavese is no longer committed to the discipline of a Communist Party engaged in Cold War manoeuvres and compromises – a discipline which, although self-imposed, he found highly uncongenial. But he was, nevertheless, strongly influenced by his political experience and, as a result, his later works have an historical and political (but not party-political) dimension that the earlier ones lacked. Gioanola in fact sees that there are two sides to Pavese, the 'witness to that mal du siècle to which no one is immune' and also the one characterized by 'an almost Christian openness in love for his neighbour and a renewing social commitment' (Gioanola 1972, 12–5). But he seems to limit the latter side of Pavese to finding expression in his essays and letters, rather than in his narrative works. I suggest that both sides of Pavese find expression in *La luna e i falò*, which thus turns out to be a richer and more complex work than is often thought.

Il carcere (which was written between November 1938 and April 1939, although not published until 1948) is based on Pavese's traumatic experience of *confino* at Brancaleone Calabria. Gioanola describes it as the most autobiographical of Pavese's novels (Gioanola 1972, 191), and Pavese himself discusses it in terms of a 're-evocation' of his life at that time (Pavese 1968, 596). But although it describes the experience of *confino*, it has nothing to say about Italian history or politics, and offers no account of the living conditions of the southern peasantry. It is a view of *confino* only as expressed by a highly egocentric individual, in which prison and *confino* are primarily bold and striking metaphors of a condition of solitude in which the protagonist, Stefano, systematically cultivates self-sufficiency as the essentially sterile kind of maturity to which he feels destined. It is difficult to view this tale as part of a 'ciclo storico', in spite of Pavese's claim. One needs only to compare it with *Cristo si è fermato a Eboli* to realise just to what degree the story excludes whatever does not contribute to Stefano's progress in solitude.

Il compagno (written in 1946) and *La casa in collina* (1947–8) need not concern us here, although both engage directly with political end ethical issues. The former is set in Turin and Fascist Rome and deals with the 'conversion' of Pablo from a superficial and pleasure-seeking life-style to political commitment in the ranks of the militant left. The latter is set in the country but deals with the ethical issue of commitment (or non-commitment) to armed resistance in 1943 (Moloney 1990).

La luna e i falò is in part the story of a migrant's return. As such, it naturally has certain features in common with other accounts of the return home (Pellegrini 1953; Canzoneri 1973), for example in the narrator's disconcerted realisation that much has changed during his absence, and that he is out of touch with all that has happened in the intervening years. He remembers his childhood and youth, describes what he finds in the present, and learns what happened while he was away, in a novel which is brilliantly constructed on three time-planes, with the narrator's carpenter-friend, Nuto, acting as a link with both the narrator's past and also with the years of the Fascist period and the war. When the novel begins, then, the narrator has already completed a journey in geographical space: now he must embark on a journey through time – a journey that reveals that he is not as experienced and mature as he had thought. His experience exemplifies the typical Pavesian novel-structure as journey as analysed by Giorgio Bàrberi Squarotti (Bàrberi Squarotti 1989).

The first-person narrator is known to us only by the nick-name of Anguilla [Eel] given to him as a boy on account of his slim and wiry physique. Since European eels cross and re-cross the Atlantic several times in the course of their lives, the name can also be seen as having a prophetic or emblematic value, anticipating his destiny, with which he will eventually have to come to terms. It is also possible that Montale's poem 'L'anguilla', which vividly celebrates the eel's powerful urge to return, may also have been a factor in Pavese's choice of name for his character (even though the Ligurian poet seems to misunderstand the eel's breeding cycle). Guj points out that 'L'anguilla', described by Glauco Cambon as a symbol of life over death, was published in Naples in a number of *Botteghe Oscure* that was republished in Rome in July 1949 only a couple of months before Pavese began to write *La luna e i falò* (Guj 1986, 42–3).

Anguilla is one of Pavese's most successful creations. Unlike Stefano of *Il carcere*, he is not simply Pavese's *alter ego* (although the fact that his friend Nuto is based on Pavese's carpenter-friend Pinolo Scaglione has encouraged autobiographical readings of the novel). Nor is his voice ever taken over by that of his author, as is that of the mechanic Berto, in *Paesi tuoi*. Pavese has given Anguilla a convincing personal history and a personality to match. He has also given him a recognisable, individual voice, which is different from that of his author. Anguilla is consistent, coherent and convincing. This does not mean that he is always an attractive or admirable character. He is at times egotistical and callous towards the poverty of others, as when he tells Nuto: 'Lascia le cose come sono. Io ce l'ho fatta, anche senza nome' [Leave things alone. I made it, even without a name]. This is the authentic voice of the self-made man though the ages. Nuto, who has a social conscience, retorts: ' Non bisogna dire, gli altri ce la facciano, bisogna aiutarli' [It's not enough to say, let the others get on with it, you have to help them] (Pavese 2000, 16).

At times, too, Anguilla is dilettante and irresponsible, as when, in Chapter IV, he gives Nuto gratuitous advice on how to organise left-wing opposition. Sometimes, he misreads situations, as when, returning for the first time to Gaminella, the farm where he grew up, he notices that there is an ox in the stable and concludes: 'Chi adesso stava nel casotto non era dunque più pezzente come noi' [the people in the cottage weren't as poor as we were any more] (Pavese 2000, 11). He could hardly be more mistaken. Only later do we learn from his conversation with Valino, the new share-cropping tenant, that the ox is the property of the farm's owner, the 'Madama della Villa', and that she makes sure that the animal has enough to eat while her tenants live lives of grinding poverty far worse than anything Anguilla had ever known while growing up with Padrino and Virgilia. In order to understand the situation fully, the attentive reader needs to put Anguilla's observations together with his subsequent conversations with Valino and Nuto. The latter at one point tells Anguilla quite sharply that in the old days he at least got enough to eat; the same cannot be said of Valino's son, Cinto, who suffers from malnutrition.

At no point does Anguilla explicitly correct his erroneous first impression. Nor does he intervene to comment explicitly on the declining living standards of the sharecropping peasantry, now being squeezed beyond the limits of endurance by a grasping landlord. Readers have to contrast Anguilla's developing perceptions for themselves; and, when they do, they discover that Anguilla himself changes and develops during the course of the narrative. Nothing could be further from his initial unthinking comment that individuals should make their own way in the world unaided than his decision to help the now orphaned Cinto by financing the operation that should straighten his twisted leg. Readers also discover that although Anguilla may not explicitly offer an interpretation of Italian history, one is implicit in the novel, and Pavese seeks express it in terms of his concept of individual destiny.

The novel's view of Italian history is naturally related to its narrative structure and to the three different time-levels on which it operates. I emphasise that

that there are three time-levels rather than a simple opposition of past and present, since it is in large measure Anguilla's exploration of the middle level, during which he was absent, in America, which leads him to come to terms with the present. In the opening chapters, Anguilla's account of his return from America after the 1939–45 war stresses his perceptions of sameness and continuity:

> Stessi rumori, stesso vino, stesse facce di una volta. I ragazzotti che correvano tra le gambe alla gente erano quelli; i fazzolettoni, le coppie di buoi, il profumo, il sudore, le calze delle donne sulle gambe scure, erano quelli. E le allegrie, le tragedie, le promesse in riva al Belbo (Pavese, 2000, 14).

> Same sounds, same wine, same faces as before. The lads running between people's legs were the same; the headscarves, the pairs of oxen, the perfume, the sweat, the women's stockings on their dark legs, were the same. And the merriment, the tragedies, the promises made on the banks of the Belbo.

Anguilla's initial perception is that he has changed, but that the peasant world has not. Seasons have past, not time: 'Per me delle stagioni erano passate, non degli anni' [As far as I was concerned, seasons had passed, not years] (Pavese 2000, 55). The very phrase 'Per me', placed strongly at the beginning of the sentence, both indicates that this is Anguilla's subjective reaction to what he sees and suggests that it may well not be validated by the author, or, indeed, Anguilla's subsequent experience. Anguilla's ignorance and dilettantism make him an unreliable narrator, a familiar figure in much modern narrative. We have to look carefully at Anguilla's view of Le Langhe as untouched by time, that is, by history, although his perception of continuity and sameness provide a useful pointer towards Pavese's perception of the disconcerting continuities of Italian history.

Anguilla is an illegitimate child from the Foundling Hospital at Alessandria, brought up by Padrino and Virgilia, who have two daughters. They give the boy a home partly for the sake of the subsidy they will receive as foster-parents and partly in order to have another male member in the family workforce. Anguilla has vivid memories of a life of poverty and hard work; but, as Nuto points out, Padrino was a tenant-farmer, not a share-cropper, and he did not have to share his crop, as Valino does. If the tenant hill-farmer leads at best a precarious existence, which can easily become impossible, the sharecropper's lot is even harsher.

Padrino's dream of a self-sufficient family unit is shattered when Virgilia dies. Cooking, washing, lighting and maintaining the fire, fetching water, gathering firewood, looking after the animals, spinning and weaving, are all time- and labour-consuming tasks, carried out by the woman of the household. Without the essential working adult female, the workforce is too small to run the farm, and the family is broken up. The local parish priest finds a place for Anguilla as 'servitore', or general farm-boy, at La Mora, a large and prosperous farm owned by the wealthy Sor Matteo.

Anguilla's period at La Mora marks his transition from childhood to youth, his introduction to the world of work and the beginning of the process of self-discovery and maturing which is still continuing when he returns. At La Mora, Anguilla sees wealth for the first time in his life. The contrast between Padrino's marginal hill farm and the fertile farm on the richer land of the plain is analogous to the situation in Fontamara, although not so extreme: La Mora is not a 'latifondo'. The situation in the novel reflects the situation in much of Italy's rural history.

The years from 1896 to 1914 had been the take-off period for agriculture in the north, thanks to capital investment and State-guaranteed profits. A more cost-effective system of agriculture came into being, although mainly confined to areas in northern and central Italy, but it also produced a rural proletariat that could be hired and fired at will. While Sor Matteo prospers, Padrino sells up and Anguilla becomes a labourer. This was typical of a period in which the number of owner-cultivators fell sharply while the overall number of landless labourers increased. But, 'la riccezza chi la fa e chi la gode'. Or, as the English north-country proverb puts it, 'Clogs to clogs in three generations'. Sor Matteo's energies and enterprise have built up his farm and his wealth. Even in his old age, his knowledge and judgment enable him to maintain his position and direct operations.

But the next generation is frivolous and superficial. Sor Matteo wants to give his daughters the social advantages he lacked. They have an education of sorts and a culture of sorts. They read novels which the young Anguilla, who is beginning to acquire a culture of his own, finds frivolous – probably Guido da Verona and Pitigrilli, very popular at the time, although their authors are not named. They play the piano. They send for seeds – no one ever tells Irene and Silvia to go and buy them themselves – in order to grow flowers, not useful crops like vegetables. We rarely see or hear of them working. Their lives are dominated by their ambition to be invited to social gatherings at Il Nido, entry to which would mark their emancipation from the soil and their acceptance by a socially higher class. They have no real purpose in life and no positive values on which to build their lives. They drift into amorous adventures – and amorous disasters. They and their equally frivolous and irresponsible boyfriends could be read as an austere comment by Pavese on that *Italietta* which took no interest in anything serious and was guilty of allowing Fascism to take power and then failing to prevent the drift into war. They represent a society without a future – which may be why they are both killed off and represented as having no offspring.

It is at La Mora that Anguilla discovers his vocation to leave Le Langhe. He moves to Genova, and the Fascist clampdown on dissent and the Special Laws of 1926 are the occasion – almost, one feels, the pretext – for him to leave for the United States. On his return, as we have seen, he comes rapidly to the conclusion that nothing has changed, that the seasonal rhythm of the peasants' labour is outside history and has not been touched by it, is unchanged and unchangeable. At this point Anguilla seems perilously close to Jahier in viewing the hill peasants as destined inevitably to a poverty that is unchanging and unchangeable.

The novel's opening thus suggests a primary concern with psychological and existential themes:

> C'è una ragione perché sono tornato in questo paese, qui e non invece a Canelli, a Barbaresco o in Alba. Qui non ci sono nato, è quasi certo; dove son nato non lo so; non c'è da queste parti una casa né un pezzo di terra né delle ossa ch'io possa dire 'Ecco cos'ero prima di nascere'... Chi può dire di che carne sono fatto? Ho girato il mondo abbastanza da sapere che tutte le carni sono buone e si equivalgono, ma è per questo che uno si stanca e cerca di mettere radici, di farsi terra e paese, perché la sua carne valga e duri qualcosa di più che un comune giro di stagioni (Pavese 2000, 9).

> There's a reason why I came back to this village, here and not to Canelli, Barbaresco or Alba. I wasn't born here, that's for sure; there's not a house or a piece of land hereabouts that I can say 'This is what I was before I was born'... Who can say what flesh I am made of? I've wandered about the world enough to know that all flesh is good and worth another, but that's why you get tired and try to put down roots, to make a bit of land and a village for yourself, so that your flesh will be worth something and last a bit more that the usual round of the seasons.

No doubt there is in that opening statement, tentative as it is, a vague and not very clearly formulated awareness that individuals do not exist in a vacuum, social or genetic, that one needs forebears and (perhaps) descendants; but there is little room for doubt that Anguilla's quest is a personal one. He wants to understand himself, not his society and its history. Ulysses-figure he may be, but he is tired of wandering and wants to settle down: 'uno si stanca e cerca di mettere radici'. One would not seriously expect such an egoist to be overly interested in others anyway.

Yet, whether he acknowledges it or not, whether he likes it or not, his identity has a social dimension and this social dimension presses itself on his attention. He can see, on the one hand, the similarities between now and then, be comforted by them, take pleasure in them: the taste of a fig, the feel of the heat coming up from the ground, the round of the seasons. On the other hand, he can also see the changes, which disconcert him since they make him realise he no longer belongs. His reluctance to visit La Mora is a clear indication of the difficulty he has in coming to terms with the changes. Even from the first chapter it is clear that Anguilla does not understand his village: 'Possibile che a quarant'anni, e con tutto il mondo che ho visto, non sappia ancora che cos'è il mio paese?' [Possible that at forty, and having seen so much of the world, I still don't understand my village?] (Pavese 2000, 3).

By chapter XIV, less than half way through the novel, Anguilla's personal quest is over, in the sense that both he and his 'paese' have changed. The experience of his childhood and youth are still inside him, as formative experiences and inner riches, but they do not constitute roots. By chapter XV he knows that he will leave again: 'la mia giornata sono adesso i telefoni, le spedizioni, i selciati della città' [my days now are the telephone, dispatching goods, city pavements] (Pavese 2000, 79). If *La luna e i falò* were the story of one man's quest to come to terms with his personal destiny, it could end there. But it doesn't. There is still that other quest which in the opening chapters was subordinate to the personal one: 'Possibile che a quarant'anni [...] non sappia ancora che cos'è il mio paese?' The remainder of the novel is devoted primarily to Anguilla's desire to understand the village, to come to terms with it as it is now, which means that he has to see its present in terms of its past, of which he is largely ignorant. The 'paese' becomes an Italy in microcosm – an Italy that has difficulty in coming to terms with its recent past.

Anguilla himself never explicitly formulates his changed purpose in those terms. Nor do the style and technique of the novel change. We still have the lyrical flow of his memories, punctuated by his conversations with Nuto, Cinto and Valino. The interwoven themes which enable one to interpret the novel in historical terms are, on the one hand, Anguilla's relationship with Cinto and, on the other, the resistance.

Anguilla finds that his former home at Gaminella is now occupied by the taciturn, surly Valino, his son Cinto, and two women: 'due donne, sottane nere, una decrepita e storta, una più giovane ossuta' [two women, black skirts, one decrepit and bent, the other younger, bony] (Pavese 2000, 32). Anguilla sees himself in Cinto, Padrino in Valino and his step-sisters in the younger woman, since Angiolina and Giulia would by now be about her age. Anguilla is mixing his time-scales in a most disturbing way: Cinto could be a young version of himself, at the age of ten, but Valino's sister-in-law is what Angiolina and Giulia would be now: 'Se in qualche luogo erano vive, dovevano avere l'età di quella donna' [If they were alive somewhere, they must be about the same age as that woman] (Pavese 2000, 32).

Whether this confusion of time-scales matters or not, the fact remains that there are significant differences between Padrino's household and Valino's. Valino, as a sharecropper, is even poorer than Padrino was, and although Anguilla may remember having scabs on his knees, and chilblains, as Cinto has, he never suffered from rickets, caused by undernourishment. When Cinto's mother lies dying, the angry and frustrated doctor tells her why her son has rickets: 'aveva detto che non era mica il latte, ma le fascine, andare scalza nella pioggia, mangiare ceci e polenta, portar ceste' [he'd said it wasn't her milk, but the bundles of firewood, going barefoot in the rain, eating beans and polenta, carrying baskets] (Pavese 2000, 34).

Valino, in fact, is a representative figure, not an isolated victim. It cannot be a coincidence that his name is (almost) an anagram of 'villano'. Even if that is the case, he has a mythical dimension: he is a Sisyphus-figure, doomed to repetitious labour and defeat (Musolino 1990).

Life for Valino is a continuous struggle with the land in order to extract from it what he can, and against the farm's new owner, the Madama della Villa. Cinto relates, with malicious glee, how they had picked the best tomatoes before the 'padrona' came, scales in hand, to claim her share. Episodes such as this portray vividly a situation of conflict and mistrust that had probably always characterised sharecropping, if Giovanni Morelli's *Libro di ricordi* (1393–1421) are typical, with their warning that thieving peasant tenants are not to be trusted. But landowners may also be prisoners of the system; Anguilla does not accept the Cavaliere's offer of hospitality because he knows that the impoverished old man would have to buy a bottle of his own wine from his tenants, who are systematically swindling him.

Traditionally, sharecroppers were considered a privileged caste, to be contrasted with those peasants who enjoyed no security on the land. This came to an end early in the nineteenth century. The 'mezzadri' won some rights in 1920, but the blackshirt squads soon restored 'normality' to the countryside (Ginsborg 1990, 26). Fascism merely papered over the cracks, and since the war did much to raise the peasants' political awareness, tensions were bound to reappear in the post-war period, which saw a constant struggle to improve contracts and conditions of work. But in 1946, the De Gaspari government stipulated that the traditional 50/50 per cent division of produce should remain in force, not the 60/40 per cent in favour of the peasants, which the 'mezzadri' had been seeking. It was not until 1947 that Segni legislated in favour of a 53/47 per cent split, with the landowner compelled to set aside 4 per cent of income for improvements. This represented a substantial defeat for the peasant movement and is the unspoken context of Pavese's novel. Anguilla's perception that seasons had passed, not years, turns out to be merely an expression of his personal delight in the sameness he discovers and his initial failure to realize that the course of history had made the peasantry more impoverished than before.

Anger and frustration are a natural and inevitable reaction to such a situation – an anger and frustration which find expression in the way individuals treat each other. Valino beats the women of his household, who call after Cinto angrily: 'Un urlo della donna dall'aia, che chiamava Cinto, voleva Cinto, malediceva Cinto' [...] [A yell from the woman in the yard, calling Cinto, wanting Cinto, cursing Cinto] (Pavese 2000, 38). Anguilla comments: 'Si sente spesso questa voce sulle colline' [You often hear that voice on the hills]. The comment indicates that this is not an isolated incident, that anger and frustration are widespread, while the present tense suggests that Anguilla is registering the phenomenon as a characteristic of post-war rural society. Valino's regular brutality towards his family is another manifestation of the same phenomenon.

The incident which provokes Valino into his final explosion of destructive rage, in which he kills his womenfolk, sets fire to the house and commits suicide, is yet another dispute with the Madama della Villa over the division of the crops.

Pavese might at this point seem to be expressing a bleakly pessimistic historical determinism, a view of rural life as a series of essentially a-historical cycles of deprivation from which only a few fortunate individuals can escape. Whatever differences there are between one cycle and another – for example between Anguilla's youth and the greater poverty of Cinto – may be attributed, as they are by Gioanola, to chance (Gioanola 1972, 370). This is to ignore the historical context.

It is, however, possible to argue also that the novel calls into question the achievements of the resistance. After all, Pavese's diary entry for 17 November 1949, already quoted, the theme assigned to *La luna e i falò* in the 'ciclo storico' is 'post-resistenza' – to which one might add 'post hoc ergo propter hoc', in the sense that the novel depicts the tensions inherent in post-war Italian society as the indirect consequences of the resistance, which Pavese never glamorises by the use of a capital R.

The resistance was, for Pavese, a civil war. In *La casa in collina* the narrator, Corrado, moves from an attitude of superior isolation to a humanitarian pacifism prompted by a deep sense of compassion for human suffering. He sees not only the resistance but all war as civil war: 'Ogni guerra è una guerra civile [...]' But he also foresees a situation in which the war will spread and thus compel even pacifists to take sides (Moloney 1990).

In *La luna e i falò*, this theme is developed further. What more natural than that the discovery of the corpses of *repubblichini* executed by partisans should lead to both an exploration of Nuto's role in the resistance and the account of Santa's death? Moreover, the village's reaction to the discovery of the corpses also enables us to date the action of the novel fairly precisely.

Anguilla returns to Italy just over a year after the end of the war, if his main memory of Genova is of its war damage. When the narrative begins, he has been 'keeping an eye' on his 'paese' for a year after an initial visit. 'Paese' in this context seems to denote not only the village but also the surrounding district with its farms. During this period, he re-establishes contact with his childhood friend and mentor, Nuto.

Nuto is contrasted with Anguilla in many ways. He shows, as Gioanola rightly says, that it is possible to achieve maturity without leaving the *paese*. He is also a man with a social conscience. It is not difficult to see some the remarks he makes at La Mora as the expression of his youthful Socialism, but in his desire, as an adult, to see money abolished, he verges on anarchism. He is certainly a pacifist, opposed to all forms of violence and cruelty, even preventing children from tormenting a lizard: 'E poi si comincia così, si finisce con scannarsi e bruciare i paesi' [Then you start that way and end up slaughtering people and burning down villages] (Pavese 2000, 8) Although in many respects a different kind of character, he also represents in this respect continuity with Corrado, in *La casa in collina*. When the war reached the Langhe, he sided with the resistance, not killing, but supplying the local partisans and tending the wounded.

The resistance was, for Nuto, above all the period when consciences were roused and choices were made. Now, with the fighting over, he does not indulge in heroics, despising those who 'si sono messi i fazzoletti l'indomani' [who put their neckerchiefs on the day after] (Pavese 2000, 65). Anguilla tells him that the Communists should have struck in 1945, while their partisan units were still armed and organised. There had been, in fact, a real fear that Communist partisans could present a serious military threat: the America National Security Council reported in February 1948 that they were 'believed to have the military capability of gaining initial control of Northern Italy' (Clarke 1989, 324; cf. Ginsborg 1990, 68). But when Anguilla asks him why the Communists had not struck while the iron was hot, Nuto merely replies: 'Io non avevo che una pialla e uno scalpello' [I just had my plane and chisel] (Pavese 2000, 27). Taken at its face value, the reply is evasive and ambiguous, seeming to imply that he had the tools of his trade and had to set about earning a living. It is, however, likely – given that in this novel every detail counts – that Pavese has invested the tools of his trade with a symbolic value, implying that reconstruction was more urgent a task than revolution. On this subject, Ruth Ben-Ghiat quotes the partisan Teresio Olivelli, who in 1944 used the image of fire to describe the transforming effect of war:

> […] we have burned all bridges: the extreme pain and suffering of the war have cleansed us of all impurities: we want to sweep away any residues. We are in a hurry to construct and reconstruct (Ben-Ghiat 2001, 203).

In the person of Nuto, Pavese is pointing to the limits of what resistance and revolution could accomplish. He brilliantly represents in fictional terms what Ginsborg calls 'the two dominant elements in working class consciousness at this time', namely 'a desire to reconstruct after the terrible damages of the war years and a widespread expectation of social and economic reform' (Ginsborg 1990, 82).

A totally negative view of the resistance is put forward by the *benpensanti* of the village, who dismiss it as a civil war instigated by murderously-inclined Communists motivated only by envy and the desire to rob them, the pillars of society, of their wealth and their land. It is not difficult to see that this desire to discredit the resistance has its roots in their determination to maintain a social order that is seen by Pavese as unjust. They affect for the dead a compassion they do not feel, for among their number are the *Signora della Villa*, who ruthlessly exploits Valino, and the parish priest, who is intent on making political capital out of the funeral of the *repubblichini*. The mood and tone of chapter XII would inevitably have brought to the minds of Italian readers the virulent and effective anti-Communist election campaign of the early months of 1948, in which the Christian Democrats had the fervent support of the Roman Catholic Church at all levels and in which parish priests preached sermons which were little more than election addresses (Ginsborg 1990, 116–17). The priest and the *benpensanti* together represent an attempt to foil any movement towards social reform and seek to restore the *status quo ante bellum*.

Valino's bonfire of his home is essentially a peasant protest – the last desperate protest of a bitterly angry and frustrated man who has no hope. Bonfires, however, are in the novel also a symbol of renewal. The peasants light bonfires on the edges of their fields in order to ensure greater fertility the following year. There is no rational explanation for the custom, but Nuto is convinced that it is effective: 'fatto sta che tutti i coltivi dove sull'orlo si accendeva i falò davano un raccolto più succoso, più vivace' [the fact remains that the fields where bonfires were lit on the edge gave a more substantial, more lively crop] (Pavese 2000, 51). Anguilla is understandably sceptical – after all, he sells fertilisers – but nevertheless it is noticeable that he sees the wartime destruction of Genova in the same terms: 'Magari è meglio così, meglio che tutto se ne vada in un falò d'erbe secche e che la gente ricominci' [Perhaps it's better this way, better for everything to go up in a bonfire of dry grass and for people to start again] (Pavese 2000, 136–7). The account of Santa's funeral pyre can be read in the same way; indeed, the novel's closing words constitute an invitation to see Santa's death as symbolising the death and destruction of an element in Italian society that had played fast and loose with Fascism and the resistance, betraying both, with the consequent possibility of renewal: 'L'altr'anno c'era ancora il segno, come il letto di un falò' [Last year there were still traces of it, like a bonfire bed] (Pavese 2000, 73).

Cinto, on the other hand, may represent a new Italy. The rickets from which he suffers can be read as representing the legacy of the past. If so, his lameness is as symbolic as Anguilla's illegitimacy. But neither resistance nor revolution, in

Pavese's view, can by itself produce a new society or guarantee a future in which truly human values can flourish. Recourse has to be had to a new ethic, as Corrado came to realise in the earlier novel. For that purpose, co-operation and education are necessary. Nuto and Anguilla co-operate to ensure Cinto's future. Nuto will give him a home and teach him a trade. Anguilla will later offer him the chance of working with him, so that he will have a choice that neither of his mentors had in their youth.

It does not follow, however, that Pavese is offering a facile optimism, or that Cinto's problems will in fact be solved. We see him on the verge of change; but we do not see that change take place. We know that Anguilla will pay for him to be examined by a doctor in Alessandria with a view to having an operation on his leg; but we do not know whether or not that operation will be successful. Moreover, Pavese reminds us that the forces of darkness and unreason – the 'selvaggio' – constantly threaten any progress that might be made. As Nuto and Anguilla take their last walk together, in the course of which Nuto finally reveals the truth about Santa's death, they pass two burnt-out houses. The first is Valino's. Mention of it seems intended to associate Cinto's future with Santa's death. The second is one that had been occupied by the partisans and burnt down by the Germans. One 'falò' was lighted during the resistance, the other after the war. Some good comes out of both. The first was part of the necessarily violent and destructive process which led to the defeat of Nazism – of the 'selvaggio' par excellence – and which, as Nuto points out, led to an awakening of the peasantry: 'Se anche i mezzadri e i miserabili del paese non andavano loro per il mondo, nell'anno della guerra era venuto il mondo a svegliarli […] perfino i tedeschi, perfino i fascisti erano serviti a qualcosa…' [Even if the sharecroppers and the poor of the area didn't go about the world, in the war year the world came and roused them […] even the Germans, even the Fascists, served a purpose] (Pavese 2000, 71). The second bonfire opens up for Cinto the possibility of a new future. But the one did not prevent the tragedy of the other, and the brief mention of the partisans' house in this final chapter, together with the reactionary attitudes of the village *benpensanti*, is a reminder that human kind's fragile achievements are always at risk.

In Pavese's early fiction, the countryside is the abode of the 'selvaggio', in the sense of the irrational and the instinctive, which may be destructive, as in the case of Talino, in *Paesi tuoi*, but is not invariably so. In his mature fiction, on the other hand, the 'selvaggio' is still to be found in the country, but now it is associated with corruption and destruction, as it is in *Il diavolo sulle colline*. War, however, reveals that the 'selvaggio' is an omnipresent threat, both in the city (as with the rat in the ruins in *La casa in collina*) and in the country (as we see with the bodies of the 'repubblichini' in *La luna e i falò*). Farming, however, involving as it does the taming and the directing of nature and consistent vigilance against the threat of 'il selvaggio', becomes a powerful metaphor for the fragility of progress. In *Il diavolo sulle colline*, the rank growth of the garden at Il Greppo, Poli's country estate, is contrasted with Orazio's family farm and the deeply satisfying order of a well-kept vineyard. When, in *La luna e i falò*, Nuto and Anguilla look at the ruins of the house at Gaminella, the latter notices that unchecked growth is beginning to break the terraces down: 'La riva ha vinto' [The terrace has won] (Pavese 2000, 164).

In *La luna e i falò*, Pavese succeeds in finding symbols which express both the ontological and the societal, symbols which sum up his existential themes but which at the same time enable him to comment incisively on Italian society in general and Piedmontese rural society and the decline of share-cropping in particular. The still unsettled years of the immediate post-war period represent for Pavese what Guido Dorso called an 'occasione storica', rich with possibilities for change which had been brought about by the destruction of the war years, although the Piedmontese novelist's optimism is infinitely more cautious and guarded than Dorso's ever was. The last word of the novel is 'falò'. Only time will tell which kind of bonfire it was, destructive or restorative, and only time will tell whether Nuto's desire to break out of the cycle of deprivation and defeat, to 'rompere le stagioni' has been realized by means of the remedial action taken by Nuto and Anguilla, who has finally, to the extent that he is capable, committed himself to others and realized his humanity.

Conclusion: New orientalisms for old?

As used by Edward Said, the term 'orientalism' refers among other things to 'the ideological suppositions, images and fantasies about a currently important and probably urgent region of the world called the Orient' (Said 1985, 14). Since the south of Italy has come to be regarded as Italy's 'Orient', several modern historians have analysed stereotypes of that region in terms of Orientalism. While one may doubt whether, in world terms, it is or was as important or urgent a region as the Orient, there is no doubt that in the Italian context it has been both. A number of writers have extended the concept of the south to include other deprived areas in the centre and north, so that the binary opposition of north-south also includes aspects of the urban-rural opposition. The formation of the usually negative stereotypes of the south and the ways in which they have been used to affirm the perceived superiority of the supposedly more progressive north have in recent years been extensively studied. There is a sense in which the novelists studied in this book anticipate the work of historians, but they do much more than challenge the traditional denigratory stereotypes of the peasantry, whether southern or northern, which had been handed down from the nineteenth century and have recently been revived and exploited by the Northern Leagues as part of their campaign to free the north, seen as industrious and profitable, from the burden of financing the south, seen as incompetent and loss-making.

Fascism presented itself as a movement bringing renewal and modernisation to a country that was in many ways backward and needed to be brought into line with the progress of northern Europe. At the same time, it presented itself as inheriting and restoring all that was good about an ancient country. Rural society and rural life were seen as possessing great virtues of patience, fortitude, industriousness and fertility, so that 'bonifica' [land reclamation] could be used as a convenient metaphor for the Fascist project. In so far as the traditional binary opposition of north versus south had always presented the south as inferior and the north, both of Italy and of Europe in general, as the superior source of civilisation and progress, there was little about this aspect of the Fascist view of Italy that was new. What was new was Mussolini's attempt to modernise Italy in the sense of industrializing and militarising it while at the same time trying to 'ruralize' the country by imposing on it what he saw as traditional rural values. The novelists I have studied challenge the Fascist project in two ways.

In the first place, they protest vigorously and movingly against the manifest injustice of the traditional structures of rural society, which keep land, and therefore wealth and power, in the hands of the minority, who consequently have no interest in promoting either agricultural reform or social and economic justice. This is the case whether that minority consists of owners of great estates, as in the case of Silone's *Fontamara* and Jovine's *Le terre del Sacramento*, or the rural middle class, as in the case of Levi's *Cristo si è fermato a Eboli*. The protest is made whether peasants are themselves landless labourers, as in Fontamara, small proprietors, as in Levi's Gagliano, or sharecroppers, as in Pavese's *La luna e i falò*. Their protest is effective because it combines familiarity with the copious literature on the subject of rural society with personal observation of the lives of local communities. In his essay, 'La narrativa e il "sottosuolo" meridionale' of 1956, Silone attributed more importance to the latter than the former:

> Può darsi che qualcuna delle espressioni più recenti della narrativa meridionale sia stata ispirata o stimolata dalla copiosa letteratura d'ordine economico e sociologico che negli ultimi sessant'anni, per opera di persone d'indiscusso valore, fu appunto consacrato allo studio della nostra 'questione meridionale' [...] (Silone 1999, 1369).

> Perhaps some of the most recent expressions of southern narrative have been inspired or stimulated by the copious literature of an economic or sociological kind that in the last sixty years has been devoted by people of undoubted merits to the study of our 'southern problem'.

But, Silone continued, it would be a mistake to 'pensare a una derivazione, o semplicemente a un accostamento della narrativa a quella pubblicistica. Verga non è derivato di sicuro dall'on. De Felice' [to think of narrative as deriving from or simply approaching political journalism. Verga certainly does not derive from the Hon. De Felice]. He stresses the importance of personal contact and experience. This point was later taken up by Steinberg, who argues that:

> History alone [...] patient sifting of documents and sensitive reading of letters and memoirs, cannot reveal the peculiarities of particular communities, for these are the very things that residents themselves take for granted (Steinberg 1986, 84).

What Balzac called, in his preface to *Le père Goriot*, 'les particularités de cette scène pleine d'observations et de couleurs locales' [the particular details of this scene full of local observations and colours] became for a time the province of the novel, which achieves its effectiveness as protest precisely because it combines historical and sociological knowledge with personal experience and observation.

The second way in which novelists challenge the Fascist project is by querying the validity of the supposed rural values of official propaganda and asserting alternative values that are seen as ethically superior – the values of true community and a natural sense of justice. The evil ideologies of Fascism and Nazism come from the north, whose traditional assumption of superiority is therefore brought into question. Novelists also respond to the Fascist and Nazi sacralisation of political discourse by having recourse to older mythologies – Christian in the case of Silone and Jovine, even more ancient in the case of Levi and Pavese, whose Piemonte becomes a classical landscape. They thus avoid the danger Thomas Hardy, for example, saw as inherent in regional fiction: what is there in it that is universal? Local settings are thereby raised to the level of the universal and the representative. Silone, like Levi, could say with conviction shortly before his death that his Abruzzo was everywhere (Rawson 1978, 34–7).

Published or, in the case of *Fontamara*, republished after the second world war, these novels contributed to two important debates. The first of these was about the issue of rural poverty – seen mainly, but not exclusively, as a southern problem – and the issue of land reform. Novels about the Fascist past, in this context, had to be read as being also about liberated Italy's current problems, with a warning not to repeat or perpetuate the injustices of the past.

In the event, there was no effective land reform in post-war Italy. In May 1948 Segni, then Minister of Agriculture, announced that the great estates would be abolished, but 'what finally transpired was not the agrarian reform, but various slices of it' (Ginsborg 1990, 131), with three agrarian reform laws being passed in 1950, affecting only land redistribution, mainly in Sicily, Sardinia, Calabria and Abruzzo. The amount of land redistributed was far from sufficient to meet peasants' needs, and, in any case, agrarian contracts of employment and tenure were not reformed. Manlio Rossi-Doria, initially a convinced supporter of the reforms, remained bitterly disappointed by their results. In addition, the government established, also in 1950, the Cassa per il Mezzogiorno, a State fund for the south. This amounted to the 'humiliating panacea of State charity' that Carlo Levi, Dorso and the Actionists did not want. Many Italians assumed that the standard of living in the south, and rural areas in general, must in consequence inevitably rise and that problems had therefore been solved. Other factors helped to divert attention away from problems that in effect remained unsolved.

The USA was not willing to take migrants on the scale of the decades after the first world war, but was willing to put pressure on other countries to do so. In 1951, a bilateral agreement between Italy and Australia came into effect and between 1954 and 1971 the Italian-born population of Australia increased from 120,000 to 290,000 (Castles 1992, 42). Argentina and Canada were also popular destinations for enterprising Italians in search of a new life and prosperity. The increasing prosperity of northern Europe also attracted them in large numbers.

Then, from 1958 until 1963, Italy's own 'economic miracle' saw waves of migrants head northwards to work in Italian industry. Nanni Balestrini's *Vogliamo tutto* (1971) is narrated by a car factory worker from Fuorni, a 'frazione' of Salerno, who works for Fiat in Turin and takes part in strikes and protest actions. The centre of discontent moved northwards and the dangerously high pressure in the southern boiler diminished noticeably.

The southern problem had not been solved: it had simply appeared to go away, and socially aware novelist turned their attention to the pressing problems of industrial society, both in the north and the south, with works such as Ottiero Ottieri's *Donnarumma all'assalto* (1959) and Goffredo Parise's *Il padrone* (1964). Sociology, moreover, acquired a human, individual dimension. Reviewing a number of recent sociological studies, Adrian Lyttleton wrote in the *Times Literary Supplement* of 4 October 1991:

> The social sciences have a bad name for abstraction, but, for all that, the new social science-inspired history of the south brings us face to face with flesh and blood individuals. The books under review frequently deal with aspects of experience which in the past have been left to the novelist; sentiment, intrigue and the objects of consumption all have their place (Lyttleton 1991, 14).

He then compares the families discussed in Paolo Macry's *Ottocento* (Turin: Einaudi, 1988) to those depicted in Tomasi di Lampedusa's *Il Gattopardo*. One could of course observe that novelists such as Silone, Levi, Jovine and Pavese were writing for a very different public from the one addressed by academic sociologists such as Marta Petrusewiez, Paolo Pezzino, Gabriella Gribaudi, Giuseppe Civile and Paolo Macry, whose books Lyttleton was reviewing. One could also observe that illiterate or semi-literate peasants, unlike the cultured families studied by Macry, left little in the way of written records – letters, diaries and memoirs – for sociologists to sift and read sensitively, although police, court and prison records might be useful sources of information for some of their number.

Ultimately, however, we do not read novels primarily for the historical information they convey and we continue to read the novelists whose works I have discussed even though the ways of life they depict have disappeared from most of western Europe. Traditional stereotypes invariably assume that change in the south must come from the more enlightened and progressive north, while accounts of the exodus from rural societies assume the superiority and greater attractiveness of the urban environment. The south and the rural are considered to be incapable of generating change. The writers about the south we have considered subvert traditional stereotypes and question conventional assumptions. Instead of merely becoming the interlocutors of northerners' essentially negative

views of the south, they achieve the remarkable feat of both articulating a profound critique of southern society and government while at the same time interpreting the south as a source of unchanging values of great worth on which a new
form of community could be based. Pavese goes even further and turns Piedmontese rural society into a microcosm of contemporary Italy.

The proper frame of reference for a history of the formation of stereotypes of
the south is the problematic of nineteenth-century 'nation building' (Dickie 1999
(2), 14–15). In that context, literature exercised the important functions of
enabling the new nation to take stock of its constituent parts and propagating
patriotic values. The harsh experience of Fascism, war, occupation and resistance
as civil war prompted a further period of stocktaking in the turbulent years after
the second world war. If Fascism did indeed represent, in Gobetti's memorable
phrase, 'the autobiography of the nation', rather than being, as Croce would have
it, a northern importation, a temporary disease in an otherwise healthy body
politic, then the history and identity of the nation needed urgently to be reconsidered. Italian society was divided, even fragmented, between traditional monar-
chism and republicans, between Christian Democrats and Communists, between
restorers and reformers. Culture – and particularly the novel – had an important
part to play in articulating alternative visions of what shape post-war ideals of
community might take. The debate lost none of its relevance in the dark 'years of
lead' between 1973 and 1980, with their urban terrorism, when 'the Italian protest
movement was the most profound and long-lasting in Europe' (Ginsborg 1990,
298).

The authors we have studied are intellectuals who have seen it as their duty to
represent, speak out and testify on behalf of the peasants of their region or, in the
case of Carlo Levi, the region he has come to consider 'his'.

By turning to mythology to universalise a moment of crisis, and by raising
questions about the nature of community, the novelists considered in this book
have sought to fulfil their obligations as intellectuals in society. But in seeking to
replace 'Italy's Orient', 'a system of representations that belong to the realm of
ideas and myths culled from texts, not from empirical reality' (Said 1991, 1), have
novelists merely replaced old orientalisms with new?

There can be no doubt that their ideas about the south or about rural society
in general have inevitably been 'culled from texts' to some extent. It is difficult to
see how it could be otherwise. Silone was very familiar with Marxist and anarchist
theory, as well as reasonably well read in nineteenth- and twentieth-century literature, although he denied having read Verga before writing *Fontamara*. Carlo
Levi had to read up about the south before writing his first article for Gobetti, on
Salandra, and continued to read widely about both the south and the philosophy
of history. Francesco Jovine researched the history of the south in considerable
detail and saw his works from *Signora Ava* onwards as providing an historical

record and interpretation of his region. Pavese was also widely read and deliberately shaped his fictions in terms of myth. Yet, as we have seen, Silone claimed to attach more importance to direct personal experience than to the influence of texts. The direct experience of the south in *confino* gave new life and a dramatic new direction to Levi's writing and painting. Jovine lived and worked in the south before he began systematically to study its problems.

There must come a point, however, at which the way we interpret what we see is modified by what we have read or by what we believe, whether or not we are aware of this process of modification. This is likely to be particularly true of politically or religiously committed writers, however much they strain to achieve detachment, relating what they write to historical or sociological research, especially if they are writing with a polemical thrust. Silone deliberately stresses the ignorance and initial selfishness of the *cafoni* of Fontamara in order to throw into greater relief the unity they later achieve. Levi wittingly or unwittingly omits any suggestion of clientelism in Gagliano and only indirectly, even inadvertently, reveals the existence of rivalries that undermine the validity of his picture of social harmony amongst the peasants. The brutishness of Pavese's Valino is dramatically highlighted, so that he is far from a typical figure.

There is a sense in which southern or rural society is described and interpreted in terms of a personal experience that is itself shaped and interpreted in terms of personal belief and ideology. That belief and ideology are in turn formed by experience both of life and of texts. The writer's vision of rural society must then itself be given expression in a written form that is at least modified by other literary texts. The influence of other novels, on Silone, from Manzoni's *I promessi sposi* to Nikolai Gogol's *Dead Souls*, has long been recognised. Levi drew on the example of travel writers, beginning with the ironic Stendhal. Jovine was strongly influenced by Manzoni, Nievo and Silone. Pavese came to write about Piemonte after the example of American novelists writing about their regions. Literary influences may also be negative: all the novelists I have discussed seek in one way or another to distance themselves from the dramatically self-indulgent D'Annunzio.

Literary works that deal with social and political issues are shaped by a complex and, I suspect, ultimately indefinable, certainly unquantifiable, process of influences. Said's 'natural' description may well be a chimera, as may Gramsci's 'national-popular' literature. Oral history may have given an opportunity for peasants' voices to be heard, but only by a minority. Even when members of the peasantry write poetry or narrative, they almost inevitably do so in a style that echoes traditional literary 'high' style, since these are in the Italian tradition the only models available to them. Giovanni Carsaniga argues convincingly that 'peasant literature' is, in the Italian context, an impossibility (Carsaniga 1985, 21–8). This may perhaps limit the value of novels as direct and authentic accounts of peasant experience, but it does not therefore follow that the accounts they give are false and devoid of historical value. Critics have repeatedly despaired of finding 'the truth' in works of history or sociology and turned instead to narrative fiction. Novels can offer truth about human behaviour, set in a specific social or historical context that is sympathetically observed and carefully interpreted. Novels of peasant crisis deal with the reality of an Italy that had become a country unknown to most of its inhabitants and which could, therefore, have been perceived as exotic and mysterious in its backwardness. Instead of confirming existing stereotypes, they offer a challenge to received ideas and a stimulus to rethink values and beliefs not only about the society described, but also about the society – northern and urban – in and by which they are read. And here lies the difference between any kind of 'Orientalism' or denigratory stereotyping and the images of southern and rural life offered by our novelists. The traditional function of stereotypes is to confirm or reinforce the observer's sense of superiority over what is observed or described. Southerners had been complicit in the process of stigmatising the south, while northerners had valued the backwardness of the south as a yardstick by which to measure their own progress. Helping the backward was even seen – by Pasquale Villari, for example, in his *Lettere meridionali* – as a necessary means by which northern intellectuals might recover their lost ideals and sense of purpose (Moe 2002, 228–34). Novelists of peasant crisis refigure perspectives by writing about peasant societies in positive terms and suggesting that they can detect in them the beginnings of a new civilization.

In the event, History moved on and peasant society in Italy has changed almost out of all recognition. There are however peasant societies in other parts of the world experiencing their own crises, such as the *sem terras*, the movement of landless people founded in Brazil in the 1980s, and the peasants of Costa Rica. Land tenure is a problem is several countries in southern Africa, while globalisation is now one of the main causes of peasant crisis. Novels of peasant crisis continue to be read in developed societies, however, and their challenge will continue to make itself heard as long as mechanised mass urban society is perceived to be alienated and alienating and humankind searches for an alternative.

References/Select Bibliography

PRIMARY SOURCES

Jovine, F. & Domeneghini, L. ca.1930	*La patria fascista. Storia di ieri e oggi.* Rome: Libreria del Littorio, [ca. 1930].
Jovine, F. 1934	*Un uomo provvisorio.* Modena: Guando, 1934.
Jovine, F. 1945	'I poveri nei romanzi di Gabriele d'Annunzio'. *Il Mercurio*, March-April 1945, pp. 106–13.
Jovine, F. 1947	'Come ho visto la società meridionale'. *La Voce*, 19 December 1947, then in Jovine 1976.
Jovine, F. 1960	*Racconti.* Turin: Einaudi, 1960.
Jovine, F. 1970	'Del brigantaggio meridionale'. *Belfagor* 25 (1970), 6, pp. 623–41.
Jovine, F. 1972	*Le terre del Sacramento.* Turin: Einaudi, 1972.
Jovine, F. 1976	*Viaggio nel Molise*, Pref. di N. Perrazzelli. Isernia: Marinelli, 1976.
Jovine, F. 1987	*Ragazza sola*, ed. F. D'Episcopo. Campobasso: Edizioni Enne, 1987.
Jovine, F. 1990	*Signora Ava.* Turin: Einaudi, 1990.
Levi, C. 1964	*Paura della libertà.* Turin: Einaudi, 1964.
Levi, C. 1965	*Cristo si è fermato a Eboli*, ed. P. M. Brown. London, Harrap, 1965.
Levi, C. 1975 (1)	*Contadini e Luigini.* Rome: Basilicata, 1975.
Levi, C. 1975 (2)	*Coraggio dei miti. Scritti contemporanei 1922–1974*, ed. G. De Donato. Bari: De Donato, 1975.
Levi, C. 1990	*Poesie inedite 1934–1946.* Rome: Mancosu, 1990.
Levi, C. 1998	*L'invenzione della verità. Testi e intertesti per "Cristo si è fermato a Eboli".* A cura di M. A. Grignani. Alessandria: Ed. Dell'Orso, 1998.
Levi, C. 2000	*Le mille patrie. Uomini, fatti, paesi d'Italia.* A cura di G. De Donato: Introd. di L. M. Lombardi Satriani. Rome: Donzelli, 2000.
Levi, C. 2001	*Scritti politici. A cura di David Bidussa.* Turin: Einaudi, 2001.
Pavese, C. 1962	*La letteratura americana e altri saggi.* Turin: Einaudi, 1962.
Pavese, C. 1966	*Lettere 1945–1950, a cura di L. Mondo.* Turin: Einaudi, 1966.
Pavese, C. 1968	*Saggi letterari.* Turin: Einaudi, 1968.
Pavese, C. 1990	*Il Mestiere di vivere 1935–1950.* Nuova edizione condotta sull'autografo. A cura di Marziano Guglieminetti e Laura Nay. Turin: Einaudi, 1990.

Pavese, C. 2000   *La luna e i falò* a cura di G. L. Beccaria. Turin: Einaudi, 2000.
Silone, I. 1933   Fontamara. Paris: Nuove Edizioni Italiane, 1933.
Silone, I. 1939   *The Living Thoughts of Mazzini* presented by Ignazio Silone. London, Toronto, Melbourne and Sydney: Cassell, 1939.
Silone, I. 1947   *Fontamara*. Rome: Faro, 1947.
Silone, I. 1948   'Abruzzo e Molise'. *Attraverso l'Italia*, vol. XIV. Milan: Touring Club Italiano, 1948, pp. 7–12.
Silone, I. 1949   *Fontamara*. Milan: Mondadori, 1949.
Silone, I. 1963   'La terra e la gente'. U. Chierici and others, *Abruzzo*. Milan: Electa, 1963, pp. 33–95.
Silone, I. 1977   'A Note on Revision'. In *Fontamara* ed. J. Rawson. Manchester: Manchester University Press, 1977.
Silone. I. 1998   *Romanzi e saggi*. Volume primo, 1927–1944, a cura e con un saggio introduttivo di Bruno Falcetto. Mondadori: Milan, 1998.
Silone, I. 1999   *Romanzi e saggi*. Volume secondo, 1945–1978, a cura e con un saggio introduttivo di Bruno Falcetto. Mondadori: Milan, 1999.

OTHER NOVELS OF RURAL LIFE

Alvaro, C. 1955   *Gente in Aspromonte*. Milan: Garzanti, 1955.
Berto, G. 1974   *Il brigante*. Milan: Rusconi, 1974.
Bonaviri, G. 1958   *La contrada degli ulivi*. Venice: Sodalizio del libro, 1958.
Borsa, M. 1920   *La cascina sul Po. Storiella semplice*. Casa ed. Risorgimento: Caddeo, 1920.
Bufalari, G. 1976   *La masseria*. Florence: La Nuova Italia, 1976.
Celletti, T. 1938   *Tre tempi*. Milan–Verona: Mondadori, 1938.
Cinelli, D. 1931   *Castiglion che Dio sol sa*. Milan: L'Eroica, 1928.
d'Ambra, L. 1931   *Il guscio e il mondo*. Milan: Mondadori, 1931.
Fucini, R. 1988   *Le veglie di Neri* & *All'aria aperta*. In *Tutti i racconti*. Florence: Salani, 1988.
Gibbon, L. G.   *Sunset Song*. London & Sydney: Pan Books, 1978.
Nievo, I. 1994   *Novelliere campagnuolo*. Milan: Mondadori, 1994.
Perri, F. 1928   *Emigranti*. Milan: Treves, 1928 (under pseudonym of Paolo Albatrelli).
Perri, F. 1943   *I conquistatori*. Rome: Libreria Politica Moderna, 1925 (under pseudonym of Paolo Albatrelli). Repub. Milan: Garzanti, 1943.
Reymont, W. 1921   *I contadini*. (I; *L'autunno*; II; *L'inverno*; III; *La primavera*; IV; *L'estate*). Aquila: Vecchioni & Florence: Novissima, 1921–32.
Sapori, F. 1935   *Sotto il sole*. Rome: Novissima, 1935.
Seghers, A. 1933   *A Price on his Head*. (Der Kopflohn. *Roman aus einem deutschen Dorf im Spätsommer 1932*. Amsterdam: Querido Verlag, 1933.
Seminara, F. 1942   *Le baracche*. Milan: Rizzoli, 1942.
Seminara, F. 1951   *Il vento nell'oliveto*. Turin: Einaudi, 1951.
Seminara, F. 1952   *La masseria*. Milan, Garzanti, 1952.
Sholokov, M. A. 1967   *And Quiet Flows the Don*. Harmondsworth: Penguin, 1967.
Soffici, A. 1912   *Lemmonio Boreo*. Florence: Libreria della Voce, 1912.

Verga, G. 1968   *I Malavoglia*. Milan: Mondadori, 1968.
Verga, G. 1969   *Tutte le novelle*. Milan: Mondadori, 2 vols, 1969.
Vittorini, E. 1988   *Conversazione in Sicilia*. Milan: Rizzoli, 1988.

OTHER SOURCES

Absolom, R., 1999   'Peasant Memory and the Italian Resistance, 1943–45'. In
                        Bosworth & Dogliani 1999, pp. 31–44.
Aliberti, C. 1977   *Come leggere 'Fontamara' di Ignazio Silone*. Milan: Mursia, 1977.
Alicata, M. 1968   'L'orologio di Carlo Levi'. *Scritti letterari*. Milan: Il Saggiatore,
                        1968, pp. 260–5.
Alvaro, C. 1935   *Terra nuova. Prima cronaca dell'Agro Pontino*. Rome: Istituto
                        nazionale fascista di cultura, 1935 (republished Milan: Lombardi,
                        1989).
Alvaro, C. 1956   'Inserzione nella contemporaneità'. In *La narrativa meridionale.
                        Quaderni di prospettive meridionali*, 1 (1956), pp. 47–9.
Annoni, C. 1974   *Invito all lettura di Ignazio Silone*. Milan: Mursia, 1974.
Arnone, V. 1980   *Ignazio Silone*. Rome: Edizioni dell'Ateneo, 1980.
Arouimi, M. 1994   'Les harmonies de la peur: Cristo si è fermato a Eboli'. *Strumenti
                        critici*, 76 (1994), 3, pp. 363–86.
Asor Rosa, A. 1975   *La cultura*. In *Storia d'Italia*, vol. IV, *Dall'unità a oggi*. Turin:
                        Einaudi, 1975.
Asor Rosa, A. 1972   *Scrittori e popolo: Il popolo nella letteratura italiana contemporanea*.
                        Rome: Samonà e Savelli, 1972.
Aurigemma, M. 1982   'Carlo Levi'. In *Novecento. Gli scrittori e la cultura letteraria nella
                        società italiana*. Ideazione e direzione G. Grana. Vol. 7, Milan:
                        Marzorati, 1982, pp. 6462–89.
Bagnasco, A. 1977   *Tre Italie. La problematica territoriale dello sviluppo italiano*.
                        Bologna: Il Mulino, 1977.
Bagnoli, P. 1984   'Ignazio Silone e Carlo Rosselli'. *Nuova Antologia*, 553 (1984),
                        2150, pp. 239–47.
Bailey, F. G. 1971   *Gifts and Poison*, ed. by F. G. Bailey. Oxford: Blackwell, 1971.
Baldassaro, L. 1995   'Paura della libertà: Carlo Levi's unfinished preface'. *Italica*, 72
                        (1995), 2, pp. 143–54.
Banfield, E. C. 1958   *The Moral Basis of a Backward Society*. Glencoe: The Free Press,
                        1958.
Banti, A. M., 2000   *La nazione del Risorgimento. Parentela, santità e onore alle origini
                        dell'Italia unita*. Turin: Einaudi, 2000.
Bàrberi Squarotti, G. 1989 'Il viaggio come struttura del romanzo pavesiano'. In Ioli, G.
                        1989.
Basso, L. 1961   *Le riviste di Piero Gobetti* a cura di Lelio Bassi e Luigi Anderlini.
                        Milan: Feltrinelli, 1961.
Beccaria, G. L. 2000   'Introduzione' to C. Pavese, *La luna e i falò*. Turin: Einaudi,
                        2000, pp. v–xxxiii.

Ben-Ghiat, R. 2001 · *Fascist Modernities. Italy, 1922–1945*. Berkeley : University of California Press, 2001.

Berger, J. 1979 · *Pig Earth*. London: Writers and Readers Publishing Cooperative, 1979.

Bevilacqua, P. 1996 · 'New and old in the Southern Question'. *Modern Italy* 1 (1996), 2, pp. 81-92.

Bevilacqua, P. 1997 · *Breve storia dell'Italia meridionale dall'Ottocento a oggi*. Rome: Donzelli, 1997.

Biasin, G. P. 1968 · *The Smile of the Gods*. Ithaca – New York: Cornell University Press, 1968.

Bigongiari, P. 1956 · 'Radici, linguaggio e stile di una narrativa'. In *La narrativa meridionale. Quaderni di prospettive meridionali*, I (1956), pp. 107–13.

Biocca, D. & Canali, M. 2000 · *L'informatore: Silone, i comunisti e la polizia*. Milan: Luni, 2000.

Bo, C. 1951 · *Inchiesta sul neorealismo*. Turin: RAI, 1951.

Bobbio, N. 1977 · *Trent'anni di storia della cultura a Torino*. Turin: Einaudi, 1977.

Bogliari, F. 1980 · *Il movimento contadino in Italia dall'unità al Fascismo*. Turin: Loescher, 1980.

Bonsaver, G. 2000 · *Elio Vittorini: The Writer and the Written*. Leeds: Northern Universities Press, 2000.

Bosworth, R. & Dogliani, ? 1999 · *Italian Fascism. History, Memory and Representation*. Basingstoke: Macmillan Press, 1999.

Brisse, A. & Rotrou, L. 1876 · *The Draining of Lake Fucino Accomplished by His Excellency Prince Torlonia*. Rome: Imprimerie de la Propagande, 1876

Bronzini, G. B. 1969 · 'Valori della cultura tradizionale del Mezzogiorno d'Italia'. *Studi storici in onore di Gabriele Pepe*. Bari: Dedalo Libri, 1969, pp. 753–72.

Bronzini, G. B. 1977 · *Mito e realtà della civiltà contadina lucana*. Matera: F.lli Montemurro editori, 1977; reprinted Galatina: Congedo editore, 1981.

Bronzini, G. B. 1996 · *Il viaggio antropologico di Carlo Levi. Da eroe stendhaliano a guerriero birmano*. Bari: Edizioni Dedalo, 1996.

Brown, P. M. 1965 · 'Introduction' and 'A Note on Fascism'. Carlo Levi, *Cristo si è fermato a Eboli*. With an introduction, notes and select vocabulary by Peter Brown. London: Harrap, 1965.

Buccini, S. 1983 · 'Rassegna di studi sul tema città-campagna nell'opera narrativa di Cesare Pavese'. *Critica Letteraria* 38 (1983), pp. 171–9.

Bullock, A. 2000 · *La famiglia Chaplin. Storia di un'epoca*. Vol. II *1913–1930: Il carteggio a cura di Allan Bullock*. Florence: Olschki, 2000.

Buonaiuti, E. 1971 · *L'anno del Risveglio. Scritti giornalistici*. Premessa di F. Zucchetti. Introduzione agli articoli del *Risveglio* di A. Crisafulli. Milan: Dall'Oglio, 1971.

Calvino, I. 1978 · *Il sentiero dei nidi di ragno*. Turin: Einaudi, 1978.

Camerino, G. A. 1982 · 'Carlo Levi'. *Letteratura italiana contemporanea*, diretta da Gaetano Mariani, vol. III. Rome: Lucarini, 1982, pp. 95–109.

Campagna, F. 1967 — *La politica della città*. Bari: Laterza, 1967.

Canziani, E. 1928 — *Through the Appenines & the Lands of the Abruzzi. Landscape and Peasant Life*. Cambridge: Heffer, 1928.

Capo, A. 1984 — *L'assalto ai latifondi; lotte contadine e riforma agraria a Capaccio-Paestum*. Casalvelino Scalo (Salerno): Galzerano, 1984.

Caracciolo, A. 1950 — *L'occupazione delle terre in Italia*. Rome: Edizioni di Cultura Sociale, n. d. (c. 1950).

Carbone, M., 1980 — *In Lucania con Carlo Levi*. Fotografie di Mario Carbone, commento di Gino Melchiorre, testo di Carlo Levi. Cosenza: Lerici, 1980.

Carducci, N. 1977 — *Invito alla lettura di Jovine*. Milan: Mursia, 1977.

Carducci, N. 1983 (1) — 'Carlo Levi: per un nuovo umanesimo'. *Contributi. Rivista della Società di Storia Patria per la Puglia*, 2 (1983), 2, pp. 47–66.

Carducci, N. 1983 (2) — 'Cristo si è fermato a Eboli tra storia e utopia'. *Contributi. Rivista della Società di Storia Patria per la Puglia*, 2 (1983), 4, pp. 7–41.

Carducci, N. 1999 — *Storia intellettuale di Carlo Levi*. Lecce: Pensa, 1999.

Carotenuto, A. 1977 — *Jung e la cultura italiana*. Rome: Asrolabio, 1977.

Carter, I. 1979 — *Farm Life in Northeast Scotland 1840–1914*. Edinburgh: John Donald, 1979.

Carsaniga, G. 1986 — 'Rocco Scotellaro or the impossibility of peasant literature'. *Spunti e ricerche* 1986 (2), 21–36.

Castles, S. 1992 — 'Italian migration and settlement since 1945'. In *Australia's Italians. Culture and community in a changing society*. Sydney: Allen & Unwin, 1992.

Catani, R. D. 1975–6 — 'Detachment and Compassion in Carlo Levi's *Cristo si è fermato a Eboli*'. *ATI Journal* 17 (1975–6), pp. 3–7.

Catani, R. D. 1979 — 'Structure and Style as Fundamental Expression. The works of Carlo Levi and their poetic ideology'. *Italica* 56 (1979), 1, pp. 110–25.

Cattanei, L. 1986 — 'Francesco Jovine: uomini e donne di un trentennio'. *Otto/Novecento* 10 (1986) 3–4, pp. 99–140.

Cattanei, L. 1990 — 'Rileggendo Carlo Levi'. *Humanitas. Rivista bimestrale di cultura* (Brescia), 45 (1990), 6, pp. 884–7.

Chiaromonte, N. 1970 — *The Paradox of History: Stendhal, Tolstoy, Pasternak and Others*. London: Weidenfeld & Nicolson, [1970].

Chu, M. 1998 — 'Sciascia and Sicily: discourse and actuality'. *Italica*, 75 (1998) 1, pp. 78–92.

Ciascia, R. 1949 — 'Mezzogiorno, Questione del'. *Enciclopedia italiana*. Rome: Istituto della Enciclopedia Italiana, vol. XXIII (1949), pp. 149–52.

Cinanni, P. 1979 — *Lotte per le terre nel Mezzogiorno, 1943–1953. 'Terre pubbliche' e trasformazione agraria*. Venice: Marsilio, 1979.

Cirese, A. M. 1976 — *Intellettuali, folklore, istinto di classe: note su Verga, Deledda, Scotellaro, Gramsci*. Turin: Einaudi, 1976.

Cirese, A. M. 1980 — *Cultura egemonica e culture subalterne. Rassegna degli studi sul mondo popolare tradizionale*. Palermo: Palumbo, 1980.

Clark, M. 1984   *Modern Italy 1871–1982*. London and New York: Longman, 1984.

Colburn F. D. 1989   *Everyday Forms of Peasant Resistance*. Avonmouth, New York & London, England: M. E. Sharp, 1989.

Colclough, N. T.1971   'Social Mobility and Social Control in a Southern Italian Village.' In Bailey 1971, pp. 212–30.

Craig, I. 1974   'Novels of Peasant Crisis'. *Journal of Peasant Studies*, 2 (1974), 1, pp. 47–68.

Crovi, R. 1960   'Meridione e letteratura'. *Il Menabò* 1960 (3), pp. 267–91.

Crupi, P. 1977   *La letteratura nello stato d'assedio. Scrittori e popolo nel Mezzogiorno*. Ravenna: Longo, 1977.

Cucchiarelli, P. &   *La scuola della libertà* a cura di P. Cucchiarelli e R. Petruzelli.
    Petruzelli, R. 1980   Rome: Edizioni Ragionamenti, 1980.

Dal Lago, E. 2001   'Rethinking the Bourbon Kingdom'. *Modern Italy*, 6 (2001), 1, pp. 69–78.

Davis, H 1984   *'La luna e i falò:* What Kind of Ripeness?' *Italian Studies* 39 (1984), pp. 79–90.

Davis, J. 1996   'Perspectives on the "Southern Question"', in C. Levy 1996, pp. 53–68.

De Bernières, L. 1997   *Captain Corelli's Mandolin*. London : Random House, 1997.

De Castris, A. L. 1961   'Realismo di Jovine'. *Convivium* 1 (1961), pp. 52–70. Then in *Novecento. I contemporanei. Gli scrittori e la cultura letteraria nella società italiana*. Ideazione e direzione G. Grana. Vol. 6, Milan: Marzorati, 1979, pp.7023–43.

De Donato, G. 1974   *Saggio su Carlo Levi*. Bari: De Donato, 1974.

De Donato, G. 1993   *Carlo Levi nella storia e nella cultura italiana*, a cura di G. De Donato. Manduria: Lacaita, 1993.

De Donato, G. 1998   *Le parole del reale. Ricerche sulla prosa di Carlo Levi* . Bari: Dedalo, 1998.

De Donato, G. 1999   *Carlo Levi. Il tempo e la durata* in *"Cristo si è fermato a Eboli"*. Rome: Fahrenheit 451, 1999.

De Donato, G. &   *Un torinese nel Sud: Carlo*
    D'Amaro, S. 2001   *Levi: una biografia*. Milano: Baldini & Castoldi, 2001.

De Felice, R. 1965   *Mussolini il rivoluzionario (1883–1920)*. Turin: Einaudi, 1965.

De Felice, R. 1966   *Mussolini il Fascista*. Vol. I, *La conquista del potere (1921–1925)*. Turin: Einaudi, 1966.

De Felice, R. 1968   *Mussolini il Fascista*. Vol. II, *L'organizzazione dello Stato fascista*. Turin: Einaudi, 1968.

De Felice, R. 1974   *Mussolini il duce*. Vol I, *Gli anni del consenso (1929–1936)*. Turin: Einaudi, 1974.

De Felice, R. 1981   *Mussolini il duce*. Vol. II, *Lo Stato totalitario (1936–1940)*. Turin: Einaudi, 1981.

de la Nieves, M. 1992   *Introduzione a Cesare Pavese*. Bari: Laterza, 1992.

De Martino, E. 1975   *Morte e pianto rituale. Dal lamento funebre antico al pianto di Maria*. Turin: Beringhieri, 1975

De Martino, E. 1987   *Sud e magia*. Milan: Feltrinelli, 1987.

D'Episcopo, F. 1978   'Don Matteo Tridone, personaggio-chiave del romanzo *Signora Ava* di Francesco Jovine'. *Studi lucani e meridionali a cura di P. Borraro.* Galatina: Congedo, 1978.

D'Episcopo, F. 1984   *Il Molise di Francesco Jovine. Narrativa e antropologia.* Campobasso: Edizioni Enne, 1984.

D'Episcopo, F. 1994   *Francesco Jovine scrittore molisano* a cura di Francesco D'Episcopo. *Atti del convegno di studi sulla figura e l'opera di Francesco Jovine*, Guardialfiera, 11 novembre 1990. Naples: Edizioni scientifiche italiane, 1994.

D'Eramo, L. 1971   *L'opera di Ignazio Silone. Saggio critico e guida bibliografica.* Milan: Mondadori, 1971.

Dickie, J. 1999 (1)   'Many Souths: Many Stereotypes'. *Modern Italy*, 4 (1999), 1, pp. 79–86. (Rev. art. on Schneider 1998.)

Dickie, J. 1999 (2)   *Darkest Italy: The Nation and Stereotypes of the Mezzogiorno 1860–1900.* Basingstoke: Macmillan, 1999.

Dorso, G., 1944   *La rivoluzione meridionale. Il Mezzogiorno d'Italia da Cavour* a Mussolini. Milan: Il Saggiatore, 1944.

Dorso, G. 1972   *La rivoluzione meridionale.* Turin: Einaudi, 1972.

Dorso, G. 1986   'Cristo si è fermato a Eboli'. In G. Dorso, *L'occasione storica* a cura di C. Muscetta. Bari: Laterza, 1986.

Edelman, M. 1999   *Peasants against Globalization. Rural Social Movements in Costa Rica.* Stamford, California: Stamford University Press, 1999.

Eliot, T. S. 1974   *Collected Poems 1909–1962.* London: Faber & Faber, 1964.

Engels, F. 1990   *The Peasant Question in France and Germany.* In Marx-Engels 1990, 27.

Faenza, L. 1975   *Fascismo e ruralismo nei 'Testi unici' di Grazia Deledda, Angiolo Silvio Novaro, Roberto Forges Davanzati.* Bologna: Alfi, 1975.

Falaschi, G. 1971   'Carlo Levi'. *Belfagor*, 26 (1971), 1, pp. 56–82.

Falaschi, G. 1978   *Carlo Levi.* Florence: La Nuova Italia, 1978.

Fanon, F. 1971   *The Wretched of the Earth.* Harmondsworth: Penguin, 1971.

Feo, M. 1986   'Tradizione latina'. In *Letteratura italiana.* Dir. A. Asor Rosa. Vol. V, *Le questioni.* Turin: Einaudi, 1986, pp. 311–78.

Ferri, F. 1964   *Lo stato operaio 1927–39.* Antologia a cura di Franco Ferri. Rome: Editori Riuniti, 1964.

Finocchiaro Chimirri, G. 1968   '*Signora Ava* di Francesco Jovine'. *Teoresi* 23, (1968), 3–4, pp. 355–89.

Foa, V. 1991   *Il cavallo e la torre. Riflessioni su una vita.* Turin: Einaudi, 1991.

Forgacs, D. 1986   *Rethinking Italian Fascism. Capitalism, Populism and Culture.* Edited by David Forgacs. London: Lawrence and Wishart, 1986.

Fortini, F. 1974   'Per uno stato civile dei letterati'. *Verifica dei poteri. Scritti di critica e di istituzioni letterarie.* Nuova edizione accresciuta. Milan: Garzanti, 1974.

Fortunato, G. 1947   *Pagine e ricordi parlamentari.* Rome: Coll. Meridionale editrice, 1947.

Fortunato, G. 1973   'La questione meridionale e la riforma tributaria' in *Il Mezzogiorno e lo Stato italiano.* Florence: Vallecchi, 1973, pp. 543–4.

Fortunato, G. 1982   *Galantuomini e cafoni prima e dopo l'unità*. A cura di G. Cingari. Reggio Calabria: Casa del Libro, 1982.

Freud-Jung 1974   *The Freud-Jung Letters*. Edited by W. McGuire. London: The Hogarth Press & Routledge and Kegan Paul, 1974.

Galanti, G. M.   *Descrizione dello stato antico ed attuale del contado di Molise con un saggio storico sulla costituzione del Regno*. Naples: Presso la Società letteraria e tipografica, 1781, 2 vols.

Gellner, E. 1988   *Plough, Sword and Book. The Structure of Human History*. London: Collins Harvill, 1988.

Genovesi, P. 1986   'Il mondo contadino nell'opera di Piero Jahier'. *Spunti e Ricerche* 2 (1986), pp. 9–20.

Giannantonio, P. 1980   '*Signora Ava* (1942) tra *I Vicerè* e *Il Gattopardo*'. *La cultura italiana negli anni '30–'45. (Omaggio ad Alfonso Gatto) . Atti del convegno - Salerno 21-24 aprile 1980*, vol. I, pp. 91-103. Naples: Edizioni scientifiche italiane, 1984.

Giardini, G. 1967   *Francesco Jovine*. Milan: Marzorati, 1967.

Gill, D. 1981   Review of White 1980. *Journal of Peasant Studies* 9 (1981), pp. 133–7.

Ginsborg, P. 1984   'The Communist Party and the Agrarian Question in Southern Italy, 1943–48'. *History Workshop Journal* 17 (1984), pp. 81–101.

Ginsborg, P. 1990   *A History of Contemporary Italy. Society and Politics 1943–1988*. London: Penguin Books, 1990.

Ginzburg, N. 1962   *Le piccole virtù*. Turin: Einaudi, 1962.

Gioanola, E. 1972   *Cesare Pavese. La poetica dell'essere*. Milan: Marzorati, 1972.

Glasser, R. 1977   *The Net and the Quest. Patterns of Community and how they can Survive Progress*. London: Temple Smith, 1977.

Goodman, D. & Redclift, M. 1981   *From Peasant to Proletarian. Capitalist developments and agrarian transitions*. Oxford: Blackwell, 1981.

Gramsci, A. 1966   *Gli intellettuali e l'organizzazione della cultura*. Turin: Einaudi, 1966.

Gramsci, A. 1974   *La questione meridionale*, a cura di F. De Felice e V. Parlato. Rome: Editori Riuniti, 1974.

Grieco, R. 1953   *Lotte per le terre*. Florence: Edizioni di cultura sociale, 1953

Grieco, R. 1956   *Battaglie per le terre e la libertà*. Rome: Editori Riuniti, 1956.

Grignani, M. A. 1998   *L'invenzione della verità. Testi e intertesti per "Cristo si è fermato a Eboli"*. Introduzione di M. A. Grignani. Testi a cura di V. Barani e M. C. Grignani. Alessandria: Edizioni dell'Orso, 1998.

Grillandi, M. 1971   *Francesco Jovine*. Milan: Mursia, 1971.

Griffin R. 1998   'The Sacred Synthesis: the ideological cohesion of Fascist cultural policy'. *Modern Italy*, 3 (1998), 1, pp. 5–23.

Guarnieri, S. 1976   *L'intellettuale nel partito*. Venice: Marsilio, 1976.

Guj, L. 1986   'The Migratory Journey of the Eel: A Path to Hope in Post-War Italy'. *Italian Quarterly* 104 (1986), pp. 37–44.

Gullo, F. 1945   'Il latifondo e la concessione delle terre incolte ai contadini. *Rinascita* 2 (1945), pp. 175–6.

Gurgo, O. & De Core, F. 1998   *Silone: l'avventura di un uomo libero*. Venezia: Marsilio, 1998.

Guttuso, R. 1967 — 'Per Carlo Levi pittore'. *Galleria. Rassegna bimestrale di cultura*, 17 (1967), 3–6, pp. 261–4.

Hanne, M. 1975 — 'Significant Allusions in Vittorini's Conversazione in Sicilia'. *Modern Language Review*, 70 (1975), pp. 75–83.

Hanne M, 1992 — 'Silone's *Fontamara*: Polyvalence and Power.' *Modern Language Notes*, 107 (1992), pp. 132–59.

Hearder, H. 1983 — *Italy in the Age of the Risorgimento 1790–1870*. London & New York: Methuen, 1983.

Higgins, D. H. 1970 — 'Functions of Structure in Carlo Levi's *Cristo si è fermato a Eboli*'. *SIS Universities Bulletin*, 2 (1970), pp. 15–20.

Hobsbawm, E. J. 1963 — *Primitive Rebels. Studies in Archaic Forms of Social Movement in the 19th and 20th Centuries*. Manchester: Manchester University Press, 1963.

Hobsbawm, E. J. 1973 — 'Peasants and Politics'. *Journal of Peasant Studies* 1 (1973–4), 1, pp. 2–22.

Hoggart, R. 1959 — *The Uses of Literacy*. Harmondsworth: Penguin, 1959.

Hongre B. & Lidsky, P. 1970 — *Le paysan dans la littérature française, réalté ou mythes? Sèvres :* Centre international d'études pédagogiques, 1970.

Howe, I. 1961 — Politics and the Novel. London: Stevens, 1961.

Il paese 1985 — Il paese di Carlo Levi. Aliano, *cinquant'anni dopo* a cura del Servizio Studi Cariplo. Bari: Cariplo–Laterza, 1985.

Izzo, D. 1967 — 'Santi borghesi e contadini nel Molise'. *Il Ponte* 27 (1967), 3, pp. 338–74.

Jahier, P. 1983 — *Con me e con gli Alpini*. Rome: Editori Riuniti, 1983.

Joll, J. 1980 — *The Anarchists*. Cambridge, Mass, Harvard University Press, 1980.

Jung, C. G. 1964 — *Civilization in Transition. The Collected Works*, vol. 10. London: Routledge & Kegan Paul, 1964.

Keith, W. J., 1988 — *Regions of the Imagination: the development of British rural fiction*. Toronto: Toronto University Press, 1988.

King, R. 1973 — *Land Reform: The Italian Experience*. London: Butterworth, 1973.

King, R. 1988 — 'Carlo Levi, Aliano and the Rural Mezzogiorno in the 1930s: an interpretative essay'. *Journal of Rural Studies* 4 (1988), 4, pp. 307–21.

Klemperer, V. 2000 — *The Language of the Third Reich. LTI – Lingua Tertii Imperii: A philologist's notebook*. London & New Brunswick: Athlone Press, 2000.

Kropotkin, P. 1972 — *Mutual Aid: A Fact of Evolution*. London: Allan Lane, The Penguin Press, 1972.

Lalli, R. 1981 — *La radice meridionale di Francesco Jovine*. Campobasso: Rufus, 1981.

Lanternari, V. 1993 — 'Da Carlo Levi a Ernesto de Martino: verso la nuova antropologia'. In De Donato 1993, pp. 213–25.

Laski, H. J. 1927 — *Communism*. London: Butterworth, 1927.

Leake, E. 2003 — *The Reinvention of Ignazio Silone*. Toronto: Toronto University Press, 2003.

Lenin, V. I. 1961   *What is to be done? Burning Questions of our Time.* In V.I. Lenin, *Collected Works*, vol. 5. Moscow: Foreign Languages Publishing House, 1961.

Lenin, V. I. 1963   *What the "Friends of the People" are and How They Fight the Social-Democrats.* In V. I. Lenin, *Collected Works*, vol. 1, *1893–1894*. Moscow: Foreign Languages Publishing House, 1963.

Levy, C. 1999   *Gramsci and the Anarchists.* Oxford – New York: Berg, 1999.

Liberale, R. 1977 (1)   *Il movimento contadino del Fucino dal prosciugamento del lago alla cacciata di Torlonia.* Rome: Edizioni dell'Urbe, 1977.

Liberale, R. 1977 (2)   'Il Fucino: la conquista della terra'. *Campagne e movimento contadino nel Mezzogiorno d'Italia dal dopoguerra a oggi.* Vol. I, *Monografie generali.* Bari: De Donato, 1977, pp. 42–57.

Lyttleton, A. 1973   *The Seizure of Power. Fascism in Italy 1919–1929.* London: Weidenfeld and Nicolson, 1973.

Lyttleton, A.1991   'A new past for the Mezzogiorno'. *Times Literary Supplement,* 4 October 1991, pp. 14–5.

Lussu, E. 1975   *Un anno sull'altipiano.* Milan: Mondadori, 1975.

Mack Smith, D. 1969   *Italy. A Modern History.* Ann Arbor: The University of Michegan Press, 1969.

Mack Smith, D. 1985   *Cavour and Garibaldi.* Cambridge: Cambridge University Press, 1985.

Maclean, A. 1986   *Night Falls on Ardamurchan.* London: Penguin Books, 1986.

Malinowski, B. 1922   *The Argonauts of the Western Pacific.* London: Routledge & Son, 1922.

Manacorda, G. 1967   *Letteratura italiana contemporanea (1940–1965).* Rome: Editori Riuniti, 1967.

Manacorda, G. 1972   *Vent'anni di pazienza. Saggi sulla letteratura italiana contemporanea.* Florence: La Nuova Italia, 1972.

Maraspini, A. L. 1968   *The Study of an Italian Village.* Paris & The Hague: Mouton, 1968.

Marcovecchio, A. 1967   'Il periplo del mondo'. *Galleria. Rasegna bimestrale di cultura,* 17 (1967), 3–6, pp. 99–109.

Martelli, S. 1970   *Francesco Jovine.* Campobasso: Casa molisana del libro, 1970.

Martelli, S. 1978   'Jovine e il brigantaggio meridionale'. *Studi lucani e meridionali* a cura di P. Borrero. Galatina: Congedo, 1978, pp. 107–33.

Martucci, R. 1999   *L'invenzione dell'Italia unita 1855–1864.* Milan: Sansoni, 1999.

Marx–Engels 6, 1976   *Manifesto of the Communist Party.* In Marx, K. & Engels, F., Collected Works, vol. 6. London: Lawrence and Wishart, 1976.

Marx–Engels 2, 1977   The Eighteenth Brumaire of Louis Bonaparte. In Marx, K. & Engels, F., *Collected Works*, vol. 2, London: Lawrence and Wishart, 1977.

Marx–Engels 27, 1990   Marx, K., Engels, F., *Collected Works*, vol. 27. London: Laurence & Wishart, 1990.

Mauro, W. 1965   Cultura e società nella narrativa meridionale. Rome: Edizioni dell'Ateneo, 1965.

Mauro, W. 1974   *Realtà mito e favola nella narrativa italiana del Novecento.* Milan: SugarCo, 1974.

McLaughlin, M. 1986 'Imagery in the Two Versions of Silone's Fontamara'. *ATI Journal*, 47, 1986, pp. 33–42.

Mercuri, L. 1979 'Introduzione' to I. Silone, *Memoriale dal carcere svizzero*. Milan: Lerici, 1979, pp. vii–xviii.

Miccinesi, M. 1979 *'Cristo si è fermato a Eboli' di Carlo Levi*. Milan: Mursia, 1979.

Miranda, J. P. 1977 *Marx and the Bible: a critique of the philosophy of repression*. London: SCM Press, 1977.

Moe, N. 2002 *The View from Vesuvius. Italian Culture and the Southern Question*. Berkeley, Los Angeles, London: University of California Press, 2002

Moloney, B. 1990 'Vittorini, Pavese and the Ethics of Armed Resistance'. In *The Shared Horizon. Melbourne Essays in Italian Language and Literature Presented to Colin McCormick*, ed. by T. O'Neill. Dublin: Irish Academic Press, 1990, pp. 185–202.

Moloney, B. 1996 'Ignazio Silone and *Il Risveglio*: the 1945 version of Silone's Fontamara'. *Italian Studies*, 51 (1996), pp. 134–66.

Moloney B. 2002 *'Fontamara* and *Cristo si è fermato a Eboli*: cases of intertextuality'. *Essays in Italian Literature and History in honour of Doug Thompson*, ed. G. Talbot & P. Williams. Dublin: Four Courts Press, 2002.

Montale, E. 1966 'Un pittore in esilio'. *Auto da fè*. Milan: Il Saggiatore, 1966, pp. 34–9.

Moseley, E. M. 1962 *Pseudonyms of Christ in the Modern Novel*. Pittsburgh, Pittsburgh University Press, 1962

Mumford, L. 1938 *The Culture of Cities*. London: Secker & Warburg, 1938.

Muscetta, C. 1953 *Letteratura militante*. Florence: Parenti, 1953.

Musolino, W. 1990 'Pavese, Camus and the Myth of Sisyphus: Among peasants and the stones of life'. *Spunti e Ricerche* 6 (1990), 35–55.

Nesti, A. 1974 *Gesù socialista: una tradizione popolare italiana 1880–1920*. Turin: Claudiana, 1974.

Origo, I. 1984 'Ignazio Silone. A study in integrity'. In *A Need to Testify: Four portraits*. London: John Murray, 1984, pp. 191–242.

Padovani, G. 1982 *Letteratura e socialismo. Saggi su Ignazio Silone*. Catania: Marino, 1982.

Pancrazi, P. 1953 'Il primo e l'ultimo Jovine'. In *Scrittori d'oggi, Serie VI*. Bari: Laterza, 1953.

Paris, R. 1977 *Il mito del proletariato nel romanzo italiano*. Milan: Garzanti, 1977.

Parkinson M. H., 1973 'The rural novel'. *A Dictionary of Modern Critical Terms*. Ed. by Roger. Fowler. London and Boston: Routledge and Kegan Paul,1973, pp. 165–6.

Pertile, L. 1986 In Forgacs 1986, pp. 162–184.

Petroni, G. 1956 'Il tema del giorno'. *La narrativa meridionale. Quaderni di prospettive meridionali* 1 (1956), pp. 69–79.

Petrusewicz, M. 1998 'Before the Southern Question: "Native" Ideas on Backwardness and Remedies in the Kingdom of the Two Sicilies, 1815– 1849'. In Schneider 1998, pp. 27–48.

Pogliano, C. 1976 *Piero Gobetti e l'ideologia dell'assenza*. Bari: De Donato, 1976.

Procaccini, A. 1986   *Francesco Jovine. The Quest for Realism.* New York, Berne, Frankfurt: Lang, 1986.

Raffa, G. P. 1997   'Carlo Levi's Sacred Art of healing'. *Annali d'italianistica* 15 (1997), pp. 203–20.

Rawson, J. 1977   'Introduction' to I. Silone, *Fontamara* edited, with introduction, notes and vocabulary by Judy Rawson. Manchester: Manchester University Press, 1977.

Rawson, J. 1978   'Fontamara: Frazione o Cosmo?' *ATI Journal* 26 (1978), pp. 34–7.

Rawson, J. 1980   'Che fare? Silone e Tolstoj'. In Cucchiarelli, P. & Petruzelli, R 1980, pp. 167–76.

Rawson, J. 1981   'Che fare?: Silone and the Russian "Chto Delat?" Tradition'. *Modern Language Review* 76 (1981), 3, pp. 556–65.

Rawson, J. 1985   'Silone's Early Fiction and its Abruzzo "Subsoil"'. *Italian Studies* 40 (1985), pp. 93–104.

Read, H. 1940   *The Philosophy of Anarchism.* London: Freedom Press, 1940.

Redfield, R. 1965   *The Primitive World and its Transformations.* Ithaca, N. Y., Cornell University Press, 1965.

Reidy, D. 1974   'Renato Fucini: Notebooks and Short Stories'. *ATI Journal* 14 (1974), pp. 13–9.

Rosato, G. 1969   'Lo scrittore e la regione. Silone dentro e fuori l'Abruzzo'. *Dimensioni* (Pescara) 13 (1969),1–2, pp. 20–3.

Rossi-Doria, M. 1956   Riforma agraria e azione meridionalista. Bologna: Edizioni agricole, 1956.

Russi, A. 1967   *Gli anni dell'antialienazione (Dall'Ermetismo al Neorealismo).* Milan: Mursia, 1967.

Russo, L. 1951   *I narratori (1850–1957).* Milan–Messina: Principato, 1951.

Sabbatucci, G. 1974   *I combattenti nel primo dopoguerra.* Rome: Laterza, 1974.

Said, E. W. 1985   'Orientalism reconsidered'. *Europe and its Others. Proceedings of the Essex Conference on the Sociology of Literature, July 1984.* Ed. F. Barker & others. University of Colchester, Essex, 1985.

Said, E. W. 1991   *Orientalism.* London: Penguin, 1991.

Salinari, C. 1967   *Preludio e fine del realismo in Italia.* Naples: Morano, 1967.

Salvemini, G. 1955   *Antologia della questione meridionale* a cura di B. Caizzi, Prefazione di G. Salvemini. Cremona: Ed. Di Comunità, 1955.

Salvemini, G. 1963   *Movimento socialista e questione meridionale* a cura di Gaetano Arfé. Milan: Feltrinelli, 1963.

Schneider, J. 1998   *Italy's "Southern Question": Orientalism in one country.* Ed. Jane Schneider. Oxford & New York: Berg, 1998.

Schweizer, G. 1976   *Bauernroman und Faschismus. Zur Ideologiekritik einer literarischen Gattung.* Tübingen: Vereinigung für Volkskunde, 1976.

Sciascia, L. 1970   'Verga e la libertà'. *La corda pazza. Scrittori e cose della Sicilia.* Turin: Einaudi, 1977, pp. 79–94.

Scotellaro, R. 1954   *È fatto giorno.* Ed. riveduta e integrata a cura di F. Vitelli. Milan: Mondadori, 1954.

Scott, J. C. 1989   'Everyday forms of resistance'. In *Everyday forms of Peasant Resistance.* Ed. Forrest D. Colburn. New York, London: Sharpe, Armontt, 1989, pp. 3–33.

Scurani, A. 1969   *Ignazio Silone*. Milan: Edizioni di "Letture", 1969. Profili di scrittori: 1.

Sereni, E. 1946   *La questione agraria nella rinascita italiana*. Rome: Einaudi, 1946.

Serpieri, A, 1925   'Il dazio sul grano e i trattati di commercio. Quel che attendono le classi agricole'. *L'Epoca*, 6 September 1925, p. 6.

Seton-Watson, C. 1967   *Italy from Liberalism to Fascism*. London: Methuen, 1967.

Shanin, T. 1971   *Peasants and Peasant Societies*. Selected Readings. Edited by T. Shanin. Harmondsworth: Penguin, 1971.

Shanin, T. 1972   *The Awkward Class: political sociology of peasantry in a developing society*, Russia 1910–1925. Oxford: Clarendon, 1972.

Snowden, F. M. 1985   *Violence and the Great Estates in the South of Italy. Apulia 1900–1922*. Cambridge: Cambridge University Press, 1985.

Sperduto, D. 1995   'Modificazioni cronologiche nel *Cristo si è fermato a Eboli*'. *Esperienze letterarie* 20 (1995), 2, pp. 89–93.

Spriano, P. 1963   *La cultura italiana del '900 attraverso le riviste*. Vol. VI, *L'Ordine Nuovo (1919–1929)*. A cura di P. Spriano. Turin: Einaudi, 1963.

Spriano, P. 1972   *Storia di Torino operaia e socialista (Da De Amicis a Gramsci)*. Turin: Einaudi, 1972.

Steinberg, J. 1986   'Fascism in the Italian South: The Case of Calabria'. In Forgacs 1986, pp. 83–109.

Tarrow, S. G. 1967   *Peasant Communism in Southern Italy*. London and New Haven: Yale University Press, 1967.

Thompson, D. 1982   *Cesare Pavese. A study of the major novels and poems*. Cambridge: Cambridge University Press, 1982.

Thompson, E. P. 1968   *The Making of the English Working Class*. Harmondsworth: Penguin Books, 1968.

Todini, G. 1979   'Francesco Jovine'. *Novecento. I contemporanei. Gli scrittori e la cultura letteraria nella società italiana*. Ideazione e direzione G. Grana. Vol. 6, Milan: Marzorati, 1979, pp. 6999–7023.

Tolstoy, L. 1934   *What Then Must We Do?* L. Tolstoy, Tolstoy Centenary Edition, vol. 14. Oxford: Oxford University Press, 1934.

Tolstoy, L. 1935   *The Kingdom of God is within you. In The Kingdom of God and Peace Essays*. L. Tolstoy, Tolstoy Centenary Edition, vol. 20. Oxford: Oxford University Press, 1935.

Tolstoy, L. 1937   What's to be done? In L. Tolstoy, *Recollections and Essays*. Tolstoy Centenary Edition, vol. 21. Oxford: Oxford University Press, 1937.

Torraca, F. 1907   *Scritti critici*. Naples: F. Perella (A. Traldi), 1907.

Van Den Bossche, B. 1999   'Il mito classico nell'opera di Cesare Pavese'. *Humanitas* 54 (1999), 4, pp. 713–34.

Van Den Bossche, B. 2001   *Nulla è veramente accaduto: strategie discorsive del mito nell'opera di Cesare Pavese*. Florence: Cesati, 2001.

Verri, P. 1964   *Del piacere e del dolore ed altri scritti di filosofia ed economia* a cura di Renzo De Felice. Milan: Feltrinelli, 1964.

Villari, P. 1979   *Le lettere meridionali ed altri scritti sulla questione sociale in Italia*. Introd. di F. Barbagallo. Naples: Guida, [1979].

Virdia, F. 1979   *Silone*. Florence: La Nuova Italia, 1979 (Il Castoro, no. 6).

Visser, N., 1996   'Authors, Narrators, and the Poetics of Radical Fiction'. *Orbis Litterarum* 51 (1996), pp. 131–47.

Walzer, M. 1989   *The Company of Critics. Social Criticism and Political Commitment in the Twentieth Century.* London: Peter Halban, 1989.

Ward, C. 1973   *Anarchy in Action.* London: Allen & Unwin, 1973.

Ward, D. 1996   *Antifascisms. Cultural Politics in Italy, 1943–46. Benedetto Croce and the Liberals, Carlo Levi and the "Actionists".* London: Associated University Presses, 1996.

Wells, M. X. 1998   'Carlo Levi e la Lucania: la parola e l'immagine'. In Grignani 1998.

White, C. 1980   *Patrons and Partisans. A Study of politics in two Southern Italian comuni.* Cambridge: Cambridge University Press, 1980.

Whyte, J. 1970   'The Evolution of Silone's Central Theme'. *Italian Studies* 25 (1970), pp. 49–62.

Zimmerman, P. 1975   Der Bauernroman. Antifeudalismus–Konservatismus–Faschismus. Stuttgart: Metzler, 1975.

Ziolkowsky, T. 1972   *Fictional Transfigurations of Jesus.* Princeton: Princeton University Press, 1972.

Index